THE SUPREME COURT'S
CONSTITUTION

THE SUPREME COURT'S CONSTITUTION

An Inquiry into Judicial Review and Its Impact on Society

Bernard H. Siegan

Transaction Publishers

New Brunswick (U.S.A.) and London (U.K.)

141017

Third printing 1993
Copyright © 1987 by Transaction Publishers
New Brunswick, New Jersey 08903

Library of Congress Catalog Number: 86-16190
ISBN: 0-88738-127-8 (cloth); 0-88738-671-7 (paper)
Printed in the United States of America

Library of Congress Cataloging in Publication Data

Siegan, Bernard H.
    The Supreme Court's Constitution.

    Includes index.
    1. United States—Constitutional law—Interpretation
and construction.   2. Judicial review—United States.
3. United States. Supreme Court.   I. Title.
KF4550.S48   1986   342.73′02   86-16190
ISBN 0-88738-127-8   347.3022
ISBN 0-88738-671-7 (pbk.)

Contents

To Sharon

Introduction

The United States Supreme Court is an unusual institution for a nation that proclaims its dedication to democratic processes. An unelected body whose nine members have been appointed for diverse reasons, it has the power to set aside laws that the vast majority of people support. Under our system, the Court is considered the guardian of the Constitution; yet that document does not specifically empower it to exercise judicial review over either federal or state legislation. Nor, assuming such power was intended, does the Constitution provide guidance on how it should be wielded.

Nevertheless, throughout our history, the Supreme Court has exerted enormous influence over American society. In the political arena, it both defines the authority of governmental branches and agencies and delineates federal and state powers.

In intellectual and cultural matters, it protects most kinds of expression from any regulation; it determines the sectarian content of education in the public schools and decides the amount of financial aid government may extend to private education.

In the social area, it decrees which controls, if any, the state may place on abortion and whether this procedure must be publicly funded. It imposes rules for school integration and determines the validity of measures according preferential treatment to minorities and women.

In the economic sphere, it decides the extent to which government may regulate the acquisition, use, and disposition of private property and, therefore, the validity of local zoning regulations.

In the criminal area, the Court rules on what government must do and prove before an accused may be found guilty and punished, and it determines when the death penalty may be imposed or if a particular punishment is excessive.

Considered collectively or even individually, these powers accord an awesome authority to this one governmental body. Supreme Court Justices often occupy their positions for long periods, and during their terms in office, each may exert more influence over the nation than any other official in government, including the president. Little cause for complaint might exist, if in exercising its power, the Court was merely implementing Constitutional mandates. Although majority opinions usually assert that the Justices are doing no more than that which the fundamental law requires, a closer analysis casts doubt on this contention.

In this book, I examine the opinions of the Supreme Court in eight different areas, and during this endeavor a conclusion will become apparent: the Court has frequently ruled either contrary to, or without guidance from, constitutional meaning and purpose. It has been more the maker than the interpreter of the law.

In this nation, constitutions are unique among legal papers in one important respect; they are specially drafted documents that allow interpreters substantial discretion. Thus, unlike a private contract, which, even when dealing with minor matters, may be quite lengthy, the United States Constitution, governing the entire nation, totals only fifteen book-size pages.

Many provisions are short, eloquently stated, and sufficiently ambiguous to allow an interpretation that was not intended. Constitutional commentators do not necessarily find this state of affairs disturbing: many believe in the "living constitution," one that continually accommodates itself to current conditions. From this perspective, the Framers' meaning and intention is subordinate to that of the Supreme Court. While this result would seem highly objectionable in a democratic society, constitutional language makes such an outcome to some degree unavoidable.

As we shall see in chapter 3, the Thirty-ninth Congress, which framed the fourteenth amendment, was well aware that terms such as *privileges and immunities, due process,* and *equal protection* are sufficiently open ended to allow the judiciary great latitude in definition. Even in the absence of these and other malleable provisions, the Constitution would not be definite enough to preclude judicial opportunism. Chapter 1 discloses how, in one decision, Chief Justice John Marshall changed the system of government in the United States by greatly increasing national authority at the expense of state powers.

Obviously missing from our Constitution is a set of rules on how it should be construed. In lieu of any provision to the contrary, the Constitution should be interpreted similarly to any other legal document—that is, in accordance with the drafters' meaning and intent. However, as previously indicated, under this standard the judiciary would still be able to exercise considerable discretion, particularly in defining the liberties of the people. Although a major purpose of the Constitution is to protect and preserve liberty, the original document and its amendments do not define the extent and nature of this commitment. The people's liberties are involved here, and they are too numerous and varied for the Framers to have specified.

Nevertheless, such discretionary interpretation is not warranted when the Framers did not intend it. The strict constructionist solution to interpretation is precise, uncompromising, and best implements neutral principles. According to this view, those who demand change must observe the constitutional mandate for amendment. Once the very difficult problems of meaning and objective have been resolved, this approach leaves room for judicial discretion solely within prescribed limits. It is most consistent with the notion that justice demands the rule of law and not of individuals. By comparison, those who refuse to be bound "by the hand of the past" confront the troublesome question of how much discretion courts should have in departing from the document's original meaning. Because no absolute answer to this question exists, omitting the restraint of strict construction accords immense authority to five of nine people who, at any one time, happen to occupy the highest judicial seats of power. They would then have unlimited power to define contemporary values and concerns, an exercise that is highly subjective.

The eight areas that I have selected for consideration in this book are ones to which I have given much study; they are not, however, the only illustrations of the Supreme Court's Constitution. For example, comparable judicial experience is evident in the interpretation given both the criminal law protections of the Bill of Rights and the commerce clause of article I, section 8. With respect to construing original meaning, the eight chapters appear representative of the Supreme Court's constitutional experience. In fact, many commentators consider American constitutional law as traditionally encompassing changes and departures from the original understanding. Each chapter of this book contains the history of particular provisions, and taken together they reveal the very wide latitude that the Supreme Court has exercised in construing the Constitution.

I believe that the information contained in this book will enable the public to understand more clearly the nature and scope of judicial review and to evaluate more appropriately its role in our society. This knowledge is important not only in understanding the national judiciary but also in evaluating the state supreme courts, which enjoy comparable authority over their fundamental laws.

1

Federalism, Implied Powers, and the Necessary and Proper Clause

Federalism is an important issue of the 1980s. It involves defining the line between federal and state powers and responsibilities. This is an issue that has troubled the nation since its inception. In the 1980s it is viewed mainly as a political matter on the premise that the Constitution imposes some, but essentially little, restraint on the power of Congress to pass laws governing the affairs of the nation, including those activities that occur solely within individual states. Consequently, anyone seeking more authority for the states must obtain it from Congress, for that is where the nation's primary political power resides.

In contrast, during the early years of the Union, considerable uncertainty existed about how much authority Congress actually possesses and how much is reserved to the states. The federal government was considered to be one of limited and enumerated powers, with Congress having only those powers delegated to it, either specifically or by necessary implication. Powers not delegated remained with either the states or the people. Thus, the national government did not have the virtual monopoly of authority that it is now assumed to possess.

Article I, section 8 sets forth specific congressional powers and in clause 18 authorizes Congress to "make all laws which shall be necessary and proper for carrying into execution the foregoing powers, and all other powers vested by this Constitution in the government of the United States, or any department or offices thereof." While the accounts of the 1787 Constitutional Convention are silent on the meaning of the necessary and proper power, the Federalists, the supporters of the Constitution in the ratification debates of 1787-89, minimized its scope. All it did, they claimed, was enable Congress to implement its enumerated authority, for otherwise that body could not fulfill its responsibilities. They argued that essentially the federal government had little more than the powers that were identified in the Constitution. They further maintained that the prohibitions in section 9 of article I barring congressional passage of certain

1

designated legislation did not imply the authority to enact measures not specifically mentioned.

These representations were very important in the history of our nation, for as James Madison maintained, had the people believed that the necessary and proper clause or any other provision significantly enlarged the federal power beyond what was specifically stated, the Constitution might never has been ratified.[1] While much contemporary opinion preferred a stronger national government than the Articles of Confederation had conferred, it was generally not favorable to substituting a powerful national government that left the states with only limited authority over their populace.[2] Ratification of the Constitution required approval by conventions in nine of the thirteen states. The vote in four states was very close: Massachusetts, 187 to 168, New Hampshire, 57 to 47; Virginia, 89 to 79; and New York, 30 to 27. North Carolina originally declined to ratify and did so only after Congress proposed the Bill of Rights.

The primary source of original meaning is the text itself. Thereafter are the debates of the Framers while in session. The ratification debates also may provide pertinent information particularly when there is agreement on the issue.

In *The Federalist Papers* both Alexander Hamilton and James Madison sought to assure the public about the scope of national power. The anti-Federalists (opponents of the proposed Constitution) contended that the central government would exercise great control over the states and the populace. Although the document contained provisions suggesting that the national authority was substantially restrained, they insisted these served to camouflage other clauses that ceded broad and unrestricted powers. In No. 33, Hamilton responds to the Constitution's opponents who focused on the necessary and proper and supremacy clauses as establishing an all powerful government. Hamilton completely rejected this view, asserting that "it may be affirmed with perfect confidence that the constitutional operation of the intended government would be precisely the same if these clauses were entirely obliterated as if they were repeated in every article."[3] Hamilton continued on to explain the necessary and proper clause:

> If there is any thing exceptionable [about the clause], it must be sought for in the specific powers upon which this general declaration is predicated. The declaration itself, though it may be chargeable with tautology or redundancy, is at least perfectly harmless.
>
> But SUSPICION may ask, why then was it introduced? The answer is, that it could only have been done for greater caution, and to guard against all cavilling refinements in those who might hereafter feel a disposition to curtail and evade the legitimate authorities of the Union.[4]

Madison was no less emphatic in castigating that which he also considered distortions about the national powers. Regarding the necessary and proper clause, he asserted in No. 44 that "[w]ithout the *substance* of this power, the whole Constitution would be a dead letter,"[5] explaining,

> [H]ad the convention attempted a positive enumeration of the powers necessary and proper for carrying their other powers into effect, the attempt would have involved a complete digest of laws on every subject to which the Constitution relates; . . .

> Had the Constitution been silent on this head, there can be no doubt that all the particular powers requisite as means of executing the general powers would have resulted to the government, by unavoidable implication. No axiom is more clearly established in law, or in reason, than that wherever . . . a general power to do a thing is given, every particular power necessary for doing it is included.[6]

By inserting this clause, the Framers removed a pretext "which may be seized on critical occasions for drawing into question the essential powers of the Union."[7]

These arguments were consistent with the general position taken by the Federalists. They vehemently denied that the Constitution created an omnipotent national government that could deprive either the states of their sovereignty in local matters or the people of their liberties. They contended that all parts of the Constitution must be read within its general context of establishing a government whose powers were designated. These powers were so clear and moderate that no need existed to provide the people or the states with special protective language such as would be contained in a Bill of Rights. In fact, said Hamilton (in No. 84), the addition of a Bill of Rights might lead to the imposition of authority that never existed:

> For why declare that things shall not be done which there is no power to do? Why, for instance, should it be said that the liberty of the press shall not be restrained when no power is given by which restrictions may be imposed? I will not contend that such a provision would confer a regulating power; but it is evident that it would furnish, to men disposed to usurp, a plausible pretense for claiming that power.[8]

The anti-Federalists' fears were groundless, for according to Theophilus Parsons of Massachusetts, a leading Federalist, who was later to become chief justice of Massachusetts, "no power was given Congress to infringe on any of the natural rights of the people by this Constitution; and should they attempt it without Constitutional authority, the act would be nullity and could not be enforced."[9] Federalists advanced similar arguments with respect to states rights.

Writing in *The Federalist* No. 45, Madison argued that the "powers delegated by the proposed Constitution to the federal government are few and defined" and that

> those which are to remain in the State governments are numerous and indefinite. The former will be exercised principally on external objects, as war, peace, negotiation, and foreign commerce; . . .The powers reserved to the several States will extend to all the objects which, in the ordinary course of affairs, concern the lives, liberties, and properties of the people and the internal order, improvement, and prosperity of the State.[10]

The operations of the federal government would be "most extensive and important in times of war and danger; those of the state governments, in times of peace and security." Madison asserted the latter would be more important than the former. The form of government contemplated by the Constitution consists of "local and municipal authorities [that] form distinct and independent portions . . . no more subject within their respective spheres to the general authority than the general authority is subject to them, within their own sphere."[11] The interests under the control of these local administrations "will form so many rivulets of influence," maintained Hamilton, that they "cannot be particularized without involving a detail too tedious and uninteresting to compensate for the instructions it might afford."[12]

The Federalist arguments about the necessary and proper clause may have persuaded some but clearly not all of the public, and understandably so. Even if Hamilton and Madison had correctly explained the intended meaning of the clause, their explanation was only an opinion about the definition of words that do not have meanings universally accepted. Other public figures held different opinions, and in time, as we shall see, the final arbiter of meaning, the U. S. Supreme Court, would also come to a different conclusion. "Undoubtedly", said Chief Justice John Marshall, "there is an imperfection in human language, which often exposes the same sentence to different constructions."[13]

This is the learning of constitutional, as well as other areas of law. I know of no experienced lawyers who, in negotiating contracts or other legal instruments, would accept on behalf of their clients the open-ended language of the necessary and proper clause. The lawyer's function in drafting a legal instrument is to remove ambiguity from the language used so that parties to and interpreters of the document know as precisely as possible what the understanding is.

To accomplish this degree of clarity, legal documents may be extremely lengthy and even so, despite the detail in explanation, doubts often arise. Each year, it seems, many kinds of business contracts and term leases become longer as lawyers seek to improve the language of provisions that are less explicit than they originally seemed.

Hamilton and Madison gave a certain meaning to the necessary and proper clause, and they were probably correct in their interpretation. They erred, however, in assuming or suggesting that other interpreters would come to a similar conclusion. This error is common in constitutional interpretation, for constitutions and amendments to them, the most important of all documents for the rule of law, are generally broadly drafted, permitting future interpreters to have as much control, or more control over meaning than did the original Framers. The Constitution consists of so much imprecise language that the result is a form of blank check to future interpreters—the individuals who, for a variety of reasons, happen to be Justices of the Supreme Court at the time the language is subject to litigation. The myriad of constitutional law decisions demonstrate how truly vague are the words contained in these documents. What is the meaning of, for example, legislative, executive, judicial, speech, press, religion, commerce, property, privileges, immunities, due process, or equal protection?

Despite this problem with interpretation, it is difficult to contest Hamilton's and Madison's conclusions that the federal government was to be very limited in power. If, as is now the situation, the states' powers had in most areas been subordinate to those of the national legislature, why was it necessary in section 8 to spell out the powers of Congress? Why did the Framers engage in extensive and sometimes vitriolic debate on whether certain powers should be authorized? An answer is found in the next chapter's account of the Framers' debate on authorizing the emission of paper money. This debate makes it apparent they believed the national government possessed only such powers as the document specifically accorded it.

The Constitutional Convention refused to empower the national government to act in many areas: to grant charters of incorporation; to create seminaries for the promotion of literature and the arts; to establish public institutions, rewards, and immunities for the promotion of agriculture, commerce, trades, and manufactures; to regulate stages on the post road; to establish a university; to encourage, by proper premiums and provisions, the advancement of useful knowledge and discoveries; to provide for opening and establishing canals; to emit bills on the credit of the United States (which then meant printing paper for circulation as currency); and to make sumptuary laws. Each of these proposals was introduced and either voted down or not further considered outside of committee.

Such an outcome is to be expected given the political orientation of that period which generally rejected strong government. The creation of a limited government is consistent with the then widely held Lockean position that the state is a necessary evil to which only powers essential to the common good should be granted.

When language is not clear, intent and purpose become important considerations in interpreting any legal document. The items listed in section 8 are not set forth as examples, but rather as specific powers, and a provision enabling their implementation, such as the necessary and proper clause, is in keeping with that purpose. The drafting of the clause, whether the language was more or less expansive than required, given the limitations of the space devoted to it is a matter of judgment about which lawyers might reasonably differ. The purpose of the language, however, is far less open to question.

Any other interpretation suggests that the Federalists were perpetuating a gigantic hoax in the ratification debates. The Federalists repeated over and over the argument that, as James Wilson expressed it, "the Congressional power is to be collected . . . from the positive grant expressed in the instrument of the union."[14] Every power not delegated to the general government was reserved and retained by the states or the people.

The speakers were, after all, the men who had drafted the instrument and who should therefore know most about it. Future interpreters would have great difficulty in rejecting or ignoring their statements, or so one would suppose. Although the evidence of intent is strongest when it is based on the Framers' words spoken during the debates on adoption, their subsequent statements should not be ignored, even if only to give credibility to the ratification process.

Concern over the extent of national powers is evident in the ratification documents on which seven states based their adoption of the proposed Constitution. Four contain clarification of these powers and five urged amendments to ensure limiting of national authority. In South Carolina, the convention declared that "no Section or paragraph of the said Constitution warrants a Construction that the states do not retain every power not expressly relinquished by them and vested in the General Government of the Union."

The Virginia delegates declared that the powers granted under the Constitution, being derived from the people of the United States,

> may be resumed by them whensoever the same shall be perverted to their injury or oppression and that every power not granted thereby remains with them and at their will; that therefore no right of any denomination can be cancelled abridged restrained or modified by the Congress by the Senate or the House of Representatives acting in any Capacity by the President or any

Department or Officer of the United States except in those instances in which power is given by the Constitution for those purposes.

The New York convention made the following declaration, which is similar to one contained in Rhode Island's ratification.

That the Powers of Government may be reassumed by the People, whensoever it shall become necessary for their Happiness; that every Power, Jurisdiction and right, which is not by the said Constitution clearly delegated to the Congress of the United States, or the departments of the Government thereof, remains to the People of the several States, or to their respective State Governments to whom they may have granted the same; And that those Clauses in the said Constitution, which declare, that Congress shall not have or exercise certain Powers, do not imply that Congress is entitled to any Powers not given by the said Constitution; but such Clauses are to be construed either as exceptions to certain specified Powers, or as inserted merely for greater Caution.

Massachusetts, New Hampshire, Virginia, North Carolina, and Rhode Island urged Congress to propose amendments to the Constitution that would limit the national powers to those "expressly delegated" (Massachusetts and Rhode Island), "expressly and particularly delegated" (New Hampshire), or "delegated" (North Carolina and Virginia) by the Constitution.[15]

These recommendations were subsequently embodied in the tenth amendment which, however, does not contain the word *expressly*, a fact leading Chief Justice Marshall to contend that its Framers (the first Congress) did not intend to exclude incidental or implied powers.[16] However, using this word might have severely confined national authority inasmuch as it had been inserted in the Articles of Confederation to achieve this very purpose. The more general terminology nevertheless manifests the antinationalist sentiment existing during the ratification period. The quoted portions of the ratification resolutions provide additional and persuasive support that some or all of these seven states might not have ratified had they construed the national powers as broad and expansive.

Constitutionality of the U.S. National Bank

Following ratification, the most important event relating to federalism and the necessary and proper clause was congressional passage in 1791 of the Bank Bill, chartering the United States National Bank as a private national corporation with shares to be held jointly by the United States and private individuals. The bank would, among other things, furnish credit to the government, serve as fiscal agent to the Treasury, and issue a uniform national paper currency based on commercial credit.[17] The proposal for the bank was submitted to Congress by Secretary of the Treasury Alexander Hamilton. All twenty members of the Senate who had been delegates to the Constitutional Convention voted for the measure, as did four of the seven delegates who were then members of the House.

Nevertheless, the legislation raised serious constitutional issues. Opponents of the bank contended that Congress did not have the authority to charter a corporation that would own and operate a national bank. To determine its constitutionality, President George Washington sought opinions from three members of his cabinet who were lawyers, Attorney General Edmund Randolph, Secretary of State Thomas Jefferson, and Treasury Secretary Hamilton. Randolph and Hamilton had been delegates to the Convention, and Jefferson, as a result of his close relationship to many of the delegates, was privy to much information about the proceedings. Because the Constitution did not specify the power in question, the issue turned on whether the necessary and proper clause created or implied sufficient authority to permit Congress to pass the Bank Bill. Both Randolph and Jefferson concluded that the clause did not provide this power, while Hamilton disagreed.

Randolph advised Washington that Congress had no powers that were not delegated to it, that the specified powers of Congress did not include the power to grant charters of incorporation, and that the necessary and proper clause added nothing substantial to Congress' powers. The latter provision, Randolph urged, should be considered "as among the surplusage which has often proceed[ed] from inattention as caution."[18] Jefferson agreed with these observations, and as Randolph had done, relied in part on the then pending tenth amendment to support his view that only those means indispensible to implementation could be implied:

> I consider the foundation of the Constitution as laid on this ground: That "all powers not delegated to the United States, by the Constitution, nor prohibited by it to the States are reserved to the states or to the people." To take a single step beyond the boundaries thus specially drawn around the powers of Congress is to take possession of a boundless field of power no longer susceptible of any definition. . . .
>
> It has been urged that a bank will give great facility or convenience in the collection of taxes. Suppose this were true: yet the Constitution allows only the means which are "*necessary*," not those which are merely "convenient" for effecting the enumerated powers. If such a latitude of construction be allowed to this phrase as to give any nonenumerated power, it will go to every one, for there is not one which ingenuity may not torture into a *convenience* in some instance *or other*, to *some one* of so long a list of enumerated powers. It would swallow up all the delegated powers, and reduce the whole to one power, as before observed. Therefore it was that the Constitution restrained

them to the *necessary* means, that is to say, to those means without which the grant of power would be nugatory. . . .[19]

In an opinion that seems totally inconsistent with the position that he took in *The Federalist* No. 33, Hamilton asserted "that the principles of construction like those espoused by the Secretary of State and Attorney General would be fatal to the just and indispensable authority of the United States." As for the necessary and proper clause:

The whole turn of the clause containing it, indicates, that it was the intent of the convention, by that clause to give a liberal latitude to the exercise of the specified powers. . . .

[The alternative] construction would beget endless uncertainty & embarrassment. The cases must be palpable & extreme in which it could be pronounced with certainty, that a measure was absolutely necessary, or one without which the exercise of a given power would be nugatory. There are few measures of any government, which would stand so severe a test. To insist upon it, would be to make the criterion of the exercise of any implied power a *case of extreme necessity*; which is rather a rule to justify the overleaping of the bounds of constitutional authority, than to govern the ordinary exercise of it. . . .

The *degree* in which a measure is necessary, can never be a test of the *legal* right to adopt it. That must ever be a matter of opinion; and can only be a test of expediency. The *relation* between the *measure* and the *end*, between the *nature* of the *mean* employed toward the execution of a power and the object of that power, must be the criterion of constitutionality not the more or less of *necessity* or *utility*.[20]

This was the kind of interpretation that the anti-Federalists warned would be made, part of the "virulent invective and petulant declamation" Hamilton had decried in No. 33.[21] Nevertheless, President Washington accepted Hamilton's advice and signed the legislation incorporating the Bank of the United States.

In contrast to Hamilton's change in perspective, Madison maintained the position that he had advanced in *The Federalist* No. 44. When the House of Representatives originally considered the Bank Bill, Madison, then a Congressman from Virginia, opposed it, arguing that the necessary and proper clause did not provide the requisite authority.

Whatever meaning this clause may have, none can be admitted, that would give an unlimited discretion to Congress.

Its meaning must, according to the natural and obvious force of the terms and the context, be limited to means necessary to the end, and incident to the nature of the specified powers.

The clause is in fact merely declaratory of what would have resulted by unavoidable implication, as the appropriate, and, as it were, technical means of executing those powers. In this sense it has been explained by the friends of the Constitution, and ratified by the State Conventions.

The essential characteristic of the Government, as composed of limited and enumerated powers, would be destroyed, if instead of direct and incidental means, any means could be used which, in the language of the preamble to the bill, "might be conceived to be conducive to the successful conducting of the finances, or might be conceived to tend to give facility to the obtaining of loans". . . .

If, again, Congress by virtue of the power to borrow money, can create the ability to lend, they may, by virtue of the power to levy money, create the ability to pay it. The ability to pay taxes depends on the general wealth of the society, and this, on the general prosperity of agriculture, manufactures, and commerce. Congress then may give bounties and make regulations on all these objects. . . .

Mark the reasoning on which the validity of the bill depends. To borrow money is made the end, and the accumulation of capitals implied as the means. The accumulation of money is then the end, and the Bank implied as the means. The Bank is then the end, and a charter of incorporation, a monopoly, . . . & c. implied as the means.

If implications, thus remote and thus multiplied, can be linked together, a claim may be formed that will reach every object of legislation, every object within the whole compass of political economy.

The latitude of interpretation required by the bill is condemned by the rule furnished by the Constitution itself.

Congress have power: "to regulate the value of money;" yet it is expressly added, not left to be implied, that counterfeiters may be punished.

They have the power "to declare war", to which armies are more incident, than incorporated banks to borrowing; yet the power "to raise and support armies" is expressly added; and to this again, the express power "to make rules and regulations for the government of armies;" a like remark is applicable to the powers as to the navy.

The regulation and calling out of militia are more appurtenant to war than the proposed Bank to borrowing; yet the former is not left to construction.

The very power to borrow money is a less remote implication from the power of war, than an incorporated monopoly Bank from the power of borrowing; yet the power is not left to implication.

But the proposed Bank could not be called necessary to the Government; at most could be but convenient. Its uses to the Government could be supplied by keeping the taxes a little in advance; by loans from individuals; by other Banks, over which the Government would have equal command; nay greater, as it might grant or refuse to these the privilege (a free and irrevocable gift to the proposed Bank) of using their notes in the Federal Revenue.[22]

McCulloch v. Maryland

In 1811, the bank's twenty-year charter terminated, and Congress refused renewal. Pressures remained high for creating another such institution, and in 1816, Congress passed legislation incorporating the second Bank of the United States. As was the case previously, the bank served as the government's principal fiscal agent, and its stock was owned by both private investors and the government.

Because of considerable public hostility to the bank, a number of states enacted legislation heavily taxing its branches, usually as a means of terminating their existence. The most famous instance occurred in 1818 when Maryland imposed a tax of 2 percent of the face value of the notes issued, or $15,000 annually, on all banks or branches of banks "not chartered by the legislature." The target of this tax was the Baltimore branch of the national bank whose local cashier, James William McCulloch, refused to pay the tax. Maryland sued in state court obtaining judgment against the cashier for the statutory penalty. On appeal, the U. S. Supreme Court in *McCulloch v. Maryland* unanimously reversed the Maryland courts.[23] This opinion written by Chief Justice John Marshall and issued on March 7, 1819, is one of the most important in the constitutional history of the United States.

The opinion deals with two questions. First, has Congress power to incorporate a bank? Second, if so, may a state tax the bank? Without evidencing any doubt or hesitation, Marshall proceeded to answer the first inquiry in the affirmative and second in the negative. In this book we consider only the first issue.

While consistently acknowledging the federal government to be one of specific powers, Marshall asserted that the Constitution allows Congress to exercise powers vastly greater than those enumerated. Congress may adopt legislation that is not prohibited and is "really calculated to effect any of the objects entrusted to the government." The degree of necessity is largely a matter for the legislature with only a very limited role for the courts. Thus he rejected Madison's and Jefferson's argument that the Constitution authorizes only those means absolutely or indispensably necessary to implement an enumerated power.

Marshall's interpretation enabled Congress to exercise virtually complete discretion in the means that it employs. Anyone who opposes a particular means has the difficult burden of proving that it is unauthorized. This interpretation bears little resemblance to the one that Madison and Hamilton presented in *The Federalist Papers* of a government whose powers are so few and so precisely defined that it lacks the authority to curtail personal liberties and most state undertakings. Indeed, Marshall viewed the national government in a far different light than had the Federalists during the ratification debates—a fact that is revealed in the following excerpts from *McCulloch v. Maryland.*

> A constitution, to contain an accurate detail of all the subdivisions of which its great powers will admit, and of all the means by which they may be carried into execution, would partake of a prolixity of a legal code, and could scarcely be embraced by the human mind. It would probably never be understood by the public. Its nature, therefore, requires, that only its great outlines should be marked, its important objects designated, and the minor ingredients which composed those objects be deduced from the nature of the objects themselves. . . . In considering this question, then, we must never forget, that it is *a constitution* we are expounding.
>
> Although, among the enumerated powers of government, we do not find the word "bank" or "incorporation," we find the great powers to lay and collect taxes; to borrow money; to regulate commerce; to declare and conduct a war; and to raise and support armies and navies. The sword and the purse, all the external relations, and no inconsiderable portion of the industry of the nation, are entrusted to its government. It can never be pretended that these vast powers draw after them others of inferior importance, merely because they are inferior. . . . But it may with great reason be contended, that a government, entrusted with such ample powers, on the due execution of which the happiness and prosperity of the nation so vitally depends, must also be entrusted with ample means for their execution. The power being given, it is the interest of the nation to facilitate its execution. It can never be their interest, and cannot be presumed to have been their intention, to clog and embarrass its execution by withholding the most appropriate means. . . . Can we adopt that construction (unless the words imperiously require it) which would impute to the framers of that instrument, when granting these powers for the public good, the intention of impeding their exercise by withholding a choice of means? . . .[24]
>
> The government which has a right to do an act, and has imposed on it the duty of performing that act, must, according to the dictates of reason, be allowed to select the means; and those who contend that it may not select any appropriate means, that one particular mode of effecting the object is excepted, take upon themselves the burden of establishing that exception.[25]

On this basis, the necessary and proper clause was not required to expand power, but could instead be considered, as the attorneys for Maryland argued, a restraint on the legislative powers to those only necessary and proper to achieve a permitted purpose. Marshall rejected this position.

> The subject is the execution of those great powers on which the welfare of a nation essentially depends. It must have been the intention of those who gave these powers, to insure, as far as human prudence could insure, their beneficial execution. This could not be done by confiding the choice of means to such narrow limits as not to leave it in the power of Congress to adopt any

which might be appropriate, and which were conducive to the end. This provision is made in a constitution intended to endure for ages to come, and, consequently, to be adapted to the various *crises* of human affairs. To have prescribed the means by which government should, in all future time, execute its powers, would have been to change, entirely, the character of the instrument, and give it the properties of a legal code. It would have been an unwise attempt to provide, by immutable rules, for exigencies which, if foreseen at all, must have been seen dimly, and which can be best provided for as they occur. To have declared that the best means shall not be used, but those alone without which the power given would be nugatory, would have been to deprive the legislature of the capacity to avail itself of experience, to exercise its reason, and to accommodate its legislation to circumstances. If we apply this principle of construction to any of the powers of the government, we shall find it so pernicious in its operation that we shall be compelled to discard it. . . .[26]

In ascertaining the sense in which the word "necessary" is used in this clause of the constitution, we may derive some aid from that with which it is associated. Congress shall have power "to make all laws which shall be necessary and *proper* to carry into execution" the powers of the government. If the word "necessary" was used in that strict and rigorous sense for which the counsel for the state of Maryland contend, it would be an extraordinary departure from the usual course of the human mind, as exhibited in composition, to add a word, the only possible effect of which is to qualify that strict and rigorous meaning; to present to the mind the idea of some choice of means of legislation not straightened and compressed within the narrow limits for which gentlemen contend. . . .[27]

We admit, as all must admit, that the powers of the government are limited, and that its limits are not to be transcended. But we think the sound construction of the constitution must allow to the national legislature that discretion, with respect to the means by which the powers it confers are to be carried into execution, which will enable that body to perform the high duties assigned to it, in the manner most beneficial to the people. Let the end be legitimate, let it be within the scope of the Constitution, and all means which are appropriate, which are plainly adapted to that end, which are not prohibited, but consist [sic] with the letter and spirit of the constitution, are constitutional. . . .[28]

Should Congress, in the execution of its powers, adopt measures which are prohibited by the constitution; or should Congress, under the pretext of executing its powers, pass laws for the accomplishment of objects not entrusted to the government, it would become the painful duty of this tribunal, should a case requiring such a decision come before it, to say that such an act was not the law of the land. But where the law is not prohibited, and is really calculated to effect any of the objects entrusted to the government, to undertake here to inquire into the degree of its necessity, would be to pass the line which circumscribes the judicial department, and to tread on legislative ground. This court disclaims all pretensions to such a power.[29]

Thus Marshall persuasively described a scheme of government that had little relation to the one established in 1789. The authority and deference that Marshall was willing to accord Congress in this opinion does not conform with his conclusions in the famous case of *Marbury v. Madison*. In *Marbury* he rejected the idea that the legislature could determine the limits of its powers.

> The powers of the legislature are defined and limited; and that those limits may not be mistaken, or forgotten, the constitution is written. To what purpose are powers limited, and to what purpose is that limitation committed to writing, if these limits may, at any time, be passed by those intended to be restrained? The distinction between a government with limited and unlimited powers is abolished, if those limits do not confine the persons on whom they are imposed, and if acts prohibited and acts allowed, are of equal obligation. It is a proposition too plain to be contested, that the constitution controls any legislative act repugnant to it; or, that the legislature may alter the constitution by an ordinary act.
>
> Between these alternatives, there is no middle ground.[30]

This reasoning is consistent with the views presented by the Federalists in the ratification debates and almost totally at variance with those set forth in *McCulloch*.

In the portion of his opinion with which we are concerned, Marshall neither considered the proceedings of the Constitutional Convention nor referred to the Federalists' arguments in the ratification debates. Moreover he made no mention of *The Federalist Papers*. Although Marshall was perhaps adhering to a contemporary practice of not delving into legislative history, in the second portion of his opinion, he does discuss sections of *The Federalist Papers* and concludes that their authors supported his position on the invalidity of the Maryland tax.[31] He could not, however, find support in them for his position on the scope of the national powers—a fact that probably explains why they are not mentioned in the first part of the opinion. Marshall also ignored the history of the Constitutional Convention that related to the federal chartering of corporations, although it would seem highly relevant to the subject at hand.

In commenting on the constitutionality of the first Bank Bill, both Jefferson and Madison stated that a proposal empowering Congress to grant charters of incorporation had been made and rejected during the Constitutional Convention. Hamilton replied that the precise nature of the proposition and the reason for its rejection were in doubt, so that no inference could be drawn bearing on the powers of Congress. No official document on this matter was available to the *McCulloch* Court. Sessions of the Convention were secret; the official journal was not published until late in 1819, after the *McCulloch* decision had been handed down. The most complete accounts are the notes that Madison made during the Convention, and these notes were not published until 1840.

Madison's notes relevant to this issue are basically confirmed by the journal and the notes taken by delegate James McHenry. According to Madison's notes, three days prior to final adjournment, Benjamin Franklin moved to add to article I, section 8: "a power to provide for cutting canals where deemed necessary." Madison moved to expand the motion "to grant charters of incorporation when the interests of the U.S. might require and legislative provisions of individual states may be incompetent." James Wilson seconded the first motion, and Edmund Randolph, the second. Like the originators of these proposals, both of these gentlemen were influential in the Convention; they subsequently served in high governmental posts, Wilson as a Supreme Court Justice, and Randolph, as Attorney General.

Franklin's motion was rejected, 8-3, and Madison wrote that the "other part fell of course, as including the power rejected."[32] Although no certainty exists about why these proposals were voted down, the episode does lend credence to the position that the Constitution does not grant Congress very extensive economic powers and more specifically that it confers no authority on that body to charter corporations. At least four active and knowledgeable members of the Convention seem to have accepted this position. Consequently, the major substance of Marshall's opinion is questionable. Moreover, failure even to consider this episode, which it is difficult to believe Marshall was not aware of, detracts from the quality of the opinion and the credibility of its author. To be sure, advocates of a position are not usually inclined to present facts favoring the opposition. However, a judicial opinion should not be partisan; it should be a reasoned explanation rather than an advocacy brief.

Commenting on the *McCulloch* decision, Albert Beveridge, Marshall's laudatory biographer declared: "In effect John Marshall thus rewrote the fundamental law of the Nation."[33] Beveridge goes on to explain that the country would benefit greatly from the construction that Marshall gave to the Constitution. However, many of the Chief Justice's contemporaries did not agree. In fact, Marshall's decision aroused a large amount of protest, ranging from those who saw it as a gross misconstruction to those who condemned it on policy grounds. The harshest criticism consisted of charges that he had turned the Constitution on its head. No doubt can exist that Marshall was aware of this protest for it had been expressed before the Court by Luther Martin, Maryland Attorney General, who had been a delegate to the Constitutional Convention.

Moreover, Marshall himself had been a delegate to the Virginia ratification convention and thus knew the nature of the debate that took place. At the Virginia Convention, George Nicholas, urging ratification, insisted that the necessary clause did not delegate any additional powers; it "only enables [the national government] to carry into execution the powers given to [it]." Edmund Pendleton agreed: "I understand that clause as not going a single step beyond the delegated powers."[34]

In his argument against the constitutionality of the Bank Bill, Martin read several extracts from *The Federalist Papers* and the debates that occurred during the Virginia and New York ratification conventions to show that the position of the Constitution's proponents was "wholly repugnant to that" relied on in support of the bank. In contrast to the arguments of its supporters, the enemies of the Constitution, asserted Martin, maintained that it contained a vast array of powers, lurking under the generality of its phraseology, which would prove highly dangerous to the liberties of the people and the rights of states unless controlled by some declaratory amendment that could negate their existence. "This apprehension was treated as a dream of distempered jealousy", said Martin as he urged the Supreme Court to prove that the Constitution's friends had not been wrong.

> We are now called upon to apply that theory of interpretation which was then rejected by the friends of the new constitution, and we are asked to engraft upon it powers of vast extent, which were disclaimed by them, and which, if they had been fairly avowed at the time, would have prevented its adoption. Before we do this, they must, at least, be proved to exist, upon a candid examination of this instrument, as if it were now for the first time submitted to interpretation. Although we cannot, perhaps, be allowed to say that the states have been "deceived in their grant," yet we may justly claim something like a rigorous demonstration of this power, which nowhere appears upon the face of the constitution, but which is supposed to be tacitly inculcated in its general object and spirit.[35]

Marshall should have understood this argument well because of his own experience in his state's ratification convention. From the accounts of that convention, it appears doubtful that the Constitution as interpreted by Marshall in the *McCulloch* case, would have been approved in Virginia. As a result of some very clever maneuvering, the Federalists had won major votes at the convention by a slender margin of 10 out of a total of 168.[36] Virginia assented to the Constitution but only with severe reservations, as previously reported. (The same had also occurred in South Carolina, New York, and Rhode Island.)

In addition, the Virginia convention recommended that Congress consider the adoption of a Bill of Rights to consist of twenty articles plus another twenty amendments to the body of the Constitution. These additions and changes would have greatly curtailed the federal power; the ten amendments subsequently made to the Constitution were "hardly a shadow"[37] of those proposed by Virginia. Beveridge reports that a large majority of Virginians was opposed to the proposed Constitution, and that most wanted nothing stronger than the weak and ineffective government of their own state.[38]

John Marshall was an extraordinarily talented thinker and writer. He had a remarkable influence on the Court; only once during his thirty-four years as Chief Justice did he file a dissenting opinion on a constitutional matter. His *McCulloch* opinion is an able and extensive dissertation on an important constitutional issue. Interestingly, it was delivered just three days after the completion of arguments—a fact indicating that it had been in preparation some time previously. Little question exists that had he been so disposed, he could have fashioned an equally impressive opinion supporting the reverse position—that the Bank Bill was not constitutional. He would have had merely to expand on the reasoning that he presented in *Marbury*, as previously quoted. However, Marshall's inclinations were nationalist, favoring a strong central government, and that leaning probably more than any other factor explains the *McCulloch* decision.

Madison, Jefferson, and Randolph were otherwise disposed, and if fate had projected them (or their appointees, in the case of the first two) into the same position of authority, the outcome would have been different. Such experiences reveal that constitutional law is quite frequently the rule of persons and not of law—a situation that, ironically, a constitutional system is supposed to preclude.

As it happens, Oliver Ellsworth resigned his position as Chief Justice after Jefferson was elected President but before he was inaugurated. Had this chronology been different, Jefferson probably would have appointed Spencer Roane as Chief Justice upon Ellsworth's resignation or death. Roane's views on "federalism" were nearly opposite Marshall's. However, like Marshall, he was able, persuasive, and fiercely dedicated to his ideas. Judging from his record as a politician and jurist, one can imagine that he could have swung a majority in his direction, or at the least greatly moderated the nationalist tone of the *McCulloch* opinion.

Perhaps, as some commentators maintain in support of Marshall's decision, a fundamental law must always be a living document, capable of growth and of keeping pace with a changing of society. Supreme Court Justices must therefore assure that the Constitution reflects this understanding. But can such responsibility include complete reversal of the most important features of the fundamental law—the core of the original concept? This question raises further thoughts about the legal process. Do legal opinions mean very much if they do not disclose the true basis of decisions? If a judge has decided that new events merit new interpretations, he or she should so advise us in order to preclude an opinion from being simply an exercise in sophistry.

Comments such as the foregoing were among the mildest directed at Marshall by critics of the *McCulloch* decision. Not surprisingly, a storm of protest erupted after this opinion was handed down. Jefferson strongly attacked it and judicial review, which, he thought, made such judicial usurpations inevitable.[39] He and other critics claimed that states' rights and localism were now subordinate to the national government. Beveridge relates the resulting outcry:

1. The country's most widely read and influential paper, the *Weekly Register*, printed the opinion in order to disparage it, giving it wider circulation than any other judicial utterance had experienced. The newspaper strongly condemned the decision and papers throughout the country echoed this criticism, with some also publishing the opinion.
2. Under an assumed name, Spencer Roane, then a judge of the Virginia Court of Appeals, wrote newspaper articles criticizing the opinion.
3. John Taylor, a highly regarded Virginia political theoretician, wrote a book denouncing and refuting John Marshall's nationalist principles. He devoted five of his 16 chapters to the *McCulloch* decision.
4. The Virginia Legislature adopted a resolution denouncing the nationalist doctrine contained in the opinion and urging constitutional amendments to prevent nationalist domination. Pennsylvania, Ohio, Indiana, Illinois, and Tennessee passed comparable resolutions.[40]

The Chief Justice was sufficiently disturbed by this criticism, particularly that from Roane, his longtime antagonist, that he took the unusual step of writing newspaper articles under the *nom de plume* of "A Friend of the Union," defending his opinion, and castigating his attackers. Two essays appeared in the *Philadelphia Union*, a leading Federalist newspaper, and nine more were subsequently published in the *Alexandria Gazette*. Marshall sought to calm the critics. He insisted that congressional power remained confined, contending that the opinion limited Congress to enacting legislation legitimately furthering specified powers. He denied that the Court had granted unlimited powers to the federal government under the pretext of having discretion in selecting the means.[41]

Perhaps because of the nationalist pressures of our society, a *McCulloch*-type decision was inevitable. Nevertheless, such a conclusion does not discharge the Supreme Court's responsibility to implement the language and meaning of the fundamental law, especially when the essence of the original understanding is involved.

Notes

1. *See* letter from James Madison to Judge Spencer Roane, September 2, 1819 in 3 MAX FARRAND, THE RECORDS OF THE FEDERAL CONVENTION OF 1787, at

435 (rev. ed. 1937) (New Haven, Conn. and London: Yale University Press, 1966).

2. *See* text accompanying *infra* notes 15, 16, 36, 37 and 38.
3. THE FEDERALIST PAPERS NO. 33 (A. Hamilton) at 202 (New York and Scarborough, Ont.: Mentor Books, 1961).
4. *Id.* at 203.
5. *Id.* at 284 (J. Madison).
6. *Id.* at 284-85.
7. *Id.* at 285.
8. *Id.* at 513-14 (A. Hamilton).
9. *Quoted in* GORDON S. WOOD, THE CREATION OF THE AMERICAN REPUBLIC 1776-1787, at 538 (Chapel Hill, N.C.: University of North Carolina Press, 1969) citing various Debates (Elliot, ed.), (Philadelphia: J.B. Lippincott Co., 1936).
10. THE FEDERALIST NO. 45 (J. Madison) at 292-93.
11. THE FEDERALIST NO. 39 (J. Madison) at 245.
12. THE FEDERALIST NO. 17 (A. Hamilton) at 119-20.
13. Ogden v. Saunders, 25 U.S. (12 Wheat.) 213, at 356 (1827) (Marshall, C. J., dissenting).
14. *Quoted in* WOOD, *supra* note 9, at 539, citing PENNSYLVANIA AND THE FEDERAL CONSTITUTION (McMaster and Stone, eds.) 143-44, 313-14.
15. THE MAKING OF THE AMERICAN REPUBLIC, THE GREAT DOCUMENTS 1774-1789, at 1009-59 (Charles Callan Tansill, ed.) (New Rochelle, N.Y.: Arlington House, 1972). The reader will note that the words *clearly* or *expressly delegated* were used in the New York, Rhode Island, and South Carolina ratifications above set forth.
16. McCulloch v. Maryland, 17 U.S. (4 Wheat.) 316, 406-8 (1819) discussed hereinafter.
17. *See* RICHARD H. TIMBERLAKE, JR., THE ORIGINS OF CENTRAL BANKING IN THE UNITED STATES 4-11 (Cambridge, Mass. and London: Harvard University Press, 1978).
18. *Quoted in* 1 WILLIAM WINSLOW CROSSKEY, POLITICS AND THE CONSTITUTION 207 (Chicago: University of Chicago Press, 1953) citing M. S. CLARKE AND D. A. HALL, LEGISLATIVE AND DOCUMENTARY HISTORY OF THE BANK OF THE UNITED STATES, at 86-91. (Washington, 1832).
19. *Opinion on the Constitutionality of the Bill for Establishing a National Bank* in 19 PAPERS OF THOMAS JEFFERSON 275, 279-80 (1974).
20. 8 PAPERS OF ALEXANDER HAMILTON 97 (1965).
21. THE FEDERALIST, *supra* note 3, at 201.
22. 2 ANNALS OF CONGRESS 1898-1901 (Gales and Seaton, Ed., 1791).
23. 17 U.S. (4 Wheat.) 316 (1819).
24. *Id.* at 407-8.
25. *Id.* at 409-10.
26. *Id.* at 415-16.
27. *Id.* at 418-19.
28. *Id.* at 421.
29. *Id.* at 423.
30. Marbury v. Madison, 5 U.S. (1 Cranch) 137, at 176-77 (1803). This decision held that a section of the Judiciary Act of 1789 authorizing mandamus actions in the U.S. Supreme Court violated article III, sec. 2, which does not enumerate such actions as part of the Court's original jurisdiction.

31. 17 U.S. at 433-35.
32. 2 FARRAND 615, at 616 (Madison's notes).
33. 4 ALBERT J. BEVERIDGE, THE LIFE OF JOHN MARSHALL at 308 (Boston and New York; Houghton Mifflin Company, 1919).
34. 3 ELLIOT'S DEBATES 245-46, 441 (Philadelphia: J.B. Lippincott Company, 1836).
35. 17 U.S. at 373 (Statement of Mr. Martin, Attorney General of Maryland).
36. 1 BEVERIDGE, *supra* note 33 at 475-76 (1916).
37. *Id.* at 477.
38. *Id.* at 321, 322, 356, 391, 469.
39. THE PORTABLE JEFFERSON 286, 994-95 (Peterson, ed. 1975).
40. 4 BEVERIDGE *supra* note 33 at 309-39.
41. *Id.* at 318-23.

2

Paper Money and Legal Tender

In replying to critics of his *McCulloch* opinion, Chief Justice Marshall emphasized that the decision was unanimous. The judicial branch was merely implementing its sworn duty of upholding the Constitution; the outcome had no relationship to the ideology or political persuasion of the Justices, who regardless of public opinion or personal interest, were preserving the Constitution.

While unanimous decisions such as *McCulloch* tend to support this theory of a judicial branch devoid of subjectivity and partisanship, concerned solely with securing the fundamental law, the four major decisions relating to the validity of paper money and legal tender paper lead to a contrary conclusion. In these cases, the opinions were divided, and, because of changes in the Court's composition, subsequent decisions conflicted with a prior one. Divided opinions reveal the absence of universal truth; appointments that lead directly to a particular outcome suggest partisanship. What is one supposed to think about the rule of law when the naming of two new Justices quickly leads to reversal of a major decision issued on the date of their appointment? Nor is confidence in the judiciary encouraged by knowlege that many businesses proceeded as if they had anticipated this reversal. Capping these faults is the fact that the Court, disregarding the Framers' intention, ruled that Congress possesses unlimited power to issue paper money and designate it legal tender.

Such is the experience of the decisions with which this chapter is concerned.

The Framers' Position on Paper Money

In recent years inflation has aroused great concern regarding the amount of money in circulation. We have learned that an inverse correlation exists between the supply of money and the value of the dollar. At present, the government, through the Federal Reserve System, is largely responsible for determining the money supply at any given period. Under authority of Congress, the national government prints, in various amounts and denominations, bills known as either Federal Reserve Notes or United States Notes each of which contains the inscription: "This note is legal tender for all debts, public and private." These notes are not redeemable in either gold or silver, and they are worth no more than their exchange value for goods and services, which, of course, fluctuates. By contrast, for a long period in the past, the government issued paper redeemable in gold or silver. The money supply was thus contained by the stock of precious metals. Without such a lever, no limit exists on the emission of money.

The power to print paper money and require its acceptance as legal tender is, of course, critical in the commerce of a country and can greatly influence the course of its economy. However, the Constitution does not specifically grant such powers to Congress.

The story of how Congress acquired unlimited authority to issue paper money and confer on it legal tender status involves the U.S. Supreme Court and some decisions that are highly controversial with respect to both the substance and the judicial disposition of the issue. It is most doubtful that the Framers intended Congress to possess such authority.

To understand this conclusion, let us turn to accounts of the 1787 Constitutional Convention, this time as they relate to the emission of paper money. In brief, in article I, section 10 the Framers expressly prohibited the states from making "any Thing but gold and silver coin a Tender in Payment of Debts" and from emitting "Bills of Credit"—the phrase that then meant paper that was intended to circulate as money and that was not redeemable in gold or silver. They did not grant these powers to Congress except for the provision in article I, section 8 that accords that body the authority to "coin money, regulate the value thereof, and of foreign coin." The states were thus denied paper emissions and legal tender authority that they had previously possessed, and the federal government was not empowered to exercise either one except as it related to coin. Nonetheless, the Supreme Court has interpreted the Constitution to allow the federal government complete discretion in issuing paper money and making it legal tender.

The authority to print paper money was an issue of great importance to the Framers, who had personal experience with the flood of depreciated notes issued by state governments and the confederacy itself, the latter in order to finance the Revolution. Although the delegates to the Constitutional Convention readily admitted that such large emissions might at times have popular and legislative support, almost everyone who spoke on the issue recognized that the power to issue money could be employed irresponsibly with adverse consequences to the country's economy.

As Professor Kenneth Dam writes, the Framers "had seen it [paper money], and the devastating effect of issuing too much of it, in detail and profusion."[1] In June, 1775, the Continental Congress began to emit bills of credit; by 1780, $100 in paper was worth only $2.50 in specie. During the following year, this paper was practically valueless—it was, as the saying goes, "not worth a Continental." Similar problems existed in the states, with Virginia currency valued in 1780 at 0.1 percent of that which it originally had been. After the demise of its paper currency, the Continental Congress was forced to depend almost entirely on bond issues that were sold in Europe.[2]

Early in the 1787 Convention, Gouverneur Morris, the prominent and influential delegate from Pennsylvania, voiced commonly held apprehensions about the tendency of legislative bodies to be irresponsible in economic matters.

> Emissions of paper money, largesses to the people—a remission of debts and similar measures, will at sometimes be popular, and will be pushed for that reason. At other times such measures will coincide with the interests of the Legislature themselves, and that will be a reason not less cogent for pushing them.

Morris warned that "were the National legislature formed and a war was now to break out, this ruinous expedient [paper money] would be again resorted to, if not guarded against."[3]

Because the power both to borrow money and to emit bills had been granted Congress under the Articles of Confederation, they were automatically extended to the new government in an early draft of the Constitution prepared by the Committee of Detail. The Articles had empowered the United States, in Congress assembled, "to borrow money or emit bills on the credit of the United States" upon the assent of nine states.[4] When the powers of the legislative branch were spelled out in the committee's draft to include the power to "borrow money, and emit bills on the credit of the U.S.," Morris moved to strike out the latter phrase. His explanation that "if the United States had credit such bills would be unnecessary: if they had not, unjust and useless" reached sympathetic ears. The motion was seconded by South Carolina's Pierce Butler.[5]

A lively discussion ensued, as recorded by James Madison, who was himself a participant and initially questioned the need for a complete limitation on emissions: "[W]ill it not be sufficient to prohibit the making them a *tender*? This will remove the temptation to emit them with unjust views. And promissory notes in that shape may in some emergencies be best."[6]

Madison's concern, presumably, was not with the issuance of bills but rather with granting them the status of a legal tender. He reflected the view of others who foresaw a time of war or other emergency that would create the need for borrowing without a backup in specie. But so long as such borrowing could be effected only through interest bonds or promissory notes that could be negotiated in trade, he felt that there would be no danger. Madison was not favorable to paper money. In *The Federalist* No. 44, he made known this antagonism in commenting on the constitutional ban on state bills of credit.

> The loss which America has sustained since the peace, from the pestilent effects of paper money on the necessary confidence between man and man, on the necessary confidence in the public councils, on the industry and morals of the people and on the character of republican government, constitutes an enormous debt against the States chargeable with this unadvised measure, which must long remain unsatisfied; or rather an accumulation of guilt, which can be expiated no otherwise than by a voluntary sacrifice on the altar of justice of the power which has been the instrument of it.[7]

Morris defended his move to eliminate the emission power: "[S]triking out the words [emit Bills, etc.] will leave room still for notes of a *responsible* minister which will do all the good without the mischief. The Monied interest will oppose the plan of Government, if paper emissions be not prohibited." Thus the power "to borrow money" would enable issuance of promissory notes, making any reference to emitting bills unnecessary. Apparently Morris believed that the absence of language authorizing emissions was enough to deny Congress this power. Neither he nor any other delegate sought to insert a specific ban. Nathaniel Gorham of Massachusetts was for striking the language without inserting a prohibition; "if the words stand they may suggest and lead to the measure." The government would not be disabled in its absence, for "[t]he power as far as it will be necessary or safe, is involved in that of borrowing."

George Mason of Virginia believed that Congress "would not have the power unless it were expressed" and feared that this result would hamstring the federal legislature in emergencies and future wars.

According to Madison's notes, only John Mercer of Maryland, "a friend to paper money," voiced strong opposition to Morris' motion. Recognizing the temper of the times, Mercer nevertheless objected that the denial of such discretionary power would create suspicion toward the government. He further cautioned that it was unwise to excite the opposition of all those who were friends of paper money. "The people of property would be sure to be on the side of the plan, and it was impolitic to purchase their further attachment with the loss of the opposite class of Citizens."

Madison summarized the position of other delegates who spoke on Morris' motion as follows:

Oliver Ellsworth of Connecticut

> thought this a favorable moment to shut and bar the door against paper money. The mischiefs of the various experiments which had been made, were now fresh in the public mind and had excited the disgust of all the respectable part of America. By withholding the power from the new government, more friends of influence would be gained to it than by almost any thing else. Paper money can in no case be necessary. Give the Government credit, and other resources will offer. The power may do harm, never good.

Edmund Randolph of Virginia, "notwithstanding his antipathy to paper money, could not agree to strike out the words, as he could not foresee all the occasions that might arise." James Wilson of Pennsylvania, however, thought that it would "have a most salutary influence on the credit of the United States to remove the possibility of paper money. This expedient can never succeed whilst its mischiefs are remembered. And as long as it can be resorted to, it will be a bar to other resources."

Pierce Butler "remarked that paper was a legal tender in no Country in Europe. He was urgent for disarming the Government of such a power."

Mason "was still averse to tying the hands of the legislature *altogether*. If there was no example in Europe as just remarked, it might be observed on the other side, that there was none in which the Government was restrained on this head."

George Read of Delaware "thought the words, if not struck out, would be as alarming as the mark of the Beast in Revelations." John Langdon of New Hampshire "had rather reject the whole plan than retain the three words ['and emit bills']."

In the end, Madison's doubts appear to have been resolved. He became

> satisfied that striking out the words would not disable the government from the use of public notes as far as they could be safe and proper; and would only cut off the pretext for a paper currency and particularly for making the bills a tender either for public or private debts.

When the vote was taken, Morris's motion to strike passed 9-2, with only New Jersey and Maryland dissenting.[8]

Subsequently, a draft of the Constitution was considered in which the clause prohibiting the states from emitting bills of credit or making anything but gold and silver a tender in payment of debts, contained the exception: without consent of Congress. However, this exception was eliminated (by a vote of 8-1 with one divided) with Roger Sherman of Connecticut remarking that the time was favorable "for crushing paper money."

Otherwise, he said, its friends would lobby Congress to enable states to emit it.[9]

Luther Martin, attorney general of Maryland, was a delegate to the Constitutional Convention. An opponent of the Constitution and a supporter of paper money, he advised his legislature about the delegates' response to Morris's motion to strike the emission power in the following words:

> Against the motion we urged, that it would be improper to *deprive* the Congress of that *power*; that it would be a novelty unprecedented to establish a government which should not have such authority; that it was impossible to look forward into futurity so far as to decide, that events might not happen that should render the *exercise* of such a power *absolutely* necessary; and that we doubted, whether, if a war should take place, it would be *possible* for this country to *defend* itself, without having recourse to *paper credit*, in which case, there would be a *necessity* of becoming a *prey* to our *enemies*, or *violating* the *constitution* of our government; and that, considering the administration of the government would be principally in the hands of the wealthy, there could be little reason to fear an *abuse* of the *power*, by an unnecessary or injurious exercise of it. But, Sir, a majority of the convention, being wise beyond every event, and being willing to risk any political evil, rather than admit the idea of a paper emission, in any *possible* event, refused to *trust* this authority to a government, to which they were *lavishing* the most *unlimited* powers of *taxation*, and to the *mercy* of which they were willing *blindly* to *trust* the *liberty* and *property* of the *citizens* of *every State* in the Union; and they *erased* that clause from the *system*.[10]

Alexander Hamilton was another of the Framers who strongly rejected federal paper money. He expressed this position in his "Report On a National Bank," written in 1790 when he was Secretary of the Treasury. Hamilton characterized paper emissions as so liable to abuse and even so certain of being abused that the government ought never to trust itself "with the use of so seducing and dangerous an expedient."[11]

During the ratification debates the ban on state powers to issue legal tender paper was discussed with the Federalists generally in support. The anti-Federalists seemed mostly in opposition, although many prominent and influential leaders on their side agreed with the Federalists on this issue. Evidently little or nothing was said relating to the ban on national paper money emissions.[12] Among the harshest critics of paper money were Chief Justice Marshall and Justice Joseph Story, both of whom were strongly Federalist and commented unfavorably on state paper money experiences.[13]

The Framers could have expressly prohibited this power to the Congress. In so doing they would have fully substantiated Justice Stephen Field's belief that the debates established "with moral certainty" their intent to forbid legal tender notes.[14] (Field made this comment in a dissenting opinion delivered in 1884.) Their insertion of emission and legal tender prohibitions on the states might suggest a different treatment for the federal government. However, the states had possessed and utilized these powers prior to the Convention, while the newly created national government had only those powers that were vested in it. The fact that a power was not prohibited did not imply that it was authorized. Any other construction would have made the federal government one of virtually unlimited power, for relatively few powers were specifically denied. The question arises: if the enumeration of powers was meaningless in this situation, why did leading delegates bother both to discuss and remove the power to emit bills of credit and to dispute whether other powers should be enumerated or eliminated?[15] Nevertheless, by not forbidding the power, the Framers did make its exercise possible under Justice Marshall's exceedingly broad interpretation of the necessary and proper clause.

Although Madison's account is sparse, it does allow certain conclusions:

1. The Framers sought substantial limitations on Congress's power to emit paper money. Almost every speaker quoted by Madison assumed that this authority did not have to be expressly forbidden in order that it not be denied to Congress. Speakers with this perspective came from seven different states. Luther Martin's statement confirms this position.
2. The same conclusion applies to Congress's imparting the quality of legal tender to paper money. Only Madison and Butler had spoken critically of legal tender during the debates, but that circumstance does not suggest a different view on the part of the others. An opponent of paper money would be even more antagonistic toward it being given the status of legal tender. Because its acceptance was required, paper with this designation would receive widespread circulation, intensifying the problem of monetary dilution. Giving government power to make paper legal tender would also augment its authority over the economic system, an unsatisfactory outcome for most delegates.
3. Because the power was not banned, Congress could print paper money and designate it legal tender under its necessary and proper power (article I, section 8, clause 18) once the required relationship to an enumerated power had been established. (See Chapter 1 for discussion of necessary and proper power.)
4. In order to accord appropriate recognition to the Framers' purposes, "necessary and proper" in this case should mean not merely "needed or convenient" but rather something akin to "essential and indispensable." The Framers seem to have the same hostile view toward paper money that Federalists of the period generally had. They would certainly have been opposed to emissions merely to achieve political advantage, preferential treatment for debtors, or practical convenience in the operation

of government. A typical constitutional formulation appears applicable in the matter: provided a link to an enumerated power has been established, Congress is empowered to issue unbacked paper money and designate it as legal tender, but only under very special circumstances or conditions.

5. The Framers' deliberations and vote had no bearing on government promissory obligations, which could be issued under the borrowing power.

The High Court and Paper Emissions

Fundamental law on paper money and legal tender was established in three U.S. Supreme Court opinions. The first determined that Congress has authority to print paper money,[16] while the other two held that it has power to make the paper a legal tender in payment of private debts, in time of both war and peace.[17]

Veazie Bank v. Fenno concerned a federal statute passed in 1869 imposing a 10 percent tax on notes issued for circulation by any state bank. The purpose of the tax was to eliminate issuance of these notes, which were then widely used as currency. In his opinion upholding the law, Chief Justice Salmon P. Chase wrote that Congress could utilize the tax as a means to secure a sound and uniform currency for the country, for that body has constitutional powers to provide for a national currency.

> It cannot be doubted that under the Constitution the power to provide a circulation of coin is given to Congress. And it is settled by the uniform practice of the government and by repeated decisions, that Congress may constitutionally authorize the emission of bills of credit. It is not important here to decide whether the quality of legal tender, in payment of debts, can be constitutionally imparted to these bills; it is enough to say, that there can be no question of the power of government to emit them; to make them receivable in payment of debts to itself; to fit them for use by those who see fit to use them in all the transactions of commerce; to provide for their redemption; to make them a currency, uniform in value and description, and convenient and useful for circulation. These powers, until recently were only partially and occasionally exercised.[18]

Chase cited none of the "repeated decisions." I am not aware that any have been discovered. He also did not discuss historical background. Notwithstanding his assertion, the Supreme Court had never actually decided the emission question. On about twenty separate occasions prior to the Civil War, Congress had authorized the Treasury Department to issue small amounts of notes to pay governmental debts. These notes which bore specified interest amounts and due dates, were based on the national credit and were therefore different from a paper emission. Because the latter has no basis in government credit, the accuracy of Chase's statement about prior "uniform practice" is doubtful. Moreover, the assertion that "uniform practice" can make legal the illegal conduct of emitting paper money is hardly consistent with or comforting to a society dedicated to the rule of law.

Subsequent decisions accepted Chase's above quoted statements as setting forth constitutional law on Congress's emission power. Yet his conclusions not only are incorrect but also ignore totally the historical background.

The Chief Justice reserved the legal tender question for another day, which arrived shortly with the court's consideration of *Hepburn v. Griswold*.[19] centuring on the constitutionality of the Legal Tender Act of 1862.

Legal Tender Litigation During the Civil War

On 25 February 1862, in the midst of the Civil War, Congress passed an act authorizing the issuance of $150 million of "notes" redeemable only in six-percent, twenty-year bonds and not in gold or silver coin and providing that these notes should "be lawful money and a legal tender in payment of all debts, public and private, within the United States," except for duties on imports and interest on the public debt, which were still payable in specie. This paper and others of similar character issued subsequently became known as greenbacks because of their distinctive color. They constituted the kind of paper money that was so fervently condemned during the Constitutional Convention and whose issuance was not specifically authorized in the Constitution. Accordingly, the stage was set for a major decision by the U. S. Supreme Court.

The legal issue arose as a result of a promissory note executed by Mrs. Hepburn on 20 June 1860 to pay Mr. Griswold $11,250 on 20 February 1862. At the time that she made the note, and on the date of its maturity, the only form of money that could be lawfully tendered in payment of private debts was gold or silver coin.

The holder of the promissory note subsequently filed suit to collect on it. In March 1864, Hepburn tendered the holder greenbacks issued under the Act in the amount of $12,720, which included principal, accrued interest, and some court costs, in full satisfaction of her note. The payment was refused. The greenbacks were then tendered to the Court, which found the tender good and the debt fully discharged.

Throughout this litigation the value of a dollar in gold was more than the value of a dollar in U.S. notes. At that time a dollar in gold meant the physical amount of gold that was designated a dollar before the Civil War. From mid-1864 to early 1865, this amount of gold was worth more than $2 in notes and was close to that figure at the time of Hepburn's tender. The holder denied that Congress had the power to make the greenbacks a legal tender in payment of debts, which, when contracted, were payable only in gold or silver coins. The U.S. Supreme Court ruled 4-3 (or possibly more correctly 5-3, as we shall learn later) that Congress had no such authority and that, therefore, the Act of 25 February 1862 was unconstitutional with respect to existing contracts.

The case concerned solely the matter of legal tender. The printing of paper money without this requirement was no longer an issue, for in the *Veazie Bank* opinion Chase had stated that Congress could authorize the emission of paper money.

In brief, the majority opinion in *Hepburn*, written by Chief Justice Chase, reasoned as follows:

1. The Constitution does not specifically or by implication empower Congress to make any form of currency other than gold and silver coin a legal tender in payment of debt. The necessary and proper clause also does not provide such authority. While acknowledging the existence of a federal power to issue notes not designated as legal tender, Chase concluded that the government derived no additional benefit from such a designation and consequently that it was not a means appropriate, plainly adapted, or really calculated, to fulfill express powers—Chief Justice Marshall's *McCulloch* formulation.[20] It added nothing to the utility of the notes and if it facilitated the circulation of the notes, it debased the currency to a much greater degree. Moreover, a law not made in pursuance of an express power, operating to impair the obligations of contract is inconsistent with Marshall's *McCulloch* standard, that a necessary law be within the "spirit of the Constitution"—in this instance, maintaining the sanctity of private contracts.
2. *Hepburn* involved retroactive application of the Act and therefore implicated constitutional protections. The law was inconsistent with the letter and spirit of the fifth amendment's taking clause which provides that private property shall not be taken for public use without just compensation since the law appropriated property from one group for the benefit of another.

In addition, it violated the due process clause of the fifth amendment, mandating that no person shall be deprived of life, liberty, or property without due process of law. According to Chase, the provisions of this clause (as well as of the others contained in the fifth amendment) "operate directly in limitation and restraint of the legislative powers conferred by the Constitution." The legal tender law had deprived holders of contracts for payment of monies of a portion of their property.

The legal tender question was highly controversial during the post-Civil War period, with many important figures voicing different opinions on the legislation's merit and validity. Perhaps no one was more intimate with the issue than the author of the majority opinion, who had been secretary of the treasury at the time of the Act's adoption by Congress. In that capacity, Secretary Chase had advised Congress that reluctantly but decidedly he had come to the conclusion that the legal tender clauses were a necessity and that he supported them earnestly. Later (in *Knox v. Lee*, discussed hereafter) he explained that in principle he was actually averse to the legal tender clause but that he was concerned about the delay in passage of the bill which also authorized issuance of U.S. notes. Passage had been delayed by differences of opinion on the question of making the notes a legal tender. Although Chase had strongly urged Congress to adopt the bill because of the fiscal difficulties that the federal government was experiencing, he subsequently acknowleged that the paper could and should have been issued without the status of legal tender.[21]

The three dissenters per Justice Samuel F. Miller contended that the necessary and proper clause provides ample authority for the legislation. Although Miller, like Chase, considered the issue to be governed by *McCulloch*, he emphasized a different aspect of that opinion. To satisfy the *McCulloch* standard, he noted that Congress had decided that preservation of the Union mandated the issuance of currency as legal tender; the law was consequently "a necessity in the most stringent sense in which that word can be used." "Can it be said," he wrote, "that this provision cannot conduce towards the purpose of borrowing money, of paying debts, of raising armies, of suppressing insurrection?" Miller rejected Chase's interpretation of *McCulloch*, arguing in contrast that the decision required that great deference be accorded Congress's determination of that which is necessary and proper. He objected to application by courts of their perceptions of "justice" and "constitutional spirit" in passing on the constitutionality of congressional legislation.

The *Hepburn* opinions were issued on 7 February 1870. At that time, Justice Robert Cooper Grier was no longer a member of the Court, having resigned at the end of January. However, he had been a member on 27 November 1869 when the case was decided in conference and was expected to be on the Court on January 27 when the decision was originally to have been delivered. (The eleven-day delay occurred to allow the dissenters to prepare their views.) At the end of his opinion, the Chief Justice stated that Grier had concluded that the legal tender clause, if properly construed, had no application to debts contracted prior to its enactment; however, under the construction given to the Act by the other Justices, he concurred in the opinon that the clause, so far as it made U.S. notes a legal tender for such debts, is not constitutional. Thus, although when the case was actually decided, five of the eight Justices subscribed to Chase's opinion, a majority of the number authorized by statute when the decision was finally delivered did not so concur.

On the date that *Hepburn* was delivered, President Ulysses S. Grant nominated William Strong of Pennsylvania and Joseph P. Bradley of New Jersey to be Justices. When they had been confirmed and taken their seats, they joined the three dissenters to grant Attorney General Ebenezer Hoar's motion for further argument of the constitutional validity of the legal tender clause in cases still undecided. Subsequently, on 1 May 1871, in *Knox v. Lee*, the legal tender statute was sustained by a vote of 5-4 as to both preexisting and subsequent obligations with Justice Strong delivering the majority opinion and Justice Bradley entering a concurring opinion. Chief Justice Chase and Justices Nathan Clifford and Field wrote dissenting opinions.

For the most part, the opinions covered the same ground as had *Hepburn*. However, the *Knox* majority did air two positions that had not been previously discussed. The first was the historical background, and the second, the legitimacy of the Court's relatively quick reversal of the earlier case. Justice Strong perceived no problem to reopening any constitutional decision that may have been reached in error. Moreover, *Hepburn* was delivered by a divided Court, that had fewer than the legally mandated number of Justices. On the other side, Chase found the reversal unprecedented in the history of the Court, produced without any change in the opinions of those who had constituted the majority in the earlier case. Justice Clifford noted that at the time of the actual decision, the number of Justices on the Court was no less than provided for by existing law. Both he and Chase took the position that *Hepburn* was decided by a 5-3 majority.

Although Strong did not write on the historical background, Bradley did. The latter commented that when the Constitution had been adopted, the employment of bills of credit was deemed a legitimate means for financing government and that according them the quality of a legal tender was entirely discretionary with the legislature. This assertion may have been correct, but it does not deal with the Framers' proscription of this power. Bradley countered that the evidence of the Framers' intentions was not pertinent: "They chose to adopt the Constitution as it now stands, without any words either of grant or restriction of power and it is our duty to construe the instrument by its words, in the light of history of the general nature of government, and the incidents of sovereignty." The views of particular delegates "cannot control the fair meaning and general scope of the Constitution as it was finally framed and now stands." Because the power to issue bills of credit is inherent in sovereignty, it may be restrained only by express prohibition.

Despite the fact that Bradley was a very competent jurist, in this instance accepting his reasoning is very difficult. His position is totally at variance with the constitutional plan of a limited government that is evidenced by the Framers' debates on striking the paper money power. Both the Framers and the ratifiers operated on the theory that the government of the United States was a unique creation, bound by a Constitution setting forth its powers and limitations. Had the public believed that the national government, notwithstanding the express terms of the Constitution, possessed the same powers that other sovereign governments did, ratification would have been jeopardized.[22] To remove doubts that the national government had unknown or unspecified powers, the nation adopted the tenth amendment, which provides: "The powers not delegated to the United States by the Constitution, nor prohibited by it to the States, are reserved to the States respectively, or to the people."

The majority's arguments fail in this light. Justice Field remarked that the causes that led to the reversal of *Hepburn* "are patent to everyone" and that they had little to do with legal or historical analysis. The power of appointment rather than of logic was decisive. Accordingly, the appointments of Strong and Bradley are among the more controversial made to the nation's highest tribunal.

On the date that *Hepburn* was announced, the Court was two Justices short of the authorized number. At that time, President Grant's administration and most Republican Congressmen and other party leaders strongly supported the legal tender legislation. It was not likely that the President would appoint, or the Senate approve, a nominee to the Court who regarded the law as unconstitutional. This fact is evident from the position that many political and business leaders took on the *Hepburn* decision, proceeding on the basis that it would in short course be overturned.[23]

At the time of appointment, Strong and Bradley were considered staunch legal tender advocates, and neither would disappoint expectations that *Hepburn* was to be short-lived. Strong's views on the legal tender question had been judicially expressed when he helped sustain the Legal Tender Act by a bare majority while sitting on the Pennsylvania Supreme Court. Much comment has been made about Bradley's committing himself to this position in order to obtain nomination and confirmation.[24] While these allegations are of historical interest, they are not relevant to the outcome of the legal controversy, for no one with a different perspective would have been appointed. In fact, finding a qualified Republican with a contrary view might have been difficult. Professor Charles Fairman writes that seventy judges took part in sixteen state decisions on the constitutionality of the legal tender statute. With the exception of one New York appeals judge, all Republicans sustained the statute, while the Democratic judges regarded it as invalid.[25]

Final Validation of Greenbacks

The final solution in the legal tender controversy came in *Juilliard v. Greenman*, delivered on 3 March, 1884. Two congressmen agreed to settle their differences over the validity of greenbacks by setting up a contrived case under the Act of 1878, which required that greenbacks redeemed or otherwise received by the Treasury be reissued by it. Juilliard sued Greenman for $5,100.00, which he complained was still owing on the sale of 100 bales of cotton at an agreed price of $5,122.90. Greenman replied that he had satisfied this debt. In addition to $22.90 in gold coin, he had tendered $5,100.00 in greenbacks, which plaintiff refused to accept in payment. Unlike the situation in *Hepburn* and *Knox*, no war or emergency conditions existed to justify the mandate of the 1878 statute. The question for the Court was whether Congress has a constitutional power to make the greenbacks a legal tender in payment of private debts in time of peace as well as of war. In an opinion written by Justice Horace Gray, eight Justices replied in the affirmative with only Justice Field dissenting. The outcome was predictable: Except for Field, all Justices who had previously expressed opposition had died; their replacements were favorable to legal tender currency.

Justice Gray concluded that Congress possessed unlimited power to issue unredeemable paper money and designate it as legal tender. In effect, then, the Framers had totally wasted their efforts debating the issue and voting overwhelmingly to strike from the Constitution the power to emit bills of credit.

> We are irresistably impelled to the conclusion that the impressing upon the treasury notes of the United States the quality of being a legal tender in payment of private debts is an appropriate means, conducive and plainly adapted to the execution of the undoubted powers of Congress, consistent with the letter and spirit of the Constitution and, therefore, within the meaning of that instrument, "necessary and proper for carrying into execution the powers vested by this Constitution in the Government of the United States."

> Such being our conclusion in matter of law, the question whether at any particular time, in war or in peace, the exigency is such, by reason of unusual and pressing demands on the resources of the government, or of the inadequacy of the supply of gold and silver coin to furnish the currency needed for

the uses of the government and of the people, that it is, as a matter of fact, wise and expedient to resort to this means, is a political question, to be determined by Congress when the question of exigency arises, and not a judicial question, to be afterwards passed upon by the courts.[26]

According to Gray, the Framers' adoption of the motion to strike the paper money power "is quite inconclusive" in determining their intentions with respect to the greenback currency. The following are the supporting points that he made in order of their presentation together with my comments on them:

The philippic delivered before the Assembly of Maryland by Mr. Martin, one of the delegates from that state, who voted against the motion, and who declined to sign the Constitution, can hardly be accepted as satisfactory evidence of the reasons or the motives of the majority of the Convention.[27]

However, Martin's statement is important because it essentially corroborates the account that Madison presents.

Some of the members of the Convention, indeed, as appears from Mr. Madison's minutes of the debates, expressed the strongest opposition to paper money. And Mr. Madison has disclosed the grounds of his own action, by recording that "This vote in the affirmative by Virginia was occasioned by the acquiescence of Mr. Madison, who became satisfied that striking out the words would not disable the government from the use of public notes, so far as they could be safe and proper; and they would only cut off the pretext for a paper currency, and particularly for making the bills a tender, either for public or private debts." But he has not explained why he thought that striking out the words "and emit bills" would leave the power to emit bills, and deny the power to make them a tender in payment of debts.[28]

In the quoted passage, Madison uses three separate terms— public notes, paper currency, and bills—that the Justice considered as synonyms, but that in Madison's day had differing meanings. Notes meant, for Madison, promissory obligations of the government and not paper money, whereas he seems to have used the terms *paper currency* and *bills* synonymously. Under these definitions, Madison's remarks are entirely coherent. Professor Dam suggests that Gray's failure to differentiate notes from the rest stems from the fact that during the Civil War period both the 1861 demand obligations and the 1862 legal tender paper were called "notes." The term *bills of credit* had by then long disappeared from the common language.[29]

And it cannot be known how many of the other delegates, by whose vote the motion was adopted, intended neither to proclaim nor deny the power to emit paper money, and were influenced by the argument of Mr. Gorham, who "was for striking out, without inserting any prohibition," and who said: "if the words stand, they may suggest and lead to the emission." "The power, so far as it will be necessary or safe, will be involved in that of borrowing."[30]

Gorham's remarks were made on two separate occasions in the debate, and by running them together, Gray incorrectly sets forth the speaker's position. The last sentence appears in response to George Mason's apprehensions that Congress "would not have the [emissions] power unless it were expressed." Mason further "observed that the late war could not have been carried on, had such a prohibition existed." Gorham replies in effect that Mason need not worry. Congress would have the power to obtain funds "so far as it will be necessary or safe" under the borrowing power, presumably by way of promissory obligations. Gorham appears to acknowledge that unnecessary or unsafe emissions would not be authorized if the motion carried.

Gorham's earlier comments are not necessarily in conflict. Madison's account, although very short, is sufficient to allow the following interpretation of the delegate's views. Gorham supported Morris's motion to strike because (perhaps among other reasons) "if the words stand they may suggest and lead to the emission." Striking the words would limit the power; consequently, no need existed for "inserting any prohibition." The central government would be able to emit promissory paper "as it will be necessary or safe" pursuant to the borrowing power. Possibly, Morris feared that a specific prohibition might interfere with such application of this power.[31]

To be sure, there is no record attesting to the purposes and motives of the prevailing side on the motion to strike. Nevertheless, the evidence and circumstances as previously recounted are quite convincing that the Framers substantially limited Congress's paper emissions.

> And after the first clause of the 10th section of the 1st article had been reported in the form in which it now stands, forbidding the States to make anything but gold or silver coin a tender in payment of debts, or to pass any law impairing the obligation of contracts, when Mr. Gerry, as reported by Mr. Madison, "Entered into observations inculcating the importance of public faith, and the propriety of the restraint put on the States from impairing the obligation of contracts, alleging that Congress ought to be laid under the like prohibitions," and made a motion to that effect, he was not seconded.[32]

Elbridge Gerry made his motion on 14 September, three days before final adjournment and considerably after the Convention had voted to strike the emission power on 16 August. The Convention's closing days were the occasion for many such last efforts to change provisions, most of which failed. Gerry subsequently refused to sign the Constitution—because, among other reasons, of the inclusion of the necessary and proper clause—and called instead for a new convention. Near the end of the Convention, Gerry was clearly at odds with most of the other delegates. The episode reveals nothing about the Framers' intent with respect to paper money.

> As an illustration of the danger of giving too much weight, upon such a question, to the debates and the votes in the Convention, it may also be observed that propositions to authorize Congress to grant charters of incorporation for national objects were strongly opposed, especially as regarded banks, and defeated [citations]. The power of Congress to emit bills of credit, as well as to incorporate national banks, is now clearly established by decisions to which we shall presently refer.[33]

One is tempted to reply that two wrongs do not make a right. The fact that the Court incorrectly decided prior cases does not of itself justify consciously erring further in the instant situation. Moreover, none of the earlier decisions bound the Court on the matter of legal tender in peacetime.

Having thus eliminated the Framers' discussions from consideration, Gray confronted only the question of ascertaining a source for the legal tender power. He found that a relationship existed between it and the powers to coin money and to regulate interstate and foreign commerce and the value of domestic and foreign coins. A still closer relationship was found in the power "to borrow money on the credit of the United States." Gray held that these powers are coextensive. How does the designation of legal tender for paper used to pay private debts relate to the borrowing of money by government? Justice Field could find no relationship. The words "to borrow money" should, he argued, be interpreted as they are when employed in charters of municipal bodies or private corporations or in contracts of individuals. Gray disagreed that the Court was bound to this ordinary course of interpretation. The words "to borrow money," vesting a power in the national government for the safety and welfare of the people, should not "receive that limited and restricted interpretation and meaning which they would have in a penal statute, or in an authority conferred, by law or by contract, upon trustees or agents for private purposes."[34]

This remarkable statement is not comforting to persons committed to the rule of a written constitution. Presumably all terminology in the Constitution is intended to protect public safety and welfare, and under Gray's interpretation, little of it would be immune from judical fiat. The words "to borrow money" may not be completely clear, but they are nevertheless relatively certain as the language goes. Surely they are more definite than is the terminology ordinarily thought of as requiring judicial discretion—for example, due process, equal protection of laws, and privileges and immunities. Gray's theory of interpretation would convert most of the Constitution to a kind of due process clause.

To be sure, Gray was not the first Justice to interpret loosely Congress's money emissions powers. As he observed, by the time of *Juilliard*, the Court had construed the Constitution as empowering Congress to emit paper money and to provide for its circulation as currency (short of giving it the quality in time of peace of legal tender for private debts). On this occasion Gray relied chiefly on the inherent character of sovereignty to resolve the remaining issue of wartime versus peacetime powers.

> The power, as incident to the power of borrowing money and issuing bills or notes of the government for money borrowed, of impressing upon those bills or notes the quality of being a legal tender for the payment of private debts, was a power universally understood to belong to sovereignty, in Europe and America, at the time of the framing and adoption of the Constitution of the United States.[35]

Gray thus applied the rationale espoused by Justice Bradley in *Knox* except that the former confined it to interpreting the borrowing power. Both are equally defective. As an historical matter, paper emissions such as the greenbacks had no relationship to this power. The Constitution's phrase "to borrow money" had its origin in the Articles of Confederation, which used this or similar wording three times and always in conjunction with the power to emit bills of credit. This sequence of language indicates that the Articles' framers regarded the two powers as distinct and separate, that contrary to Gray's assertions, the power to borrow differed from and did not include the power to emit paper money. The Framers operated under like assumptions, striking the emissions power and leaving the borrowing power as drafted. This exercise would have been meaningless if they had believed that the newly created national government automatically possessed the emissions and legal tender powers.

Justice Gray's presentation and the foregoing critique of it lead to this brief summary in conclusion of the chapter. Although it is not possible to prove that the Framers intended to prohibit totally the emissions power, neither can it be shown that this authority is under normal peacetime conditions incident to any enumerated power. In striking the power, the Framers made certain it would not be irresponsibly and unnecessarily applied. Congress could emit paper money and make it legal tender only when to do so was necessary and proper to implement a specified power and this standard requires the existence of very special conditions or circumstances.

The impact of this distortion of the Constitution is considerable. Under the Court's rulings, none other than political restraint exists on the amount of the United States' money supply. This is not a very secure anchor when compared to that provided by tying the supply to the nation's ownership of gold and silver. As a result, the country faces the same perils of a potentially inflated currency that the Framers experienced in their period and sought to avoid for the future.

Notes

1. Dam, *The Legal Tender Cases*, 1981 *Sup. Ct. Rev.* 367, 383.
2. *Id.* at 383-84, CHESTER WHITNEY WRIGHT, ECONOMIC HISTORY OF THE UNITED STATES 2nd ed., 179-85, 191-92 (New York, Toronto, London: McGraw-Hill, 1949).
3. 2 MAX FARRAND, THE RECORDS OF THE FEDERAL CONVENTION OF 1787, at 76, 299 (rev. ed. 1937)(New Haven, Conn. and London; Yale University Press, 1966). *See* WRIGHT *supra* note 2.
4. 2 FARRAND at 168.
5. *Id.* at 308-9.
6. *Id.* at 309.
7. THE FEDERALIST PAPERS NO. 44 (J. Madison) at 281-82 (New York and Scarborough, Ont.: Mentor Books, 1961).
8. 2 FARRAND at 309-10. *See* further discussion on the Framers' intentions in text accompanying *supra* notes 3-6.
9. 2 FARRAND at 439.
10. 3 FARRAND at 205-6.
11. Directed to the Speaker of the House of Representatives, December 31, 1790.
12. JACKSON TURNER MAIN, THE ANTIFEDERALISTS, 7, 165-67, 218-70 (Chapel Hill, N.C.: University of North Carolina Press, 1961).
13. Sturgis v. Crowninshield, 17 U.S. (4 Wheat.) 122, 204-6 (1819); 2 JOSEPH STORY, COMMENTARIES ON THE CONSTITUTION *sec.* 1371 (New York: Da Capo Press, 1970).
14. Juilliard v. Greenman, 110 U.S. 421, 451 (1884)(Field, J., dissenting).
15. *See* Chapter 1 *supra* for a more extended discussion on this issue.
16. Veazie Bank v. Fenno, 75 U.S. (8 Wall) 533 (1869).
17. Knox v Lee, 79 U.S. (12 Wall) 457 (1871) and Juilliard v. Greenman, 110 U.S. 421 (1884).
18. 75 U.S. at 548.
19. 75 U.S. (8 Wall) 603 (1870).
20. *See* Chapter 1 *supra.*
21. CHARLES FAIRMAN, RECONSTRUCTION AND REUNION, 1864-88, PART ONE, 6 HISTORY OF THE SUPREME COURT OF THE UNITED STATES 684-87 (New York: Macmillan, 1971).
22. *See* Chapter 1 *supra.*
23. FAIRMAN, *supra* note 21, at 767-71.
24. *Id.* at 719-38.
25. *Id.* at 700.
26. 110 U.S. at 450.

27. 110 U.S. at 443.

28. *Id.*

29. Dam *supra* note 1, at 387-88. Dam cites Chief Justice Marshall's definition in Craig v. Missouri, U.S. (4 Pet.d) 410, 424, 432, 434-35 (1830) as well as that of Justice Johnson who dissented in the case (at 441).

30. 110 U.S. at 443.

31. Because of his earlier remarks Gorham has also been interpreted as not wishing to withdraw the emissions power, Dam *supra* note 1, at 386 n. 94, in which case his comments are not explanatory of the majority position.

32 110 U.S. at 443-44.

33. 110 U.S. at 444.

34. *Id.*

35. 110 U.S. at 447.

3

Economic and Property Rights

During approximately the last four decades the Supreme Court has relegated economic liberty—the right to produce and distribute goods and services—to a place of very low priority. However, in recent years this position has come under strong attack. A host of distinguished economists and academicians are asserting that the freedoms involved in economic activities deserve no less recognition than do those related to other pursuits.[1] These scholars argue that no significant philosophical, moral, or pragmatic reasons justify the greater protection that the Court grants the marketplace of ideas than that which it grants the marketplace of goods and services.

Despite this changing perception, the United States Supreme Court has not significantly altered its policy towards economic activities that do not involve other specially protected liberties. Only once since 1936 has the Court invalidated a statute as violating economic rights, and subsequently it reversed that decision.[2]

The Court generally observes this hierarchy of rights: At the top are the rights of expression, religion, sexual privacy, and voting; at the bottom are economic rights and hovering somewhere above the latter are the rights of property ownership, as embodied in the eminent domain clause of the fifth amendment. Federal law accepts in practice the belief of former Justice William O. Douglas that under the Constitution "free speech, free press, free exercise of religion are placed separate and apart; they are above and beyond the police power; they are not subject to regulation in the manner of factories, slums, apartment houses, production of oil and the like."[3]

This priority has a highly significant impact on society. Consider, as an example, the hundreds of federal and state regulations barring or curtailing entry into a business or occupation. An individual or corporation aggrieved by such laws has the almost impossible burden of proving that the government's action is unconstitutional. By contrast, when the press is restricted, the government, not the private party involved, must assume the arduous task of proving that the law or regulation is constitutional. With laws regulating property ownership, the federal courts also presume constitutionality and again the burden is on the aggrieved party to overcome this presumption. Accordingly, legislation in one area is examined under the presumption of validity and in the other under the presumption of invalidity.

In this respect the Burger Court differs little from the Warren Court, and many otherwise critical constitutional commentators approve this part of the Burger record. On the one hand, when economic or social legislation is in question, these writers insist that the courts should not substitute their judgments for those of Congress and state legislatures on the wisdom of public policy. On the other, they support the principle that in the case of legislation curbing speech, press, religion, or sexual privacy, the basic issue is whether the legislature has acted arbitrarily in restraining exercise of the liberty in question. They contend under our system of government, the courts are obligated to perform this role.

Although few will disagree with the former perspective, it is not critical to the judicial review of a statute. Economic legislation invariably takes from one group and gives to another. In these cases, as in those involving first amendment rights or sexual privacy, the important question for the justices to decide is whether the legislature is unjustifiably depriving people of their liberties.

During the period between 1897 and 1937, the Supreme Court frequently struck down economic legislation on the ground that it deprived people of liberty without due process of law. The Court reached its decisions pursuant to a doctrine known as "substantive due process." This concept was ultimately doomed in part because under it some welfare legislation was declared unconstitutional. Probably no group of justices has ever been the object of so much criticism as have been these early proponents of substantive due process. Yet these justices sought to uphold economic liberties much as civil libertarians strive to uphold intellectual and political rights, and (as we shall see subsequently) with at least as much, if not more, constitutional sanction.

The point can be made by considering the records of Justices Oliver Wendell Holmes, Jr. and Louis Brandeis, history's most illustrious opponents of substantive due process. Both were eager to strike down duly enacted speech and press restrictions on the ground that they violated constitutional rights—precisely the argument advanced by the substantive due process Justices in invalidating economic and social legislation.

Instead of being a contest between authoritarians and libertarians, as some authors suggest, the controversy was between two groups of judges who interpreted the Constitution differently. Many historians are strongly sympathetic to the beliefs of Holmes and Brandeis, and they have idealized these men as heroic fighters for freedom against reactionary judges.

However, an examination of the cases scarcely supports such a conclusion. In opining that the Supreme Court should not enter the sphere of economic and social policy, Holmes would have conferred almost unrestrained power in this area on Congress and state legislatures. He would have largely eliminated judicial review for the persons affected, thus leaving their fate to such mercies as legislators were willing or able to dispense.

Brandeis agreed with Holmes, often supporting his own position with economic reasoning. Although known in history as a strong supporter of individual liberties, Brandeis tended to believe that government is almost always right when it restricts economic and property interests and almost always wrong when it does the same to intellectual and political matters.

Both the Warren and the Burger Courts have struck down economic and social legislation that also infringed on the more prized liberties. Those enterpreneurs whose commercial activities can be regarded as within the speech, press, privacy, and gender guarantees of the Constitution are granted judicial protection. However, the economic or social importance of the activity is not decisive. That which counts is whether a majority of the Court is willing to fit it within a protected constitutional category.

Let me illustrate the change in judicial perspective on economic restraints that has occurred over the years by considering the now highly controversial decision in *Lochner v. New York* (1905) and contrasting it with more recent case of *Minnesota v. Clover Leaf Creamery Co.* (1981).[4] In furtherance of the discussion, reference will also be made to *Euclid v. Ambler*,[5] which validated zoning. First the *Lochner* case.

Lochner

In 1895, New York enacted, as part of a measure establishing sanitary and other working conditions for bakeries and confectioneries, a provision limiting to sixty the number of hours an employee in such establishments could "be required or permitted" to work each week, with a maximum of ten hours a day. The defendant employer had been indicted for a violation of this provision and found guilty by the trial court. The defendant demurred to the indictment, chiefly on the ground that the law violated his liberty under the due process clause of the fourteenth amendment. In a 5-4 decision the Supreme Court agreed with Mr. Lochner, setting forth this standard for determining the constitutionality of economic legislation:

> The act must have a . . . direct relation, as a means to an end, and the end itself must be appropriate and legitimate, before an act can be held to be valid which interferes with a general right of an individual to be free in his person and his power to contract in relation to his own labor.

The majority opinion observed that the Court had previously upheld a Utah law limiting employment in underground mines and smelters to eight hours a day except in emergencies. However, because the New York law covered a situation considered by the majority far less perilous to health, and because it allowed no exceptions, it was distinguishable from the Utah statute. As Justice John Marshall Harlan noted, the Court would have come to an opposite conclusion had the law limited employment to eighteen hours a day, for working this longer period would indeed be detrimental to health. Moreover, the opinion implied that the other parts of New York law relating to sanitary working conditions were a valid exercise of police power. After reviewing the statute and precedents, the majority concluded that New York did not have sufficient justification to regulate the working hours of bakery employees. In fact, the majority noted, the law could well be harmful, for limitations upon hours result in reduced wages—a situation that "might seriously cripple the ability of the laborer to support himself and his family." Under current decisions a similar statute would unquestionably be declared constitutional by the U.S. Supreme Court.

The Clover Leaf Case

To illustrate existing law in the area of economic liberty, consider the *Clover Leaf Creamery Co.*, a case decided by the Supreme Court in January 1981. In 1977, Minnesota's legislature had enacted a statute banning the retail sale of milk in plastic, non-returnable, non-refillable containers. The sale of milk in paperboard cartons was not affected. According to its text, the statute was designed to promote resource conservation, ease solid waste disposal problems, and conserve energy. However, a Minnesota District Court found that the "actual basis" for the prohibition of plastic milk bottles "was to promote the economic interests of certain segments of the local dairy and pulpwood industries at the expense of the economic interests of other segments of the dairy industry and plastic industry." The legislature had acted in behalf of private and not public interest. The district court thus held that the law violated the equal protection clause of the U.S. Constitution. The Minnesota Supreme Court affirmed this ruling on the ground that the statute was irrational: "The evidence conclusively demonstrates that the discrimination against plastic, non-refillable containers is not rationally related to the act's objectives."

Nevertheless, the U. S. Supreme Court reversed the decision, voting 7-1 that the law did not violate equal protection. For the majority, Justice William J. Brennan relied on precedents holding that state economic laws will be sustained unless they either are totally senseless or infringe upon some specially protected liberty. In sharp contrast to the *Lochner* standard, Brennan asserted that challengers have the burden of convincing courts "that the legislative facts on which [a] classification is apparently based could not reasonably be conceived to be true by the governmental decisionmaker."

Zoning

The standard of review established for zoning cases is more rigorous than is the minimal scrutiny applied in the *Creamery* case, but not by very much. The Court continues to adhere to Justice George Sutherland's 1926 *Euclid* opinion, which reversed a lower court decision that zoning is the taking of property in violation of the fourteenth amendment. In *Euclid*, the district court had proceeded on the long prevailing theory that property ownership is a substantive right under the due process clause and thus may be limited only under few and special circumstances. Zoning, the lower court determined, could hardly be considered of that character. However, by a 6-3 majority the Supreme Court disagreed and upheld zoning in principle, placing the burden on land owners to show that a particular ordinance was unreasonable and arbitrary. "Before these [zoning] ordinances can be declared unconstitutional, [they must be shown to be] clearly arbitrary and unreasonable, having no substantial relation to the public health, safety, morals or general welfare."

In *Lochner*, *Creamery*, and *Euclid* the Court neither sought the intention of the framers of the fourteenth amendment nor cited precedent containing such information. Remarkably, the Court has never conducted any extensive inquiry into the framers' intentions with respect to the material freedoms.

Responding to the dearth of research, this chapter examines the relevant background and debates on the framing of section 1 of the fourteenth amendment with particular emphasis on *Lochner*. The evidence is very persuasive that *Lochner* was a legitimate interpretation of original meaning and that the current standards enunciated in *Creamery* and *Euclid* are not supported by the amendment's history.

Our inquiry will concentrate on both section 1 of the fourteenth amendment and the Civil Rights Act of 1866; for interpretative purposes the two cannot be separated. The former was framed by the Thirty-ninth Congress in 1866 and ratified by three-fourths of the states by 1868. Although the framers may have considered other sections more important, only sections 1 and 5 of the amendment have been judicially significant, and they read as follows:

> *Section 1.* All persons born or naturalized in the United States, and subject to the jurisdiction thereof, are citizens of the United States and of the State wherein they reside. No State shall make or enforce any law which shall abridge the privileges or immunities of citizens of the United States; nor shall

any State deprive any person of life, liberty, or property, without due process of law; nor deny to any person within its jurisdiction the equal protection of the laws.

Section 5. The Congress shall have the power to enforce, by appropriate legislation, the provisions of this article.

Civil Rights Act of 1866

While opinion is divergent as to the full meaning of section 1, commentators do agree that at the least, it was intended to authorize passage of and constitutionalize the Civil Rights Act of 1866—that is, to assure that the latter's provisions were permitted by the Constitution and to place its safeguards beyond the power of any subsequent Congress to repeal. The chief purpose of this Act was to provide federal protection for the emancipated blacks in the exercise of certain enumerated liberties. However, it applied to all the states and benefitted other people as well. Sections 1 and 2 of the Act which are pertinent to this examination, provide as follows:

> *Section 1.* That all persons born in the United States, and not subject to any foreign Power, excluding Indians not taxed, are hereby declared to be citizens, of the United States; and such citizens, of every race and color, without regard to any previous condition of slavery or involuntary servitude, except as a punishment for crime whereof the party shall have been duly convicted, shall have the same right, in every State and Territory in the United States, to make and enforce contracts, to sue, be parties, and give evidence, to inherit, purchase, lease, sell, hold, and convey real and personal property, and to full and equal benefit of all laws and proceedings for the security of person and property, as is enjoyed by white citizens, and shall be subject to like punishment, pains and penalties, and to none other, any law, statute, ordinance, regulation or custom, to the contrary notwithstanding.

> *Section 2.* That any person who, under color of any law, statute, ordinance, regulation, or custom, shall subject, or cause to be subjected, any inhabitant of any State or Territory to the deprivation of any right secured or protected by this Act, or to different punishment, pains, or penalties on account of such person having at any time been held in a condition of slavery or involuntary servitude, except as a punishment for crime, whereof the party shall have been duly convicted, or by reason of his color or race, than is prescribed for the punishment of white persons, shall be deemed guilty of a misdemeanor, and, on conviction, shall be punished by fine not exceeding one thousand dollars, or imprisonment not exceeding one year, or both, in the discretion of the Court.[6]

Section 3 gave lower federal courts original and the Supreme Court appellate jurisdiction. It provided for removal to the federal courts of suits or prosecutions under the Act that had been commenced in state courts.

Section 4 directed district attorneys, marshals, and other federal officials to institute proceedings against violators. The balance of the statute contained other provisions relating to enforcement.

In the Senate, the Civil Rights Bill was introduced on 29 January 1866 by its author, Senator Lyman Trumbull of Illinois, chairman of the Judiciary Committee, and on 1 March, in the House by Representative James F. Wilson of Iowa, chairman of its Judiciary Committee. Both were Republicans, members of the party that held substantial majorities in the two bodies. Forty-two Republicans and 10 Democrats occupied the Senate, and 145 Republicans and 46 Democrats were in the House. At that time the eleven states that participated in the recent rebellion were not represented. The Republicans overwhelmingly supported the Civil Rights Act both initially and after President Andrew Johnson's veto. The Democrats opposed it.

Determining legislative intent can at times be an arduous undertaking. How does a court decide what motivated the 128 representatives and 33 senators who favored the joint resolution proposing the fourteenth amendment? Only a small fraction spoke in the debates. Moreover, speakers with particular concerns emphasized these aspects and ignored others. However, legislatures function to produce laws that generally reflect the members' will. Because every legislator cannot be knowledgeable on every measure or every issue, legislatures operate primarily through committees that are supposed to study and understand their assigned areas. Consequently, individual members often defer to committee members. For some lawmakers, a vote may for the most part represent an expression of confidence in a committee or its members that author or support a measure. They may go along without fully considering or understanding some parts of a bill if they are satisfied that the authors generally mirror their own concerns. Committee majorities may also reflect the party line, which can control certain lawmakers. When voting, lawmakers are probably aware that explanations of committee chairmen or other specially interested members will be considered important by courts interpreting legislation.

For these reasons, this chapter will be most concerned with the explanations and positions of floor managers and other leading proponents of the measures under study.

Section 1 of Trumbull's bill was much amended before its final passage. It emerged less racially oriented than when first introduced. The following is Trumbull's original section 1, showing the subsequent changes:

> *Section 1.* That all persons [of African descent] born in the United States *and not subject to any foreign Power, excluding Indians not taxed*, are hereby declared to be citizens of the United States, [and there shall be no discrimina-

tion in civil rights or immunities among the inhabitants of any State or Territory of the United States on account of race, color, or previous condition of slavery; but the inhabitants] *and such citizens* of every race and color, without regard to any previous condition of slavery or involuntary servitude, except as a punishment for crime whereof the parties shall have been duly convicted, shall have the same right *in every State and Territory in the United States*, to make and enforce contracts, to sue, be parties, and give evidence, to inherit, purchase, lease, sell, hold, and convey real and personal property, and to full and equal benefit of all laws and proceedings for the security of person and property, *as is enjoyed by white citizens*, and shall be subject to like punishment, pains and penalties, and to none other, any law, statute, ordinance, regulation, or custom to the contrary notwithstanding.[7]

Trumbull found authority for his bill in section 2 of the thirteenth amendment, giving Congress power to enforce "by appropriate legislation" section 1, which abolished slavery. The bill would make the amendment meaningful by securing practical freedom for the former slaves. "Of what avail will it now be that the Constitution of the United States has declared that slavery shall not exist, if in the late slaveholding States laws are to be enacted and enforced depriving persons of African descent of privileges which are essential to freemen?"[8] By conferring citizenship, the bill entitled former slaves to exercise those rights guaranteed to citizens by the Constitution. A statute depriving a citizen of civil rights secured to other citizens constitutes "a badge of servitude which, by the Constitution, is prohibited."[9]

To determine what those rights were, Trumbull referred to judicial decisions defining article IV, section 2, (commonly referred to as the comity clause), which declares that "The citizens of each State shall be entitled to all privileges and immunities of citizens in the several States." He concluded that the decision most elaborate upon this clause and containing the settled judicial opinion (except possibly for being excessive on rights of suffrage) was that delivered by Supreme Court Justice Bushrod Washington in *Corfield v Coryell,* an 1823 Federal Circuit Court case.[10] Cited at various times in the debates on the Civil Rights Act and the fourteenth amendment, Washington's famous pronouncement on the meaning of the privileges and immunities clause of article IV follows:

We feel no hesitation in confining [the constitutional provision to] these expressions to those privileges and immunities which are, in their nature, fundamental; which belong, of right, to the citizens of all free governments, and which have, at all times been enjoyed by the citizens of the several states which compose the Union, from the time of their becoming free, independent, and sovereign. What these fundamental principles are, it would perhaps be more tedious than difficult to enumerate. They may, however, be all comprehended under the following general heads: Protection by the government;

the enjoyment of life and liberty, with the right to acquire and possess property of every kind, and to pursue and obtain happiness and safety; subject nevertheless to such restraints as the government may justly prescribe for the general good of the whole. The right of a citizen of one state to pass through, or to reside in any other state, for purposes of trade, agriculture, professional pursuits, or otherwise; to claim the benefit of the writ of habeas corpus; to institute and maintain actions of any kind in the courts of the state; to take, hold and dispose of property, either real or personal; and an exemption from higher taxes or impositions than are paid by the other citizens of the state, may be mentioned as some of the particular privileges and immunities of citizens, which are clearly embraced by the general description of privileges deemed to be fundamental: to which may be added, the elective franchise, as regulated and established by the laws or constitution of the state in which it is to be exercised. These, and many others which might be mentioned, are, strictly speaking, privileges and immunities, and the enjoyment of them by the citizens of each state in every other state, was manifestly calculated (to use the expressions of the preamble of the corresponding provision in the old articles of confederation) "the better to secure and perpetuate mutual friendship and intercourse among the people of the different states of the Union." But we cannot accede to the proposition . . . that, under this provision of the constitution, the citizens of the several states are permitted to participate in all the rights which belong exclusively to the citizens of any other particular state. . . .[11]

Senator Trumbull observed that Justice Washington's definition included all the rights set forth in the proposed legislation. Thus the bill did no more than protect the "fundamental rights belonging to every man as a free man, and which under the Constitution as it now exists we have a right to protect every man in."[12] Actually, Washington's opinion concerned citizens of one state engaged in activities in another; Trumbull's position was that their rights should be no less in their own states than outside them.

Representative Wilson offered a similar interpretation.[13] He likewise asserted that the law, instead of creating rights, merely enforced the fundamental rights to which citizens already were entitled under the Constitution, quoting also from Justice Washington's construction of article IV's privileges and immunities clause.[14] The congressman emphasized the basic character of the bill's protections and identified them as natural rights.[15]

In addition to arguing as Trumbull did that the Act was authorized under the thirteenth amendment, Wilson contended that Congress had implied powers under the Constitution to protect fundamental liberties of United States citizens from abridgment by the States. Establishing such authority was necessary inasmuch as the Act affected all the states and might apply to other than those whom Congress could protect under the authority of the amendment.[16] According to the Congressman, the "great fundamental civil rights which it is the true office of Government to protect" were named in the celebrated commentaries of England's Sir William Blackstone and New York's Chancellor James Kent. Both declared that the three absolute rights of individuals were personal security, personal liberty, and personal property. All the liberties set forth specifically or generally in the proposed Civil Rights Act, Wilson concluded, were either embodied in these rights or necessary for their enjoyment.[17]

Continuing this theme later in the debates, Wilson asserted that the fifth amendment's due process clause guarantees the rights contained in the bill and that Congress has implied authority to set aside state laws abridging their exercise.

> An amendment to the Constitution [provides] that "no person shall be deprived of life, liberty, or property without due process of law.". . . . These are the rights to which this bill relates having nothing to do with subjects submitted to the control of the several States.
>
> The citizen is entitled to the rights of life, liberty, and property. Now, if a State intervenes and deprives him, without due process of law, of these rights, as has been the case in a multitude of instances in the past, have we no power to make him secure in his priceless possessions? When such a case is presented, can we not provide a remedy? Who will doubt it?[18]

Opponents of the legislation focused on the serious constitutional problems that it raised. First, there was the questionable relationship between the goal of the thirteenth amendment—to eliminate slavery—and the goal of the bill—to eliminate discrimination. Second was the issue of how the proposed law could apply to blacks or whites who were free and thus never affected by the amendment. Third, the opposition contended that under the *Dred Scott* decision,[19] Congress did not have authority to confer citizenship on former slaves. Fourth, opponents argued that Congress could not require the states to observe provisions in the Bill of Rights, for that document was solely a limitation on the federal government. And fifth, opponents doubted that Congress had power to penalize persons who in good faith obeyed state laws. To survive challenge, it was evident that the legislation required a firmer constitutional foundation, which in time the fourteenth amendment provided.

In the congressional debates, specific economic rights were mentioned either as belonging to the freedmen or as being denied to them in the South. Senator Trumbull said that all men have the right to make contracts, to buy and sell, and to acquire and dispose of property.[20] Senator Howard of Michigan asserted that the freedman must be able to earn and purchase property and to benefit by the "fruits of his toil and his industry."[21] Representative Thayer of Pennsylvania was concerned that the freedmen have the ability to contract for their labor and to purchase a home and have the liberty to enjoy the ordinary pursuits of civilized life.[22] Representative Lawrence of Ohio stated that all citizens have the right to make contracts to "secure the privilege and the rewards of labor."[23] Representative Windom of Minnesota was also concerned that all citizens have the right to contract for their labor, to enforce the payment of their wages, and to have the means of holding and enjoying the "proceeds of their toil."[24]

Trumbull and Windom gave examples of statutes (known as the Black Codes) abridging the rights of freed blacks, that would be outlawed by the Act. Mississippi, for instance, had passed a statute authorizing local officials to prevent freedmen from carrying on independent business and compelling them to work only as employees. It also barred freedmen from holding, leasing, or renting real estate. In addition, Georgia and South Carolina prohibited any Negro from buying or leasing a home.[25] Representative Cook was alarmed by laws "that a man not supporting himself by labor shall be deemed a vagrant, and that a vagrant shall be sold."[26]

Such conditions persuaded Congress to limit certain legislative powers of the rebellious states. But Congress went much further in the Civil Rights bill, imposing it on all states for the benefit of individuals other than former slaves. However, the legislators were not interested in stripping the states of all powers in the racial area. A considerable amount of congressional debates centered on the language that had originally been inserted in section 1, after the provision on citizenship, and that remained in the measure adopted by the Senate, stating that "there shall be no discrimination in civil rights or immunities . . . on account of race, color, or previous condition of slavery." Proponents of the proposed act in both Houses insisted that neither this provision nor any other part of the legislation related to political rights, social privileges, voting, officeholding, jury service, or school integration. However, primarily because the foregoing language was sufficiently extensive to risk this interpretation, the judiciary committee voted to eliminate it while the measure was pending in the House. Representative Wilson thought that the deletion did not materially change the bill; "but some gentlemen were apprehensive that the words we propose to strike out might give warrant for a latitudarian construction not intended."[27] The Senate accepted the amendment.[28] With this language omitted, the bill was much more confined in application. The change also diminished its racial orientation, giving it a broader libertarian character.

The congressional debates evidence the existence of dual goals for the civil rights legislation—to secure an equality of rights for blacks as well as for other citizens. Senator Trumbull viewed the bill as affecting state legislation generally, quoting in his introductory statements from a note to Blackstone's *Commentaries*: "In this definition of civil liberty it ought to be understood, or rather expressed, that the restraints introduced by the law should be equal to all, or as much so as the nature of things will admit."[29] He subsequently denied that the bill would benefit black men exclusively.

> It applies to white men as well as black men. It declares that all persons in the United States shall be entitled to the same civil rights, the right to the fruit of their own labor, the right to make contracts, the right to buy and sell, and enjoy liberty and happiness; . . . [The only object] is to secure equal rights to all the citizens of the country, . . .[30]

Nevertheless, Trumbull sought to minimize the actual impact.

> If the State of Kentucky makes no discrimination in civil rights between its citizens, this bill has no operation whatever in the State of Kentucky. Are all the rights of the people of Kentucky gone because they cannot discriminate and punish one man for doing a thing that they do not punish another for doing?[31]

Trumbull expressed essentially the same views in his speech urging the Senate to override President Johnson's veto. Again he emphasized the legislation's racial objectives and acknowledged its applicability to the rest of the population. The following indicates that the statute would impose a reasonableness standard on state legislation:

> The bill neither confers nor abridges the rights of any one, but simply declares that in civil rights there shall be an equality among all classes of citizens, and that all alike shall be subject to the same punishment. Each State, so that it does not abridge the great fundamental rights belonging, under the Constitution, to all citizens, may grant or withhold such civil rights as it pleases; all that is required is that, in this respect, its laws shall be impartial.[32]

In his introductory statement Wilson asserted that "the entire structure of this bill rests on the discrimination relative to civil rights and immunities made by the States on 'account of race, color, or previous condition of slavery.'"[33] He thought that the thirteenth amendment empowered Congress to protect such rights. However, he recognized that the measure might have a broader application and proceeded to argue that Congress had authority to enforce the rights of others as well. Enacting the statute was also necessary "to protect our citizens, from the highest to the lowest, from the whitest to the blackest, in the enjoyment of the great fundamental rights which belong to all men."[34]

The Civil Rights Act was entitled "A bill to protect all persons in the United States in their civil rights and to furnish means for their vindication." Congressmen other than the bill's floor managers interpreted it in a manner corresponding to this title.

Representative John Bingham, Republican of Ohio (about whom a great deal more will be said later), viewed the measure as affecting the entire nation. It was not proposed

> simply for the protection of freedmen in their rights for the time being in the late insurrectionary States. That is a great mistake. It applies to every State in the Union, to States which have never been in insurrection, and is to be enforced in every State in the Union, not only for the present, but for all future time, or until it shall be repealed by some subsequent act of Congress. It does not expire by virtue of its own limitation; it is intended to be permanent.[35]

In a lengthy speech urging the House to override the President's veto, Representative Lawrence asserted that the bill would have a very broad impact. He claimed that it would protect every citizen in the exercise of fundamental liberties. "It is scarcely less to the people of this country than Magna Charta was to the people of England."[36] The legislation required that "whatever of certain civil rights may be enjoyed by any shall be shared by all citizens in each State and in the Territories."[37]

Representative Broomall of Pennsylvania also interpreted the legislation broadly, asserting that "its terms embrace the late rebels, and it gives them the rights, privileges, and immunities of citizens of the United States."[38] The bill would help "secure protection to the loyal men of the South" who were victims in their person and property of oppression and prosecution in Southern states only because of their loyalty to the Union; "loyal men who . . . have had their property confiscated by the State courts, and are denied remedy in the courts of the reconstructed South" would deservedly be accorded federal protections.[39]

Representative Raymond of New York construed the Act as "securing an equality of rights to all citizens of the United States, and of all persons within their jurisdiction."[40] Although he favored its principles,[41] he voted against the bill because of his belief that Congress lacked authority to enact it.[42] Senator Davis of Kentucky (an opponent of the measure) contended that the bill broke down the legal system in all the states, "so far not only as [to] the negro, but as any man without regard to color is concerned."[43] Representative Thayer (a supporter) asserted that the "bill [would extend] these fundamental immunities of citizenship to all classes of people in the United States."[44] Senator Hendricks of Indiana (an opponent) stated that the bill would provide "that the civil rights of all men, without regard to color, shall be equal."[45] Congressman Kerr of Indiana (an opponent), believed that under the measure "Congress may, then, go into any State and break down any State constitutions or laws which discriminate in any way against any class of persons within or without the State." It would be able to "determine for each State the civil *status* of every person, of any race or color, who should elect to settle therein."[46]

Representative Shellabarger of Ohio (a supporter), noted that the bill was limited to protecting citizens from deprivations on account of race or color. He used the term *race* synonomously with nationality. If the bill has not passed, he argued, the states would be able to adopt discriminatory measures against, for example, Germans. In such an eventuality "this Government [would be] in this position of utter helplessness"[47] Representative Hill of Indiana (a supporter), sought unsuccessfully to amend the bill by excepting from its protection "those who have voluntarily borne arms against the Government of the United States or given aid and comfort to the enemies thereof." Evidently he thought that the bill protected these individuals.[48] Senator Cowan of Pennsylvania (an opponent), contended that the bill

> confers . . . upon everybody native born in all the States, the right to make and enforce contracts, because there is no qualification in the bill, and the very object of the bill is to override the qualifications that are upon those rights in the States. . . . The power given . . . by this bill is unlimited as to persons, and it is equally unlimited as to contracts."[49]

Some speakers considered only the effect on emancipated persons and did not comment on the statute's meaning for the rest of the population. Senator Howard of Michigan (a supporter), insisted that the bill was confined to eliminating discrimination on the basis of race or color.[50] Opponents Senator Guthrie of Kentucky and Representative Eldridge of Wisconsin indicated that this was also their understanding.[51] Senator Stewart of Nevada (a supporter), asserted that the bill did no more than strike at the renewal of any attempt to return the freedmen to slavery or peonage. Senator Henderson of Missouri (a supporter) thought that its sole object was to break down the system of oppression in the seceded states.[52]

These narrow interpretations are difficult to reconcile with abolitionist doctrine that emphasized legal equality generally and not just with respect to race. The former abolitionists, who were very influential in Republican ranks, had as a goal that "slaves and and free Negroes . . . receive legal protection in their fundamental rights along with all other human beings."[53] They had long comprehended the moral and practical problems of isolating their pleas for legal equality to one area. Because the result would be to limit the powers of government, this perspective was highly acceptable in the generally laissez-faire climate of the Republican Party. The explanations of the bill by both Trumbull and Wilson reflected these important philosophical concerns and appealed to the vast majority of their party who shared them.

Moreover, narrow interpretations of the Act are not confirmed in its language; by its terms, it benefits others than black citizens. Referring to the citizenship provision in his veto message, President Johnson remarked that it also included and made citizens "the Chinese of the Pacific States, Indians subject to taxation, the people called Gypsies, as well as the entire race designated either as blacks, people of color, negroes, mulattos, and persons of African blood."[54] In his response Trumbull did not deny this interpretation, dismissing the point as insignificant to the major thrust of the law.[55] Johnson could have gone much further in describing the inclusiveness of the measure. Most whites were also "persons born in the United States" and therefore as "such citizens of every race and color" entitled to "the same right in every State and Territory . . . as is enjoyed by white citizens." This last phrase does not affect the composition of the benefitted group, for it relates only to the safeguards provided. In the case of whites, it would mean "as is enjoyed by [other] white citizens." If white citizens then generally enjoyed the protected liberties, a state could not deny them without good cause to other people born in the United States, either individuals or groups.[56]

As originally drafted, the Senate bill contained only the qualification "the same right"; the words "as is enjoyed by white citizens" were added in the House Judiciary Committee in an amendment offered by Chairman Wilson. His reasoning was that "unless these qualifying words were incorporated in the bill, those rights might be extended to all citizens, whether male or female, majors or minors. So that the words are intended to operate as a limitation and not as an extension. . . ."[57] This intent meant that courts passing on claims of women and minors would have to consider a state's common or statute law relating to their entitlement to civil rights. (For women and minors the outcome would depend on the rights involved and for minors alone, on the age of majority.) Thus the phrase "as is enjoyed by white citizens" was a standard by which to determine state compliance with the Act.

In the instance of native born white citizens, the words "shall have the same rights . . . as is enjoyed by white citizens" would likewise constitute a standard by which state legislation treating particular individuals or groups differently than others would be judged. Thus the Act would affect state economic regulation denying the protected citizens, black or white, the right to contract freely for various purposes, such as employment, business, or property. For a statute to survive attack, a court would have to find that the affected citizens were not treated unequally—in essence, that the law was justified—as would later be required during the *Lochner* period.

The Civil Rights Act easily passed Congress. Thirteen senators spoke to its merits, most not finding any; fourteen discussed it in the House, again mostly in opposition. The bill passed the Senate on 22 February, by a vote of 33-12 and on 13 March, the House, by a vote of 111-38. Thereafter, on 6 April, the Senate voted to override President Johnson's veto by a margin of 33-15, and the House did the same on 9 April, by a vote of 122-41.

The Thirty-ninth Congress also passed the Freedmen's Bureau Bill, intended to protect for a limited period the rights of emancipated slaves in the formerly rebellious states then controlled by the Union forces. Trumbull introduced the legislation on the same day that he presented the Civil Rights Bill. President Johnson also vetoed the Bureau Bill, which was upheld, and Congress subsequently passed a modified version, which survived another veto. Each version protected against deprivation of the same rights enumerated in section 1 of the Civil Rights Act, again evidencing Congress' high priority for property and economic freedoms.[58]

Fourteenth Amendment: Bingham's Early Version of Section 1

Prior to the House debates on the Civil Rights Bill, the select Joint Committee on Reconstruction voted to submit to Congress a resolution proposing a fourteenth amendment to the Constitution. Committee member Rep. Bingham of Ohio, its primary author, first presented this resolution to the House on 26 February 1866. It was introduced concurrently in the Senate but never considered by that body. The Ohio legislator who later became the principal author of the major provision in the final version of the fourteenth amendment, was dubbed by Justice Hugo Black "the Madison of the first section of the Fourteenth Amendment."[59] This earlier version of that which was to become the second sentence in section 1, provided as follows:

> The Congress shall have power to make all laws which shall be necessary and proper to secure to the citizens of each State all privileges and immunities of citizens in the several States, and to all persons in the several States equal protection in the rights of life, liberty, and property.

The first part was worded to incorporate article IV, section 2, while the second used terminology not found elsewhere but reflecting the due process language in the fifth amendment. According to the Ohio representative, the amendment would enable Congress to apply fundamental rights contained in the Constitution to the states. "Every word of the proposed amendment is today in the Constitution, save the words conferring the express grant of power upon the Congress of the United States." The framers had omitted inserting authority for Congress to enforce against the states "the great canons of the supreme law." The amendment would, Bingham said, arm Congress "with the power to enforce the Bill of Rights as it stands in the Constitution today."[60] It encompassed no more than those safeguards granted by two provisions of the Constitution, the privileges and immunities clause of article IV and the due process clause of the fifth amendment.[61]

At this and various other times, Bingham used the term *Bill of Rights* to include all liberties protected in the Constitution: This, as he said on occasion, was the "immortal Bill of Rights," thus as other abolitionists were inclined to do,[62] according it a natural rights connotation. At other times, to be sure, he confined the term to the first eight amendments.

An opponent of the Civil Rights Act, the Congressman believed that a constitutional amendment was required before Congress could impose civil rights restraints on the states. The House, although not disposed toward the general structure of the proposed amendment, refused to table it, and on 28 February after some debate, postponed consideration by a vote of 110-37, until the second week of April. Bingham voted with the majority. The measure was never taken up again and was eventually replaced by the final version.

The problem with this earlier version was that instead of prohibiting state action infringing on liberties, the amendment placed the obligation entirely on Congress, granting it that which was considered either excessive or ill-defined authority over the states and enabling future Congresses to change policy. The final version of the fourteenth amendment was drafted to meet this concern. Consistent with the form of other constitutional protections, it prohibited certain state action, and its original purposes could be negated not by the will of another Congress but only by another amendment.

From Bingham's perspective, the amendment would have made the Civil Rights Act unnecessary. He rejected the statute in part because it removed some inherent state powers and centralized them in the federal government.[63] In contrast, his proposed amendment would greatly advance freedom and yet maintain the federal-state balance. "The care of the property, the liberty, and the life of the citizen . . . is in the States, and not in the Federal Government. I have sought to effect no change in that respect in the Constitution of the country."[64] Under the amendment, state authorities would have to answer nationally only if "they enact laws refusing equal protection to life, liberty or property."[65]

The Ohio legislator explained that the equal protection provision of the amendment applied the due process guarantee to the states. He equated these two concepts; each comprehended the other. There could be no liberty without equality and vice versa. On initial consideration this position might appear untenable, for many commentators believe that irreconcilable tension exists between liberty and equality. Governments impose myriad laws and regulations that achieve the latter at the expense of the former. This version of equality is statist, to be brought about by the adoption of laws that make people alike in their condition. However, the libertarian version, which was advanced by Bingham and espoused by John Locke, among others, is based on the rejection or elimination of laws that treat people unequally. For Bingham, equality before the law meant that all laws should apply equally and that no person or group should be favored or denied. When government limits the liberties of certain individuals, it also denies them equality with others not so incapacitated.[66]

Bingham was far from alone in this thinking. For a great many years prior to the Civil War, abolitionists had maintained that the fifth amendment's due process clause required that the laws treat equally with respect to life, liberty, and property all persons similarly situated.[67] Legislation treating certain people in a different or special way without adequate cause—therefore unequally—was found to be violative of due process in a number of judicial decisions prior to the Civil War.[68] Subsequent to ratification of the fourteenth amendment, courts employed either or both the due process and the equal protection clause to nullify legislation arbitrarily denying liberties to individuals or groups. To preserve a statute under either clause, a state had to show that sufficient reason existed to account for the differential treatment.[69]

Commentators have referred to some of Bingham's positions as "peculiar," but apparently they were not then so regarded and they greatly influenced the drafting of section 1. On the floor of the House, his colleagues frequently acknowledged him to be a highly competent constitutional lawyer. That congressional leaders held him in esteem is also evident from his appointment to the influential Reconstruction Committee and from the important role he exercised on it, becoming chairman during the third session of the Fortieth Congress. A prominent and influential Congressman in 1866, the Ohio representative has been described as radical, moderate, and conservative.[70] Although he had roots in the antislavery movement, unlike most of its congressional activists he opposed the Civil Rights bill, both as a whole and that portion of it eliminated prior to passage, that forbade discrimination in civil rights and immunities.

Bingham is a much admired figure, yet he does not lack critics. However, like many of his Republican colleagues, he advanced antislavery political theory and the constitutional interpretations that accompanied it. Contemporary commentators have little trouble finding fault. His lengthy speeches are not always clear in meaning or thought. Moreover, his interpretations of some constitutional issues are at great variance with modern thinking, making him even more difficult to comprehend.

Bingham articulated his views on the issues with which the three major guarantees of section 1 are concerned in two speeches presented before Congress—one in 1857,[71] and the other in 1859.[72] His later addresses to the Thirty-ninth Congress reveal similarity in position. Bingham customarily viewed privileges and immunities and due process in natural rights terminology, each as insulating human freedom from government oppression. In his 1857 speech, he defended the power of Congress to control slavery in the Territories, while in 1859 he attacked Oregon's attempt at statehood because it barred freed Negroes and mulattos from settling or holding real property, and making contracts within its boundaries. Bingham also expressed ideas that later would be instrumental in framing the critical clauses of section 1.

Like Trumbull and Wilson, Bingham construed article IV, section 2 as guaranteeing fundamental rights: these rights were, he contended, natural or inherent liberties of United States citizens that were intended to be secure from violation by the states. Although this position required an interpretation that essentially eliminated the section as the comity clause between the states (as it has traditionally been regarded), it was a construction that Bingham regarded as intended, even self-evident.

A strong believer in natural rights, he maintained a distinction between them and political rights, relating the former to life, liberty, and property. Natural rights were insulated from the majority, while political rights were its product. The following are excerpts from his two speeches relating to privileges and immunities.

> I deny that any State may exclude a law abiding citizen of the United States from coming within its Territory, or abiding therein, or acquiring and enjoying property therein, or from the enjoyment therein of the "privileges and immunities" of a citizen of the United States. . . . [Pursuant to article IV, section 2, the] citizens of each State, all the citizens of each State, being citizens of the United States, shall be entitled to "all privileges and immunities of citizens in the several States." Not to the rights and immunities of the several States; not to those constitutional rights and immunities which result exclusively from State authority or State legislation; but to "all privileges and immunities" of citizens of the United States in the several states. There is an ellipsis in the language employed in the Constitution, but its meaning is self-evident that it is "the privileges and immunities of the citizens of the United States in the several States" that it guaranties [sic].
>
> Citizens of the United States . . . are entitled to all of the privileges and immunities . . . amongst which are the rights of life, liberty, and property, and their due protection in the enjoyment thereof by law. . . .[73]
>
> All free persons, then, born and domiciled in any State of the Union, are citizens of the United States; and, although not equal in respect of political

rights, are equal in respect of natural rights. Allow me, sir, to disarm prejudice and silence the demagogue cry of "negro suffrage," and "negro political
equality," by saying, that no sane man ever seriously proposed political equality to all, for the reason that it is impossible. Political rights are conventional,
not natural; limited, not universal; and are, in fact, exercised only by the
majority of the qualified electors of any State, and by the minority only
nominally.[74]

His due process orientation was of the same character. According to
Bingham, the due process guarantee of the fifth amendment secures the
natural rights for all persons, requires equal treatment by the law and
comprehends the highest priority for ownership. Note his statement that no
one shall be deprived of property "against his consent," a stronger affirmation of property rights than that contemplated in the fifth amendment,
which contains no such qualification.

Natural or inherent rights, which belong to all men irrespective of all conventional regulations, are by this constitution guarantied [sic] by the broad
and comprehensive word "person," as contradistinguished from the limited
term citizen—as in the fifth article of amendments, guarding those sacred
rights which are as universal and indestructible as the human race, that "no
person shall be deprived of life, liberty, or property but by due process of law,
nor shall private property be taken without just compensation."[75]

Who . . . will be bold enough to deny that all persons are equally entitled to
the enjoyment of the rights of life and liberty and property; and that no one
should be deprived of life or liberty, but as punishment for crime; nor of his
property, against his consent and without due compensation?[76]

It must be apparent that the absolute equality of all, and the equal protection
of each, are principles of our Constitution, which ought to be observed and
enforced in the organization and admission of new States. The Constitution
provides, as we have seen, that *no person* shall be deprived of life, liberty, or
property, without due process of law. It makes no distinction either on account of complexion or birth—it secures these rights to all persons within its
exclusive jurisdiction. This is equality. It protects not only life and liberty, but
also property, the product of labor. It contemplates that no man shall be
wrongfully deprived of the fruit of his toil any more than of his life. . . .[77]

The due process guarantee was no less important to him in 1866. Delivered in his oratorical style, the following passage from a speech urging
adoption of the early version of section 1, reveals Bingham's commitment
to a natural rights perspective holding that due process is the highest reach
of justice.

Your Constitution provides that no man, no matter what his color, no matter
beneath what sky he may have been born, no matter in what disastrous
conflict or by what tyrannical hand his liberty may have been cloven down,

no matter how poor, no matter how friendless, no matter how ignorant, shall be deprived of life or liberty or property without due process of law—law in its highest sense, that law which is the perfection of human reason, and which is impartial, equal, exact justice; that justice that requires that every man shall have his right; that justice which is the highest duty of nations as it is the imperishable attribute of the God of nations.[78]

Consistent with such beliefs, Bingham rejected any constitutional distinction between citizens and persons in safeguarding liberties. During debate on the Civil Rights legislation, he opposed substituting the word *citizen* for *inhabitant* because the former confined protections.[79]

Two other events are worthy of comment in considering Bingham's beliefs. In his maiden speech to Congress in 1856, he charged that a law passed by the Kansas Territorial Legislature, making it a felony for any free person to assert that no one has the right to hold slaves in the Territory, abridged "the freedom of speech and of the press, and deprives persons of liberty without due process of law."[80] He apparently viewed due process as protective also of activity not ordinarily associated with preservation of life, liberty, and property.

Bingham's concern for constitutionally guaranteeing property and other interests not related to race is evident in a change he sought to a draft of a proposed constitutional amendment adopted by the Reconstruction Committee and authored by Representative Thaddeus Stevens. This proposal occurred after the House postponed consideration of Bingham's early version, as already described. Section 1 of Stevens's amendment provided: "No discrimination shall be made by any State, nor by the United States, as to the civil rights of persons because of race, color, or previous condition of servitude." Bingham moved to add the following provision to the amendment: "nor shall any State deny to any person within its jurisdiction the equal protection of the laws, nor take private property for public use without just compensation." This motion lost in the committee 5-7, with three absent.[81] Presumably Bingham desired both to extend the protections of the draft amendment beyond race relations to other personal freedoms and to safeguard property from any form of confiscation.

It is doubtful that he intended to augment the section's racial protections. Stevens's section 1 was similar in language to the provision in the original Civil Rights bill forbidding "discrimination in civil rights and immunities" that the House, and subsequently the Senate, deleted.[82] Bingham had urged that action because "the term civil rights includes every right that pertains to the citizens under the Constitution, laws, and Government of this country."[83] A person given to such an understanding would hardly have thought more protection necessary for such rights than was already provided by Stevens's section 1. Nor does it seem that Bingham would have received the support that he did for his proposal from Representative Rogers and Senator Johnson—both Democrats and opponents of the Civil Rights Act—had they believed it was so directed.

The equal protection provision that Bingham proposed was in the same language that he drafted for this clause in the final version of section 1. The preceding episode indicates that equal protection relates to more than just race discrimination; it constitutes a substantive limitation on other state actions. Stevens voted to support Bingham's motion, an act indicating the former's preference for coverage beyond race relations. Subsequently, the committee deleted Stevens's section 1 and replaced it with that which is now its second sentence, which was authored by Bingham.

While he emphasized the abolition of both slavery and racial discrimination, Bingham emerges essentially as a man of libertarian convictions, committed to preserving a wide array of individual freedoms from government interference. His ideas are important not only to understanding the authorship of section 1 but also in providing insight into the thinking of the political leaders who approved it.

These were mostly members of the Republican Party. The election of 1860 brought the Republicans to national power, the party of the antislavery movement. Prominent members of the party, whether radical, moderate, or conservative, had strong antislavery convictions and sought, after emancipation, to bring former slaves into the mainstream of American society and economy. As evident from the debates on the Civil Rights Bill, their political and constitutional theories stressed equal protection of the laws. According to William H. Seward, Lincoln's secretary of state and a prominent Republican, the party stood above all else for "one idea . . . the equality of all men before human tribunals and human laws."[84] The abolitionists also advanced natural law concepts that libertarian thinkers had long supported in furtherance of an economic system dedicated to private property and free enterprise. Thus, their ideas of equality reflected the positions associated with Adam Smith and John Locke.[85] In fact, frequently their proclamations during the advocacy days prior to the Civil War sounded as if they emanated from these sources.[86]

Bingham's early version of section 1 would have enabled Congress to impose these principles on the states. In the debates on the proposed amendment, ten congressmen, divided equally between supporters and opponents, made substantive comments. No one seriously quarreled with Bingham's definitions of privileges and immunities, due process, and equal protection. Opponents, however, feared that Congress would use these concepts excessively against the states, something which Bingham vigorously denied would occur because the amendment would only authorize Congress to enforce "the Bill of Rights."

When asked by Representative Hale of New York whether the amendment was aimed solely at protecting American citizens of African descent in rebellious states, Bingham denied this intent, responding that it would apply to other states and that it would also safeguard thousands of Union supporters in the erstwhile confederacy from confiscation and banishment.[87] Subsequent discussion discloses the extent to which the amendment would govern the states. The Ohio representative asserted that the amendment would confer upon Congress a general power to secure for all persons equal protection from the states with respect to life, liberty, and property. Thus it would enable Congress to strike down the Oregon constitutional provisions that Bingham had condemned in his 1859 speech. However, Hale's New York did not require congressional intervention. Bingham was uncertain about the amendment's impact in Indiana.[88] As to real estate,

> every one knows that its acquisition and transmission under every interpretation ever given to the word property, as used in the Constitution of the country, are dependent exclusively upon the local law of the States, save under a direct grant of the United States. But suppose any person has acquired property not contrary to the laws of the State, but in accordance with its law, are they not to be equally protected in the enjoyment of it, or are they to be denied all protection? That is the question, and the whole question, so far as that part of the case is concerned.[89]

Two exchanges between Hale and Representative Stevens, who supported the measure, further clarify the intended scope of Congressional authority pursuant to the amendment. Hale charged that under the equal protection provision Congress would be able to override a state's civil and criminal legislation, establishing its own laws instead. Stevens replied that the authority was far less broad.

> Does the gentleman mean to say that, under this provision, Congress could interfere in any case where the legislation of a State was equal, impartial to all? Or is it not simply to provide that, where any State makes a distinction in the same law between different classes of individuals, Congress shall have the power to correct such discrimination and inequality?[90]

In response to Hale's assertion that Congress would be empowered to overrule the states with respect to the property rights of women, Stevens explained, "When a distinction is made between two married people or two *femmes sole*, then it is unequal legislation; but where all of the same class are dealt with in the same way then there is no pretense of inequality." Stevens' explanations would require the application of reasonableness distinctions that the judiciary later utilized under substantive due process.[91]

While their responses and examples may suggest wider coverage for the equal protection provision, both Bingham and Stevens maintained that state legislation that did not abridge fundamental liberties would not be affected.

Apparently coverage under this amendment would have been broader than that under the Civil Rights Act, in which protections are specifically enumerated. The statute would be enforced by the judiciary, while the amendment's reach would depend on the will of Congress. A state law imposing restraints only on particular persons or groups would have to be justified to Congress as either nondiscriminatory, or warranted by differences in situation or condition. Had the amendment been adopted, Congress would have been in a position to strike down the law litigated in the *Lochner* case and for essentially the same reasoning employed by the Supreme Court. In that decision, the Court was not persuaded that sufficient basis existed to except bakeries and confectioneries from the prevailing rule of freedom of employment contract. New York had passed a law affecting certain persons only, and it did not show adequate reason for this differential treatment. As we shall see in the following portion of this chapter, the final version of section 1 was sufficiently similar to the earlier one to allow for the same outcome under it in a *Lochner*-type controversy.

The Final Version

On 28 April 1866 the select Joint Committee on Reconstruction voted 12-3 (only Democrats opposing), to report out another proposed version of the fourteenth amendment whose first section had been authored by John Bingham. Section 1 consisted solely of what is now its second sentence; a prior sentence on citizenship would be added subsequently. Section 5 did not differ from the one finally approved. Representative Thaddeus Stevens presented this version to the House on 8 May, and Senator Jacob Howard introduced it to the Senate on 23 May. Both men were members of the joint committee. To better comprehend section 1's meaning, I believe it best to discuss the Senate debate prior to that of the House, and the subsequent commentary will proceed on this basis.

In part Howard explained the privileges and immunities clause by quoting from Justice Washington's opinion in *Corfield v. Coryell*. Privileges and immunities "cannot be fully defined in their exact extent and precise nature," observed the Senator, adding that Washington's interpretation does give "some intimation of what probably will be the opinion of the judiciary."[92] Howard also embraced within his definition the "personal rights guaranteed [sic] and secured by the first eight amendments of the Constitution." As examples, he identified many of the rights so safeguarded, omitting those specifically included in Washington's enumeration.[93] The clause in question had been drafted to protect "privileges and immunities of citizens of the United States" to whom the Republican leaders thought article IV, section 2 applied, even though not so stated therein. This language resolved the "ellipsis in the language"—the language omissions about which Bingham expressed concern in his 1859 speech.[94]

In a statement corresponding to Bingham's assertion made when presenting his earlier version, Howard claimed that all these restraints then bound the federal government but not the states.

> These immunities, privileges, rights, thus guarantied [sic] by the Constitution or recognized by it, are secured to the citizen solely as a citizen of the United States and as a party in their courts. They do not operate in the slightest degree as a restraint or prohibition upon State legislation. . . . [Moreover,] there is no power given in the Constitution to enforce and to carry out any of these guarantees. They are not powers granted by the Constitution to Congress, and of course do not come within the [necessary and proper] clause of the Constitution . . . but they stand simply as a Bill of Rights in the Constitution, without power on the part of Congress to give them full effect; while at the same time the States are not restrained from violating the principles embraced in them except by their own local constitutions, which may be altered from year to year. The great object of the first section of this amendment is, therefore, to restrain the power of the States and compel them at all times to respect these great fundamental guarantees.[95]

Congress would have power under section 5 to enforce these and other guarantees set forth in the amendment. While not mentioning the Act by name, presumably sections 1 and 5 taken together authorized the passage of legislation such as the Civil Rights Act.

Instead of offering separate meanings for the other two clauses, Howard lumped them together in a short explanation.

> The last two clauses of the first section of the amendment disable a State from depriving not merely a citizen of the United States, but any person, whoever he may be, of life, liberty, or property without due process of law, or from denying to him the equal protection of the laws of the State. This abolishes all class legislation in the States and does away with the injustice of subjecting one caste of persons to a code not applicable to another. It prohibits the hanging of a black man for a crime for which the white man is not to be hanged. It protects the black man in his fundamental rights as a citizen with the same shield which it throws over the white man. Is it not time, Mr. President, that we extend to the black man, I had almost called it the poor privilege of the equal protection of the law? Ought not the time to be now past when one measure of justice is to be meted out to a member of one caste while another and a different measure is meted out to the member of another

caste, both castes being alike citizens of the United States, both bound to obey the same laws, to sustain the burdens of the same Government, and both equally responsible to justice and to God for the deeds done in the body?[96]

Thus these clauses outlaw racial preferences and other class and caste legislation. Here Howard spoke of protecting legal equality, both racial and otherwise, as under the Civil Rights Act. The extent of this commitment is not defined, but because of its origins and the senator's explanation, is substantive and substantial. Not being limited by the specifics contained in the Act, its impact on the states would be greater.

Howard distinguished the privileges and immunities clause from the others in two respects. First the others applied to all persons rather than to citizens only. Second, the privileges and immunities clause imposed fundamental liberties from diminution or denial by the states, while the others forbade their unequal application by the states. The senator's failure to distinguish between the due process and equal protection clauses suggests that he, like Bingham, viewed the two as basically similar in their anti-discriminatory purposes.

The three clauses thus provided sweeping protection for fundamental liberties. Except for eliminating direct congressional oversight, the final version is similar conceptually to Bingham's earlier one. The privileges and immunities clause reads as Bingham interpreted his February version of it (and of article IV, section 2). Because he used equal protection and due process interchangeably, the addition of due process language and the alteration in equal protection wording clarified meaning and provided added safeguards. In a speech to Congress in 1871, Bingham asserted that the final version was "more comprehensive than as it was first proposed. . . . It embraces all and more than did the February proposition."[97]

Bingham's speeches reveal that he, like many of similar persuasion, employed the three concepts interchangeably to condemn oppressive state legislation. All were catch phrases of the antislavery movements. Absent from the amendment is any reference to civil rights—an omission probably attributable to the fact that the term was thought to include political rights. As previously explained, this same concern had led to the deletion of this term in the Civil Rights Act.

At the prompting of other senators, Howard subsequently offered specific changes to the amendment. One that was adopted was the addition of the definition of citizenship, which became the first sentence of section 1. In the ensuing debate, only six senators, three from each party, commented substantively on that which had by that time become the second sentence of section 1. The Republicans approved, while the Democrats opposed, the latter, concentrating their criticism on the privileges and immunities clause. The sparsity of the discussion may in part be attributable to the greater passions and concerns that other sections aroused among the senators.

Senator Poland of Vermont supported and amplified Howard's explanation. He maintained that the amendment's privileges and immunities clause "secures nothing beyond what was intended" in article IV, section 2. Inasmuch as Poland did not challenge Howard's explanation he apparently assumed like other Republicans and some Justices, that article IV, section 2 was intended to protect all fundamental liberties, including those in the first eight amendments. Poland went on to argue that many of the states had repudiated or disregarded this important clause and that investing Congress with the power to enforce it was now eminently proper and necessary. Furthermore, with slavery abolished, no valid or reasonable objection could exist to the due process or equal protection clauses. "[Both clauses are] the very spirit and inspiration of our system of government, the absolute foundation upon which it was established. [They are] essentially declared in the Declaration of Independence and in all the provisions of the Constitution." In addition this Amendment would remove all doubt about the power of Congress to enact the Civil Rights Act.[98]

Senator Howe of Wisconsin, supported section 1 as a means to combat the wrongs that the rebellious states had committed and might continue to commit. They had "denied to a large portion of the population the plainest and most necessary rights of citizenship." These included, among others, the right to hold land that had been paid for, the right to sue for wages that had been withheld, and the right to give testimony. No state should be able to deny its citizens their privileges and immunities or the equal protection of the laws.[99] Senator Henderson of Missouri chose to discuss only that part of section 1 relating to citizenship. The other clauses, he asserted, merely secured the rights that attached to citizenship in all free countries. He implied that the amendment would overcome the Black Codes that had made the Negro a "degraded outcast" deprived of the "commonest rights" of property and legal processes.[100]

Senator Davis saw no need for a new privileges and immunities clause because, he stated, article IV "comprehends the same principle in better and broader language." However, he offered no explanation for this conclusion. Davis argued additionally that due process should be left to the states where it was already assured in their constitutions. Equal protection was also their concern.[101] Senators Hendricks of Indiana and Johnson of Maryland spoke about the ambiguity of the privileges clause. The former complained that he had not heard any senator or other statesman accurately define the rights and immunities of citizenship.[102] The latter, a member of the Reconstruction Committee, disapproved of only this clause because he did not understand what its effect would be.[103] His motion to delete it was rejected. Although this limited debate may not be very revealing as to meaning, it does evidence an orientation supportive of the floor managers' explanations.

On 8 June, the joint resolution was approved, 33-11, more than the required two-thirds.

Because of the limited meaning currently given the term *privileges and immunities* as it appears in the Constitution, it may seem surprising that only a few Democrats challenged Howard's extensive definition. However, the debates relating to the fourteenth amendment reveal (as heretofore noted) that most of the Republicans probably regarded privileges and immunities as encompassing all fundamental liberties secured in the Constitution, which necessarily would include those set forth in the first eight amendments. Antislavery doctrine advanced this position.[104] Were it otherwise, the clause might secure only a portion of those liberties identified in the eight amendments—a far lesser and seemingly incoherent commitment to freedom. Moreover, Washington had indicated that his list of liberties was not final and that unnamed others were also embodied within those specified. Howard's broad definition, accordingly, remained consistent with such thinking.

Washington's interpretation differs from the one that has been accepted by the U.S. Supreme Court. Pursuant to the existing understanding, the privileges and immunities clause of article IV forbids any state from discriminating in most matters against citizens of other states in favor of its own. This clause does not stand as a guardian for fundamental rights, protecting citizens against the laws of their own or other states, as Washington would have had it. Because Republicans of the Thirty-ninth Congress mostly accepted Washington's meaning, their speeches are sometimes difficult to comprehend for those steeped in contemporary Supreme Court doctrine.

However, Howard's interpretation of privileges and immunities was not uncommon among lawyers of that period. As indicated, it was in keeping with Justice Washington's position and it appears similar to that expressed by Justice Bradley for himself and Justice Noah Haynes Swayne dissenting in the *Slaughter-House Cases*.[105] Bradley believed prior to ratification of the fourteenth amendment, the privileges and immunities of citizens of the United States consisted of all the people's liberties including those secured in the Bill of Rights and elsewhere in the Constitution, even if they were not necessarily safeguarded from limitation by the states. While he did not specifically refer to the Bill of Rights, Justice Field, in his minority opinion in the *Slaughter-House Cases*, which represented the views of all four dissenters, approved Washington's interpretation: The privileges and immunities designated by Washington are those *"which belong of right to the citizens of all free governments."*[106]

Debate in the House on section 1 was also not very extensive. In describing the contents of this section, Representative Stevens read the privileges and immunities and equal protection clauses but interestingly paraphrased the due process clause as prohibiting the states from "unlawfully depriving [citizens] of life, liberty, or property." He maintained that the provisions of that which is now the second sentence of section 1 are

> all asserted, in some form or other, in our Declaration or organic law. But the Constitution limits only the action of Congress and is not a limitation on the States. This amendment supplies that defect, and allows Congress to correct the unjust legislation of the States, so far that the law which operates upon one man shall operate *equally* upon all.[107]

Stevens explained that whatever law applied to a white man would apply to the black man precisely in the same way and to the same degree. He did not otherwise define the section, except to assert that it would maintain the principles of the Civil Rights Act in the event that the latter was repealed by another Congress. After this short explanation, Stevens went on to section 2, which he considered the most important.

Howard and Bingham, as we have seen, also viewed the Constitution as defective because it did not permit the Congress or judiciary to apply its fundamental guarantees to the states. Bingham, among others, claimed that the Civil War might have been averted if the national government could have imposed these restraints on the slaveholding states.

Probably the most powerful member of Congress, Stevens was more radical than Bingham on reconstruction policy. Thus, he sought provision to guarantee negro suffrage constitutionally, but he could not obtain enough votes for passage. Bingham did not help him in this quest. However, the two took similar positions on amending the Constitution. Stevens supported Bingham's main efforts—first on the latter's earlier version of the fourteenth and then on the Ohioan's addition to section 1 of the draft amendment that he authored. Additionally, Stevens voted to delete this section 1 in favor of the one drafted by Bingham, which now constitutes the second sentence.

The two also had similar ideas in another area that may also be revealing of their prospective on section 1. During the drafting of the fourteenth amendment, Stevens sponsored bills to support the economic interests of certain railroads against hostile state legislatures on the ground that their vested rights had been impaired. Bingham voted for these measures. Commentators have speculated about the effect of such business problems upon the drafting of the amendment.[108] It is difficult to believe that these congressmen were not aware that the broad language would be invoked in support of commercial interests.

In a speech near the close of the House debate on the proposed Amendment, Representative Bingham explained that section 1 protected by national law from abridgement or denial by a state "the privileges and immunities of all of the citizens of the Republic and the inborn rights of every person within its jurisdiction. . . ."[109] In light of the congressman's known perspectives, "inborn" most likely meant natural rights. He used the same term in his previously mentioned 1857 speech when he condemned states that "trample upon the inborn rights of humanity" and lauded those that "defend[s] the inborn rights of each against the combined power of all."[110]

In the sentence from his closing speech quoted above Bingham summed up the significance and importance of section 1. For him, privileges and immunities encompassed the fundamental liberties, including those contained in the first eight amendments. Both the due process and the equal protection clauses further secured these and other natural rights for all persons, regardless of citizenhip. "That great want of the citizen and stranger, protection by national law from unconstitutional State enactments, is supplied by the first section of this Amendment."[111]

The balance of the House debate is not very enlightening on how the representatives construed that which is now the second sentence of section 1. Much of the debate concerned other sections, with a number of legislators making no reference to section 1. In all, fewer than twenty Representatives dealt with that section. Most of the Republicans who participated mentioned its relationship to the Civil Rights Act—that the amendment supplied the necessary congressional authority either to enact it or to constitutionalize its protections against diminution or extinction by subsequent Congresses.

Some spoke about the personal protections other than those in the racial area secured by the amendment. Representative Thayer said it "simply brings into the Constitution what is found in the bill of rights of every State."[112] The equality aspects were stressed by Representatives Raymond[113] and Farnsworth;[114] Representative Miller said that the due process and equal protection clauses were within the spirit of the Declaration of Independence;[115] Representative Eckley believed that the amendment afforded "security of life, liberty, and property to all the citizens of all the States."[116]

Of the Democrats, only Representative Rogers of New Jersey (a member of the reconstruction committee) spoke extensively. He warned that the privileges and immunities clause would revolutionize the entire constitutional system by eliminating the states' powers. "All the rights we have under the laws of the country are embraced under the definition of privileges and immunities." He asserted the amendment embodies "that outrageous and miserable Civil Rights Bill."[117]

On May 10, by a vote of 128-37, the House adopted the joint resolution proposing the fourteenth amendment.

The Due Process Concept and Clause

During the debates on the Civil Rights Bill and the two proposed constitutional amendments, the term *privileges and immunities* was frequently mentioned and defined. Less attention was directed at the term *due process*, which has so much more influenced the course of the nation's laws. When the latter term was mentioned, it was always in the context of limiting governmental authority. As we have seen, this perspective was shared by Representative Bingham. He equated due process with equal protection of the laws and fundamental and natural rights. No representative disputed Bingham's explanation that the equal protection provision of his first version, which was clearly substantive in character, did no more than apply the due process clause to the states. Representative Higby specifically agreed, asserting that the language of the two guarantees "is very little different."[118]

The previous discussion of the Civil Rights Act disclosed Representative Wilson's convictions about due process. He believed that the Act merely enforced the protections of the fifth amendment's due process clause against the states.[119] Representative Thayer argued that this clause gave, by implication at least, sufficient power to Congress to pass the Civil Rights Act.[120] For Representative Baker of Illinois, the proposed due process clause was "a wholesome and needed check upon the great abuse of liberty which several of the states have practiced, and which they manifest too much purpose to continue."[121] Senator Poland and Representative Miller identified the due process and equal protection clauses with the Declaration of Independence.[122] Representative Williams of New Jersey opined that if suffrage was regarded as a property right, its deprivation would violate the due process clause.[123] Thus, for these congressmen due process of law meant a substantive guarantee of life, liberty, and property. Representative Stevens, appears to have so construed the clause in introducing the amendment in the House.

Most Republican congressmen, particularly those who had been active in or associated with the antislavery movement, held similar views. Due process was a term used often before, during, and after the Civil War. Both sides of the slavery controversy employed it to further their cause. Proslavery forces contended that slaves were property and that therefore owners were protected against their loss without due process. In contrast, beginning in the mid-1830s, antislavery activists thought of the due process guarantee as constitutionalizing their natural rights beliefs in the sanctity of life, liberty, and property.[124] They repudiated any notion that a person could be someone else's property; people possessed human property only in and to their own selves. The fifth amendment's due process clause accordingly, obligated the national government to secure this property in the territories.

The due process concept was a major verbal weapon for the abolitionists. H. J. Graham observes that due process

> was snatched up, bandied about, "corrupted and corroded," if you please, for more than thirty years prior to 1866. For every black letter usage in court, there were perhaps hundreds or thousands in the press, red schoolhouse, and on the stump. Zealots, reformers, and politicians—not jurists—blazed the paths of substantive due process.[125]

Thus the political parties committed to eradicating slavery used the term to advance their position. In 1843 the Liberty Party platform declared that the fifth amendment's due process clause legally secured the inalienable rights referred to in the Declaration of Independence.[126] The 1848 and 1852 platforms of the Free Soil Party contended that the clause served both as a restraint on the federal government and an obligation that it enforce the inalienable rights enumerated in the Declaration.[127] More significant, according to the 1856 and 1860 platforms of the Republican Party, the clause denied Congress the power to allow slavery to exist in any territory in the Union. "It becomes our duty to maintain [the due process provision] of the Constitution against all attempts to violate it."[128] Some of those involved in the drafting or consideration of the Republican platforms probably would later, as members of Congress or in other political roles, be responsible for framing or adopting the fourteenth amendment. In the 1856 political campaign, "due processs of law" was a leading catch phrase of Republican orators.[129]

Due process advocacy was not confined to the antislavery movement. When the fourteenth amendment was being framed, insurance and other corporations submitted large numbers of petitions to Congress permeated with due process of law reasoning, urging federal relief from state legislation depriving them of property and economic freedoms.[130] Commentators have noted the commonality of interest between corporate and antislavery groups: Each thought it would benefit from the imposition of due process, just compensation, and privileges and immunities restraints on the states. Accordingly, both lobbied for these positions.[131] The abolition of slavery eliminated the argument over ownership of the person, and both sides of this controversy could thereafter promote personal freedom under the same reasoning.

This general perception of due process was reflected in the courts. Although the contours of due process are never precise, in 1866 it was nevertheless a definable legal concept, and to this extent the framers of the amendment spoke with clarity, obviating inquiry into their intentions. By that time, it was accepted that due process related to required processes and procedures in civil law. In this respect, it was a substantive restraint on legislatures, forbidding them from passing these kinds of oppressive laws. Considerable precedent also existed that due process of law went much further and protected ownership. In 1857, Chief Justice Roger B. Taney invoked substantive due process as one basis for his decision in the *Dred Scott* case. Taney held that Congress had no power to prohibit slavery in specified areas because the "powers over person and property . . . are not only not granted to Congress, but are in express terms denied, and they are forbidden to exercise them."[132] Taney explained this "express" limitation as follows:

> And an act of Congress which deprives a citizen of the United States of his liberty or property, merely because he came himself or brought his property into a particular Territory of the United States, and who had committed no offence [sic] against the laws, could hardly be dignified with the name of due process of law.[133]

On this point, the Chief Justice was supported by the two Justices who concurred in his opinion. This opinion did not represent the first time that Taney had accepted substantive due process. In speaking for the Court in *Bloomer v. McQuewan*[134] (1852), he had asserted that a special act depriving licensees of their right to use property protected by patent "certainly could not be regarded as due process of law."[135] However, the case was resolved on other grounds.

Substantive due process was a viable concept among U.S. Supreme Court Justices at the time the fourteenth amendment was framed and ratified. In an 1865 federal circuit court case, United States Supreme Court Justice Grier, held that a Pennsylvania statute repealing a railroad corporation charter, violated the state constitution's due course of law provision.[136] After the framing of the amendment, the first High Court ruling on due process was *Hepburn v. Griswold*,[137] issued 7 February 1870 by a Court then consisting of seven members, all appointed prior to Congress' action. For the majority of four, Chief Justice Chase determined (among other matters) that holders of contracts for payment in dollars entered into prior to the effective date of the Legal Tender Act of 1862, were deprived by that Act of their property in violation of the fifth amendment's due process guarantee. Although Justice Grier was by then no longer sitting on the Court, he had been a member when the case was decided in conference on 27 November 1869, at which time he concurred with the majority.

When the contract in *Hepburn* was executed, gold and silver coin was the only form of money that could be lawfully tendered in payment of private debts. To obtain funds for the war effort, the Act authorized the issuance of paper notes, not redeemable in gold or silver coin, and provided that with certain exceptions these notes should "be lawful money and a legal tender in payment of all debts, public and private, within the United States." While the litigation was pending, the value of dollars in coin exceeded that in notes. The majority concluded that the due process clause protects holders of the contracts in question. According to Chase, the clause (as well as other provisions of the fifth amendmen) operates "directly in limitation and restraint of the legislative powers conferred by the Constitution."

> The only question is, whether an act which compels all those who hold contracts for the payment of gold and silver money to accept in payment a currency of inferior value deprives such persons of property without due process of law.
>
> It is quite clear, that whatever may be the operation of [the Legal Tender Act], due process of law makes no part of it. Does it deprive any person of property? A very large proportion of the property of civilized men exists in the form of contracts. These contracts almost invariably stipulate for the payment of money. And we have already seen that contracts in the United States, prior to the act under consideration, for the payment of money, were contracts to pay the sums specified in gold and silver coin. And it is beyond doubt that the holders of these contracts were and are as fully entitled to the protection of this constitutional provision as the holders of any other description of property.[138]

Justice Miller, for the minority of three, did not deny that the clause was a substantive limitation on the legislature. Rather, he objected that the effect on holders was incidental to the purpose of Congress to further the war effort. President Grant subsequently appointed two Justices who on 1 May 1871, in *Knox v. Lee*,[139] joined with the three dissenters to reverse *Hepburn*. Writing for the majority in *Knox*, Justice Strong applied the same analysis to the due process issue as Miller had, and Chase followed his prior interpretation.

Justice Swayne dissented in *Hepburn*, and he and newly appointed Justice Bradley voted with the majority in *Knox*. Neither, however, should be considered antagonistic to substantive due process. On the contrary, both contended in their dissents in the *Slaughter-House Cases*, decided the following year (and to be discussed subsequently), that the fourteenth amendment's due process clause secured property and economic interests. On the issue of protecting vested property interests, these Justices would probably have agreed with the four who made up the *Hepburn* majority. In *Knox*, Bradley filed a concurring opinion, arguing that Congress was empowered to enact the disputed legislation. He did not discuss due process directly. Presumably, Swayne, who did not file a separate opinion in either case, agreed.

Decided in 1872, the *Slaughter-House Cases* was the next major decision involving due process. In 1869, Louisiana's legislature granted a twenty-five year exclusive privilege to a private corporation that it had created to operate a regulated livestock and slaughterhouse business within a specified area of about 1150 square miles, comprising New Orleans and two other parishes. The privilege required that all cattle brought into this area for commercial purposes, be slaughtered by the corporation or on its facilities. On a vote of 5-4, the U.S. Supreme Court upheld the monopoly as not violative of the fourteenth amendment or any other provision of the Constitution. With respect to the due process clause, Miller said for the majority, that "under no construction of that provision that we have ever seen" can the restraint imposed on the butchers be held to be a deprivation of property within the meaning of that provision.[140]

The four dissenters protested that the objective of the fourteenth amendment was to give the Court precisely the power to strike down measures such as the Louisiana statute that encroached upon the ability of citizens to acquire property and pursue business. In his dissent for the four person minority, Field relied on the meaning of the privileges and immunities clause and did not discuss due process.[141] However, Justice Bradley, in his separate dissenting opinion concurred in by Jusice Swayne, did comment on the concept, stating that "a law which prohibits a large class of citizens from adopting a lawful employment, or from following a lawful employment previously adopted, does deprive them of liberty as well as property, without due process of law."[142]

It is surprising that Field and another dissenter, Chief Justice Chase, did not find that the statute violated the due process clause. Field who agreed with Chase's opinions in *Hepburn* and *Knox* became in time the Court's strongest champion of substantive due process.[143] A leading abolitionist, Chase, long prior to his appointment to the Court, had advanced the due process concept to support antislavery theory and goals.[144] Justice Clifford concurred in Miller's opinion in the *Slaughter-House Cases*, but he also agreed with Chase in the two legal tender cases.

Nor should Justice Miller's opinion in the *Slaughter-House Cases* label him as an opponent of substantive due process. A literal reading of Miller's language suggests no more than that due process did not encompass the activities in question. Miller did not contend that vested property rights were outside the scope of substantive due process. That Miller was inclined to include such rights is revealed by his decision in a case that was submitted in briefs at the time that the *Slaughter-House Cases* were argued but that remained undecided until the following year.[145] In this case, Iowa's statewide prohibition law, which had been enacted in 1851, came under attack as a violation of due process. Miller wrote that a statute prohibiting the sale of property raised "a very grave question" under the fourteenth amendment's due process clause. However, Miller decided that the case did not present this issue.

It is not difficult to conclude that during the period when the Amendment was framed and ratified, a majority of the Supreme Court would have held that due process protected property ownership.

At the state level, due process clauses were also applied to strike down legislative interferences with property. The leading pre-Civil War decision on due process at the state level is *Wynehamer v. People*,[146] an 1856 New York case in which a state penal statute forbidding the sale of intoxicating liquors owned at the time of enactment (except for medicinal and religious purposes) and requiring their destruction under certain circumstances, was declared to violate the state constitution's due process clause. New York's highest court held that the clause protected the prerogatives of ownership—that is, said one Justice, while some regulation is possible, "where [property] rights are acquired by the citizen under the existing law, there is no power in any branch of the government to take them away."[147]

Thomas M. Cooley, the most influential commentator during the period following the ratification of the amendment, also asserted that due process secured property rights. In the first edition of his famous book on constitutional limitations, published in 1868,[148] he concluded that government can violate due process by the limitations it imposes

> and not any considerations of mere form. . . . When the government, through its established agencies, interferes with the title to one's property, or with his independent enjoyment of it, and its act is called in question as not in accordance with the law of the land, we are to test its validity by those principles of civil liberty and constitutional defence which have become established in our system of law, and not by any rules that pertain to forms of procedure merely. . . . Due process of law in each particular case means, such an exertion of the powers of government as the settled maxims of law sanction, and under such safeguards for the protection of individual rights as those maxims prescribe for the class of cases to which the one in question belongs.[149]

Cooley concedes that any branch of government may limit private rights to property, but only within certain bounds.

> The chief restriction is that vested rights must not be disturbed; but in its application as a shield of protection, the term "vested rights" is not used in any narrow or technical sense, as importing a power of legal control merely, but rather as implying a vested interest which it is equitable the government should recognize, and of which the individual cannot be deprived without injustice.[150]

The Justice goes on to discuss those property interests protected by due process (or its equivalent, law of the land) clauses. Thus, according to this authoritative commentator, due process at the time that the fourteenth amendment came into being provided substantive safeguards for property interests; he rejected the view that in civil matters it had no more than procedural significance.

The Fourteenth Amendment and Lochner

In 1872, United States Supreme Court Justice Stephen Field explained that section 1 of the fourteenth amendment "was intended to give practical effect to the declaration of 1776 of inalienable rights." Writing for himself and the other three dissenters in the *Slaughter-House Cases*, he asserted that it "secures the like protection to all citizens . . . against any abridgement of their common rights [by the States]."[151] The foregoing study of section 1 supports Field's conclusion. This section was drafted to accord maximum protection for liberty at the state level. Each clause of its second sentence was directed toward this end, and collectively they constitute a formidable barrier against state excesses and oppressions.

Although this general commitment is quite plain, it does not reveal which activities are safeguarded and to what extent. This issue may not be resolved for many areas, but it can be satisfied for the liberties about which this chapter is concerned—those relating to property and economics. In the civil area these were liberties of highest concern to the men responsible for framing section 1 of the fourteenth amendment—a fact that is evident from the views that they expressed, the laws they passed, and the authorities on whom they relied. For example, the Civil Rights Act of 1866, Justice Washington's definition of privileges and immunities, and the commentaries of Blackstone and Kent (the most quoted and respected legal scholars), all emphasize the importance in a free society of ownership and enterprise and the liberties required to make them meaningful. Little doubt can exist that people supporting the doctrines advanced in these materials would strive to secure economic freedoms in the fourteenth amendment. Support for this assertion can be summarized briefly as follows:

1. Section 1 of the amendment established the principles of the Civil Rights Act in the Constitution so that they could not be repealed by a subsequent Congress. The Act protected against discriminatory treatment the rights of most United States citizens "to make and enforce contracts . . . [and] to inherit, purchase, lease, sell, hold and convey real and personal property."
A major purpose of the Act was to enable the former slaves to exercise economic freedom without being subject to restraints special to them. The Act was drafted to provide this protection for native born citizens under the Blackstonian position, expounded in the debates by Senator Trumbull, that "any statute which is not equal to all, and which deprives any citizen of civil rights, which are secured to other citizens, is an unjust encroachment upon his liberty."
2. According to Justice Washington, the privileges and immunities belonging to citizens of all free governments include "the enjoyment of life and liberty, with the right to acquire and possess property of every kind" and with respect to citizens of one state "the right . . . to pass through, or to reside in, any other state for purposes of trade, agriculture, professional pursuits [and] to take, hold and dispose of property, either real or personal." Although Washington did not specifically refer to it, freedom of contract would be included in the property rights that he did mention. Contracts are a form of property in that they are an asset or acquisition that can be purchased, held, and sold. They are requisite also for the acquisition, use, and transfer of real and personal property.[152] Both Senator Trumbull and Representative Wilson explained that all the rights set forth in the Civil Rights Act were included in Washington's definition.
3. The debates disclose that Sir William Blackstone and Chancellor James Kent were highly authoritative for the Thirty-ninth Congress on the powers and purposes of government. The former declared that "the principal aim of society is to protect individuals in the enjoyment of those [three] absolute rights," which were to personal security, personal liberty, and private property. For Blackstone, the right to property meant the "free use, enjoyment, and disposal [by the owner] of all his acquisitions, without any control or diminution, save only by the laws of the land." The legislature could acquire private property but only by giving the owner "full indemnification and equivalent for the injury thereby sustained."[153] Kent wrote that "the right to acquire and enjoy property [is] natural, inherent, and unalienable."[154] Both commentators maintained that legislative restraints over private activity that could not be justified were invalid.

The legitimacy of the *Lochner* review should be considered in light of this background. Resolution of this issue should not differ under section 1 of the fourteenth amendment from that which it would under the Act, for the former incorporates the latter. The question in *Lochner* was whether the state, under the circumstances involved, could regulate the terms of certain employment contracts. The Civil Rights Act secured the "right . . . to make and enforce contracts," a provision directly applicable to the *Lochner* situation. Indeed, the Thirty-ninth Congress drafted the Act to protect, among other things, the right of emancipated blacks to contract freely for the purchase and sale of goods and services. Specifically, the legislators sought to eliminate state laws that regulated the terms of employment for blacks because these laws limited work opportunities. Such identifiable purposes became general ones applicable to other individuals and groups both under the language of the Act and the fourteenth amendment.

The defendant in *Lochner* was an employer who complained that the New York statute deprived him and other bakery employers of the right to contract with employees for more than ten hours of work per day, or a total of sixty per week. Had the statute been confined to black employers, little question could exist that it would have invited inquiry under the Act, and the state would have had the burden of justifying different treatment for black employers. Because the Act is a legal equality statute applicable to all citizens without regard to race, the state would have had the same obligation under the Act had white citizens been similarly restricted.

Pursuant to the explanations given by Bingham and Stevens, a similar burden would have been borne by the state under the original version of section 1, which had been presented to Congress in February.[155] Because the final version provides no less protection against the states, it would likewise safeguard the bakery employers.

The constitutional outcome should not differ even if it is assumed that the Act was confined solely to racial discrimination, as some contend it was. The liberties enumerated in the statute were of great concern to the Thirty-ninth Congress or they would not have been named in both the Act and the Freedmen's Bureau Bill. It is most unlikely that Congress would have secured them under the statutes but not under the Constitution. Thus it would be very odd indeed if the Congress did not intend to safeguard liberty of contract under section 1.

The charge that *Lochner* is a lawless construction of the due process clause is grounded in part on the supposition that in the 1860s due process related only to procedure and not to substance. However, no indication exists in the relevant debates that Bingham and his fellow Republicans so confined it. Among other things, they equated due process with equal application of the laws. The equal protection provision of Bingham's initial version of section 1 was premised on this understanding. For them, due process essentially meant protection against government oppression, which could take many forms.

However, at that time, the courts did not accord this interpretation to the due process guarantee. During the period in question, most U.S. Supreme Court Justices regarded due process as a safeguard for vested property or other material interests but did not extend this protection further into the economic area to include liberty of contract. In time and for good reason, the Supreme Court eliminated this distinction.

The paramount idea of due process—that government may not deprive people of their fundamental rights—has been a part of Anglo-Saxon law since King John accepted the Magna Carta in 1215. Chapter 39 thereof provides essentially that no freeman shall be arrested, detained in prison, deprived of his freehold, outlawed, banished, or in any way molested unless by the lawful judgment of his peers and by the law of the land. In time due process became synonymous with the law of the land. Thus, state constitutions usually contained either law of the land or due process clauses. Over the years, English and American courts have expanded the meaning of due process to include contemporary concerns for the preservation of liberty, at times going no further than protecting process and procedures.

Understandably, due process did not remain limited to securing vested interests. Deciding the issue on a case-to-case basis, as is typical of American jurisprudence, the Supreme Court enlarged the protections of the due process clauses to include, by 1897, the liberty to contract for the production, distribution, and sale of goods and services. In *Allgeyer v. Louisiana*,[156] Justice Peckham explained the unanimous ruling:

> The liberty mentioned in [the due process clause of the fourteenth amendment] means not only the right of the citizen to be free from the mere physical restraint of his person, as by incarceration, but the term is deemed to embrace the right of the citizen to be free in the enjoyment of all his faculties; to be free to use them in all lawful ways; to live and work where he will; to earn his livelihood by any lawful calling; to pursue any livelihood or avocation, and for that purpose to enter into all contracts which may be proper, necessary and essential to his carrying out a successful conclusion the purposes above mentioned.[157]

Due process does not bar all governmental restraints in the area it affects; rather it forbids only unjustified restraints. This approach is consistent with long held English-American conceptions about the limits of governmental powers. Thus, Blackstone defined civil liberty as "no other than natural liberty so far restrained by human laws (and no farther) as is necessary and expedient for the general advantage of the public."[158] So too, Justice Washington asserted that the fundamental liberties that he designated belonged of right to citizens of all free governments but were "subject nevertheless to such restraints as the government may justly prescribe for the general good of the whole."[159] Congressman Bingham accepted this idea with the likely clarification that a very high burden of proof be borne by the government in justifying a restraint.

Conclusion

While it involved only the due process provision, the inquiry conducted by the United States Supreme Court in *Lochner* is consistent with the framers' understanding of each of the three clauses in the second sentence of section 1. Because both "privileges and immunities of citizens of the United States" and "equal protection of the laws" were provisions not previously construed by the courts, the framers' intent should be controlling.

Interpreting the due process clause is more difficult for it already had judicial meaning when the amendment was framed. By the time of *Lochner*, however, the definition, which in the 1860s went no further than to include vested rights, had, in the normal course of adjudication, expanded to comprehend contracts of employment. This development is neither antagonistic to the basic rationale of due process nor an unrealistic extension in meaning. Constitutional adjudication does not preclude sensible movement in interpretation. Thus, when *Lochner* was decided, the constitutional outcome should have been the same, whether the Justices relied on earlier judicial interpretation or the framers' meaning of due process.

Unlike the others, this chapter concerns the Supreme Court's failure to implement its responsibility by enforcing certain rights. The usual grievance against the Court relates to its excesses—creating powers and rights—usually criticized as judicial activism. Failure to implement existing rights is no less an error than enforcing non-existent rights. The Constitution can be transgressed either through omission or commission. Chief Justice Marshall asserted that his court should "never . . . enlarge the judicial power beyond its proper bounds, nor fear[ed] to carry it to the fullest extent that duty required."[160]

Notes

A portion of this chapter appeared in Siegan, *Rehabilitating Lochner*, 22-2 & 3 San Diego L. Rev. 453 (1985). Copyright 1985 San Diego Law Review Association. Reprinted with permission.

1. See MILTON FRIEDMAN, CAPITALISM AND FREEDOM (Chicago and London: University of Chicago Press, 1962); Milton & Rose Friedman, *Free to Choose* (New York and London: Harcourt Brace Jovanovich, 1979); Coase, *The Market for Goods and the Market for Ideas*, 64 AMER. ECON. REV. 384, (1974); Director, *The Parity of the Economic Market Place*, 7 J. LAW & ECON. 1 (1964); F. A. Hayek, *The Constitution of Liberty*, 32-35 (Chicago,: Henry Regnery, 1972); McCloskey, *Economic Due Process and the Supreme Court: An Exhumation and Reburial*, 1962 SUP. CT. REV. 34; Bernard H. Siegan, ECONOMIC LIBERTIES AND THE CONSTITUTION (Chicago and London: University of Chicago Press, 1980).
2. Morey v. Dowd, 354 U.S. 457 (1957), *rev'd* New Orleans v. Dukes, 427 U.S. 297 (1976).
3. Beauharms v. Illinois, 343 U.S. 250, at 286 (1952).
4. Lochner v. New York, 198 U.S. 45 (1905); Minnesota v. Clover Leaf Creamery Co., 449 U.S. 456 (1981).
5. Euclid v. Ambler Realty Co., 272 U.S. 365 (1926).
6. Act of 9 April 1866, ch. 31, 14 Stat. 27.
7. *See* CONG. GLOBE, 39th Cong., 1st sess. 474 (1866) Deletions are within brackets and additions are in italics.
8. *Id.*
9. *Id.*
10. 6 F. Cas. 546 (C.C.E.D. Pa. 1823) (No.3,230).
11. *Id.* at 551-52.
12. CONG. GLOBE, 39th Cong., 1st Sess. 476 (1866).
13. *Id.* at 1117-19.
14. *Id.* at 1117-18.
15. *Id.* at 1117.
16. *Id.* at 1118.
17. *Id.* at 1118-19.
18. *Id.* at 1294.
19. Dred Scott v. Sandford, 60 U.S. 393 (1857).
20. CONG. GLOBE, 39th Cong., 1st Sess. 475 (1866).
21. *Id.* at 504.
22. *Id.* at 1151.
23. *Id.* at 1833.
24. *Id.* at 1159.
25. *Id.* at 1160, 1759.
26. *Id.* at 1124. Some commentators have asserted that the extent of the oppression of blacks was exaggerated. H. FLACK, THE ADOPTION OF THE FOURTEENTH AMENDMENT 96 (Baltimore: John Hopkins University Press, 1908); Bickel, *The Original Understanding and the Segregation Decision*, 69 HARV. L. REV. 1, 13 (1955).
27. CONG. GLOBE, 39th Cong., 1st Sess. 1366 (1866).
28. *Id.* at 1413.
29. *Id.* at 474.
30. *Id.* at 599.
31. *Id.* at 600.
32. *Id.* at 1760. That a reasonableness standard would apply in implementing the statute is also evident in some remarks of Missouri Senator Henderson. In responding to assertions that by conferring citizenship on certain Indians, the

states would lose power to adopt regulations governing their activities, Henderson stated that the states would continue to have power to determine among other things whether the person was competent to make contracts, as in the case of minors and lunatics. *Id.* at 572. *See also* Representative Wilson's explanations to the same effect later in the text.

33. *Id.*, at 1118.
34. *Id.*
35. *Id.* at 1292.
36. *Id.* at 1832.
37. *Id.*
38. *Id.* at 1263.
39. *Id.* at 1265.
40. *Id.* at 2502.
41. *Id.* at 1267.
42. *Id.*
43. *Id.* at 598.
44. *Id.* at 1153.
45. *Id.* at 601.
46. *Id.* at 1268.
47. *Id.* at 1293-94.
48. *Id.* at 1154.
49. *Id.* at 1782.
50. *Id.* at 504.
51. *Id.* at 601, 1155.
52. *Id.* at 1785, 3034.
53. J. TENBROEK, EQUAL UNDER LAW 118 (London: Collier Books, 2nd printing 1969). *See also* H. J. GRAHAM, EVERYMAN'S CONSTITUTION 168-71 (New York: Norton 1968).
54. CONG.GLOBE, 39th Cong., 1st Sess. 1679 (1866).
55. *Id.* at 1757.
56. In 1860, the total resident population of the United States was 31,513,000 of which 4,138,697 were foreign born. The figures for 1870 were 39,905,000 and 5,567,229, respectively. THE STATISTICAL HISTORY OF THE UNITED STATES FROM COLONIAL TIMES TO THE PRESENT, at 8 and 117 (New York: Basic Books, 1976). Because of the small percentage of foreign born, implementation of the Act's provisions would be little disturbed by the existence of this group. The Civil Rights Act can also be read as not qualifying the enumerated rights (contracts, suit, etc.) with the phrase "as is enjoyed by white citizens." This language would then apply only to the portion relating to "proceedings for the security of person and property." However, my construction of the Act would not change under this interpretation, although others may consider it as strengthening the view that the Act affected whites. In McDonald v. Santa Fe Trail Transportation Co., 427 U.S. 273 (1976), the United States Supreme Court found that the Civil Rights Act of 1866 applied to the civil rights of whites as well as non-whites. The case concerned alleged discrimination against whites.
57. CONG. GLOBE, 39th Cong., 1st Sess. App. 157 (1866).
58. *Id.* at 318, 209-10. The second Freedmen's Bureau Act was carried over a veto on 16 July 1866.
59. Adamson v. California, 332 U.S. 46, 74 (1947)(Black, J., dissenting).

60. CONG. GLOBE 39th Cong., 1st Sess. at 1088-89 (1866).
61. *Id.* at 1089.
62. J. TENBROEK *supra* note 53, at 128 and 215.
63. CONG. GLOBE 39th Cong., 1st Sess. 1292 (1866).
64. *Id.*
65. *Id.* at 1090.
66. "Though . . . all men by nature are equal, I cannot be supposed to understand all sorts of equality. Age or virtue may give men a just precedency. Excellency of parts and merit may place others above the common level. Birth may subject some, and alliance or benefits others, to pay an observance to those to whom Nature, gratitude, or other respects, may have made it due; and yet all this consists with the equality which all men are in respect of jurisdiction or dominion one over another, which was the equality . . . being that equal right that every man hath to his natural freedom, without being subjected to the will or authority of any other man." J. LOCKE, OF CIVIL GOVERNMENT, Ch. VI, Sec. 54. The same perspective is set forth in considerable depth in F. A. HAYEK, THE CONSTITUTION OF LIBERTY, 85-102 (Chicago: Henry Regnery Co., 1960). According to Hayek, the "great aim of the struggle for liberty has been equality before the law." *Id.* at 85. "Equality before the law and material equality are therefore not only different but in conflict with each other; and we can achieve either the one or the other, but not both at the same time." *Id.* at 87.
67. *See* J. TENBROEK, *supra* note 53, at 51-56. The idea was common to a great many other Republicans of the period. *See* Crosskey, *Charles Fairman, "Legislative History", and the Constitutional Limitations on State Authority*, 22 UNIV. CHI. L. REV., 1, 17 (1954).
68. *See* R. L. MOTT, DUE PROCESS OF LAW (Indianapolis: Bobbs-Merrill Co., 1926, pp. 256-76.
69. *See Id.* at 275-299. The similarity of the two clauses is discussed by Chief Justice Earl Warren in Bolling v. Sharpe, 347 U.S. 497, 499 (1954).
70. Kelly, *The Fourteenth Amendment Reconsidered*, 54 MICH. L. REV. 1049, 1052 (1956) (radical); M.L. BENEDICT, A COMPROMISE OF PRINCIPLE (New York: Norton, 1974) (conservative); B.B. KENDRICK, THE JOURNAL OF THE JOINT COMMITTEE OF FIFTEEN ON RECONSTRUCTION (New York: Columbia University Press, 1914) (moderate).
71. CONG. GLOBE, 34th Cong. 3d Sess. App. 135 (1857).
72. CONG. GLOBE, 35th Cong. 2d Sess. 981 (1859).
73. *Id.* at 984.
74. *Id.* at 985.
75. *Id.* at 983.
76. *Id.* at 985.
77. CONG. GLOBE, 34th Cong. 3d Sess. App. 140 (1857).
78. CONG. GLOBE, 39th Cong., 1st Sess. 1094 (1866).
79. *Id.* at 1292.
80. CONG. GLOBE, 34th Cong. 1st Sess. App. 124 (1856).
81. B.B. KENDRICK, *supra* note 70, at 85.
82. CONG. GLOBE, 39th Cong., 1st Sess. 1366, 1413 (1866).
83. *Id.* at 1291.
84. 4 W. SEWARD, WORKS 302 (G. Baker ed. 1884) *quoted in* Nelson, *The Impact of the Antislavery Movement upon Styles of Judicial Reasoning in Nineteenth*

Century America, 87 HARV. L. REV. 513, 537 (1974). However, to acquire popular support, the Republican 1860 platform did advocate a high protective tariff and free homesteads.

85. Among the rights to which the abolitionists gave prime attention were those of property and contract. Abolitionists urged that these liberties be extended to all people, for they were natural rights that would enable the dependent poor to become financially secure and thus independent. Nelson *supra* note 84, at 555-57. On the economic views of the named men, *See* K.I. VAUGHN, JOHN LOCKE, ECONOMIST AND SOCIAL SCIENTIST (Chicago: University of Chicago Press, 1980); A. SMITH, THE WEALTH OF NATIONS (New York: The Modern Library, 1937). Blackstone explained the common law as supportive of these ideas of limited government: "[Civil liberty] is no other than natural liberty so far restrained by human laws (and no farther) as is necessary and expedient for the general advantage of the public. Hence we may collect that the law, which restrains a man from doing mischief to his fellow citizens, though it diminishes the natural, increases the civil liberty of mankind: but every wanton and causeless restraint of the will of the subject, whether practised by a monarch, a nobility, or a popular assembly, is a degree of tyranny. Nay, that even laws themselves, whether made with or without our consent, if they regulate and constrain our conduct in matters of mere indifference, without any good end in view, are laws destructive of liberty . . . [T]hat constitution or frame of government, that system of laws, is alone calculated to maintain civil liberty, which leaves the subject entire master of his own conduct, except in those points wherein the public good requires some direction or restraint." 1 W. BLACKSTONE COMMENTARIES *121-22.

86. J. TENBROEK, *supra* note 53, sets forth these examples:
The call for the Macedon antislavery convention of 8-10 June 1847 provided that
1. The true foundation of civil government is the equal, natural and inalienable right of *all men*—and the moral obligation, resting on the entire community to secure the free exercise of these rights, including life, liberty, and pursuit of happiness, to each individual, in his person and his property, and in their management.
3. The sole and indispensable business of civil government is to secure and preserve the natural and equal rights of all men unimpaired, to prevent and redress, violations of original rights. And the benefits of government are not purchased by giving up any portion of our natural rights for protection of the rest.
5. All monopolies, class legislations, and exclusive privileges are unequal, unjust, morally wrong, and subversive of the ends of civil government.
6. The primary and essential rights of humanity are, the right to occupy a portion of the earth's surface. . . .
9. The right of self-ownership includes, of necessity, the right of each individual to the direction and to the products of his own skill and industry, and the disposal of those products, by barter or sale, in any portion of the earth where a purchaser can be found. These original and natural rights, civil government may neither infringe or impair; and all commercial restrictions therefore (except the wise and needful prohibition of immoral and criminal traffic, which no man has a natural right to engage in) are unjust and oppressive.

10. "A tariff for the protection of one particular branch of industry, so far as it reaches its end, is an unjust tax upon one portion of the community for the benefit of another. . . ." (*Id.* at 138 n.2, 142 n.7.)

At the Honeoye Liberty Mass Meeting, held 29 December 1846 through 1 January 1847, a declaration of sentiments was unanimously adopted containing similar assertions and also included the following: "The rightful power of all legislation is to declare and enforce our natural rights and duties, and take none of them from us. . . . The idea is quite unfounded, that, on entering society, we give up any natural right." *Id.* at 142 n.7.

87. CONG. GLOBE, 39th Cong., 1st Sess. 1065 (1866).
88. *Id.*
89. *Id.* at 1089.
90. *Id.* at 1063.
91. *See id.* at 1064 (additional comments of Rep. Hale).
92. *Id.* at 2765.
93. *Id.*
94. *See supra* text accompanying note 73.
95. CONG. GLOBE, 39th Cong., 1st Sess. 2765-66 (1866).
96. *Id.* at 2766.
97. CONG. GLOBE, 42d Cong., 1st Sess. App. 81, 83-85 (1871).
98. CONG. GLOBE, 39th Cong., 1st Sess. 2961 (1866). See also *infra* text accompanying notes 105 and 106.
99. *Id.* at App. 219.
100. *Id.* at 3031, 3034-35.
101. *Id.* at 240.
102. *Id.* at 3039.
103. *Id.* at 3041.
104. J. TENBROEK *supra* note 53, at 122-131.
105. 83 U.S. (16 Wall.) 36, 111, 116-17 (1872) (Bradley, J., dissenting).
106. *Id.* at 76.
107. CONG. GLOBE, 39th Cong., 1st Sess. 2459 (1866).
108. H.J. GRAHAM *supra* note 53, at 465-466.
109. CONG. GLOBE, 39th Cong., 1st Sess. 2542 (1866).
110. CONG. GLOBE, 34th Cong., 3d Sess. App. 136 (1857).
111. CONG. GLOBE, 39th Cong., 2543 (1866).
112. *Id.* at 2465.
113. *Id.* at 2502.
114. *Id.* at 2539.
115. *Id.* at 2510.
116. *Id.* at 2535.
117. *Id.* at 2538.
118. *Id.* at 1054. Bingham was asked by Representative Rogers "What do you mean by 'due process of law'?" He replied that "the courts have settled that long ago, and the gentleman can go read their decisions." In view of the definition Bingham had given the concept, it is difficult to consider his answer to the question as being serious or reasoned.
119. *See supra* text accompanying note 18.
120. CONG. GLOBE, 39th cong., 1st Sess. 1152 (1866).
121. *Id.* App. at 256.
122. *Id.* at 2961, 2510.

123. *Id.* at 1063.
124. J. TENBROEK *supra* note 53 at 119-22; KELLY *supra* note 70, at 1053-55; H. J. GRAHAM *supra* note 53, at 242-65. Concerning the early abolitionist arguments that would later be advanced under due process concept, *See* A. L. HIGGINBOTHAM, JR., IN THE MATTER OF COLOR, 329-32 (New York: Oxford University Press, 1978).
125. H.J. GRAHAM *supra* note 53, at 250. "Over the next thirty years [from 1834], due process as a substantive conception, became part of the constitutional stock in trade of abolitionism." J. TENBROEK *supra* note 53, at 121. "In comparison with the concept of equal protection of the law, the due process clause was of secondary importance to the abolitionists. It did, however, reach a full development, and by virtue of its emphasis in the party platforms, a widespread usage and popular understanding." *Id.* at 119-20.
126. *Id.* at 139. The Liberty Party was formed in 1840 and dedicated to antislavery. In 1844, its presidential candidate received 60,000 votes. It continued strong in local elections in 1846 but united in 1848 with the anti-slavery Whigs and Democrats to form the Free-Soil Party. THE COLUMBIA ENCYCLOPEDIA 1212 (1963).
127. J. TENBROEK *supra* note 53, at 140-41, nn.3 & 4. This party came into existence during 1847-48 and polled 300,000 votes. Its 1852 candidate for president received over 150,000 votes. It was absorbed into the new Republican Party in 1854. THE COLUMBIA ENCYCLOPEDIA *supra* note 126, at 767.
128. J. TENBROEK *supra* note 53, at 141, nn.5 & 6.
129. H.J. GRAHAM *supra* note 53, at 80.
130. *Id* at 83-88.
131. *Id.* at 81.
132. Dred Scott v. Sandford, 60 U.S. 393, 450 (1857).
133. *Id.*
134. 55 U.S. 539 (1853).
135. *Id* at 553.
136. Baltimore v. Pittsburgh & C.R.R., 2 F. Cas. 570, (C.C.W.D. Pa., 1865) (No. 827).
137. 75 U.S. 603 (1870). This case is discussed more extensively in chapter 2.
138. *Id.* at 624.
139. Knox v. Lee, 79 U.S. 457 (1871).
140. 83 U.S. at 81. "To reach the conclusion of Justice Miller and the majority, one must disregard not only all antislavery and all anti-race discrimination theory from 1834 on, but one must ignore virtually every word said in the debates of 1865-66." H.J. GRAHAM *supra* note 53 at 319.
141. 83 U.S. at 83.
142. 83 U.S. at 122.
143. B. SIEGAN, *supra* note 1, at 53-54.
144. J. TENBROEK *supra* note 53, at 61-63; H.J. GRAHAM *supra*, note 53, at 255 and 301, n. 18.
145. Bartemeyer v. Iowa, 85 U. S. 129 (1873).
146. 13 N.Y. 378 (1856). This decision was not followed in other states, probably for the most part because of the sensivity of the liquor issue. For a survey of pre-fourteenth amendment cases involving due process or law of the land provisions, *see* B. SIEGAN, *supra* note 1, at 24-46; R.L. MOTT, *supra* note 68, at 256-77, 275-99.

147. 13 N.Y. at 393.
148. T.M. COOLEY, A TREATISE ON THE CONSTITUTIONAL LIMITATIONS (New York: Da Capo Press, 1972).
149. *Id.,* at 356.
150. *Id.,* at 357-58.
151. 83 U.S. at 105.
152. There should be little doubt that Bingham and his colleagues would have accepted John Marshall's position that the right of contract is a natural right, Ogden v. Saunders, 25 U.S. 213, 346-47 (Marshall, C.J., dissenting).
153. 1 BLACKSTONE, *supra* note 85, at *120, 134-35.
154. 2 J. KENT, COMMENTARIES ON AMERICAN LAW 1 (New York: DaCapo Press, 1971). "There have been modern theorists, who have considered . . . [the] inequalities of property, as the cause of injustice, and the unhappy result of government and artificial institutions. But human society would be in a most unnatural and miserable condition, if it were instituted or reorganized on the basis of such speculation. The sense of property is graciously implanted in the human breast, for the purpose of rousing us from sloth, and stimulating us to action; and so long as the right of acquisition is exercised in conformity to the social relations, and the moral obligations which spring from them, it ought to be sacredly protected. The natural and active sense of property pervades the foundations of social improvement. It leads to the cultivation of the earth, the institution of government, the acquisition of the comforts of life, the growth of the useful arts, the spirit of commerce, the productions of taste, the erections of charity, and the display of the benevolent affections." *Id.* at 256-57.
155. See *supra* text accompanying notes 87-91, 97.
156. 165 U.S. 578 (1897).
157. *Id.* at 589.
158. W. BLACKSTONE, *supra* note 85, at *121.
159. Corfield v. Coryell, 6 F. Cas. 546, 552 (C.C.E.D. Pa. 1823) (No. 3,230). *See also supra* text accompanying note 11.
160. *Quoted by* JAMES BRADLEY THAYER, OLIVER WENDELL HOLMES AND FELIX FRANKFURTER ON JOHN MARSHALL 85 (Chicago: University of Chicago Press, Phoenix ed., 1967).

4

Classification on the Basis of Race: Education and Preferential Treatment

As discussed in the preceding chapter, section 1 of the fourteenth amendment provides a broad sphere of security for citizens and others against state impositions and oppressions. The present chapter deals with the extent to which the amendment protects against classification on the basis of race, and is confined to two subjects of current interest: education and preferential treatment.

The prior chapter explained that section 1 incorporates and increases the protections of the Civil Rights Act of 1866. The inquiry at hand will relate to this statute and, in addition, to the "residue" of section 1. The subsequent discussion will show that with respect to racial protections, the amendment as originally intended is nearly coterminous with the Act. How far did the statute extend? According to Senator Trumbull and Representative Wilson, its floor managers, the statute solely comprehended civil rights and not social privileges, voting, office holding, jury service, public schooling, or other political rights. Trumbull constantly emphasized that the bill "does not propose to regulate the political rights of individuals; it has nothing to do with the right of suffrage, or with any other political right." He rejected any amendment specifically excepting suffrage because it would only confuse a measure concerned with civil rights.[1] Rights created by the political process were not civil rights. He quoted Blackstone, among others, to explain civil rights and their relation to natural rights. "Civil liberty is no other than natural liberty, so far restrained by human laws and no further, as is necessary and expedient for the general advantage of the public."[2] Again quoting from Blackstone's *Commentaries*, Trumbull explained that these restraints (unlike those limiting political rights) should fall equally on all.[3]

Representative Wilson maintained the same position. Citing several sources including Blackstone and Kent, Wilson explained that civil rights were the natural rights of man and that they concerned life, liberty, and property. Perhaps most important to his explanation was this definition from Bouvier's *Law Dictionary* limiting the applicability of the term:

"Civil rights are those which have no relation to the establishment, support or management of government."

Accordingly, "civil rights and immunities" (the wording used in the original civil rights bill and subsequently eliminated) could not mean "that in all things civil, social, political, all citizens without distinction of race or color, shall be equal."[4] The requirement thus did not apply to suffrage, juries, or schools.

> [S]uffrage is a political right which has been left under the control of the several states, subject to the action of Congress only when it becomes necessary to enforce guarantee of a the republican form of government. Nor do they mean that all citizens shall sit on the juries, or that their children shall attend the same schools.[5]

Matters of this nature, Wilson subsequently affirmed, were not "within the control of Congress," and therefore were not affected by the statute. The bill has "nothing to do with subjects submitted to the control of the several states."[6]

Such assurances did not convince John Bingham that the Civil Rights Bill originally introduced in the House was limited, and, as previously reported, he supported the successful effort to remove the clause on civil rights and immunities.[7] He defined civil rights much more broadly than did Trumbull or Wilson to "include every right that pertains to the citizen under the Constitution, laws and Government of this country," including political rights. Use of the original terminology would "reform the whole civil and criminal code of every state government," since "there is scarcely a State in this Union which does not, by its constitution or by its statute laws, make some discrimination on account of race or color between citizens of the United States in respect of civil rights."[8]

Bingham differed with Trumbull and Wilson on definition, but like them he did not desire to subordinate the political authority of the states to the Civil Rights Act. His thinking on amending the Constitution was similarly directed. This fact can be ascertained from the comments that he made on the proposed original and final versions of section 1. Commenting on the former, the Ohio congressman observed that the care of the property, liberty, and life of the citizen is in the states: "I have sought no change in that respect."[9] Bingham said that instead he wished solely to enforce the Bill of Rights against the states, enabling them otherwise to continue implementing their constitutional responsibilities, which he explained in part by quoting Chancellor Kent.

> The judicial power of the United States is necessarily limited to national objects. The vast field of the law of property, the very extensive head of equity

jurisdiction, the principal rights and duties which flow from our civil and domestic relations, fall within the control, and we might also say the exclusive cognizance of the state governments. We look essentially to the state courts for protection to all these momentous interests. They touch, in their operation, every chord of human sympathy and control of our best destinies. . . .[10]

In his speech urging passage of the final version of the amendment, Bingham reiterated his purpose, to protect individual rights and not otherwise to interfere with state powers:

Allow me, Mr. Speaker, in passing, to say that this amendment takes from no State any right that ever pertained to it. No State ever had the right, under the forms of law or otherwise, to deny to any freeman the equal protection of the laws or to abridge the privileges or immunities of any citizen of the Republic, although many of them have assumed and exercised the power, and that without remedy. The amendment does not give, as the second section shows, the power to Congress of regulating suffrage in the several States.[11]

Bingham had long differentiated between natural and political rights. He rejected "political equality to all" in his 1859 speech on the ground that this goal is impossible to achieve. Moreover, "political rights are conventional, not natural; limited, not universal [and] under absolute control of the majority."[12]

Bingham's position in this respect, like those of Trumbull and Wilson, represented the majority in Congress. It could not be otherwise. These congressional leaders would have been foolhardy to have sustained and emphasized a perspective on a pending measure that was not acceptable to most of their colleagues. The reader will recall Wilson explaining that the words "civil rights and immunities" had been deleted to avoid "a latitudinarian construction not intended."

Some members of the House thought, in the general words of the first section in relation to civil rights, it might be held by the courts that the right of suffrage was included in those rights. To obviate that difficulty and the difficulty growing out of any other construction beyond the specific rights named in the section, our amendment strikes out all of those general terms and leaves the bill with the rights specified in the section.[13]

With the exception of the assurance that the persons protected were "to be entitled to the full and equal benefit of all laws and proceedings for the security of person and property, as is enjoyed by white citizens," section 1 of the Act was confined to enumerated safeguards. Despite its apparent potential for a "latitudinarian" construction, Wilson, stated that the assurance related only to the protection of life, liberty, and property. "As is enjoyed by white citizens" did not enlarge, but instead qualified, the scope of the Act's protection; otherwise persons not intended to be secured—for example, women and minors—would be included.[14]

When Ohio Representative Delano asked Wilson whether the clause (to be entitled, etc.) conferred upon the emancipated blacks the right of being jurors, Wilson replied that it did not. Nor was it intended to upset the laws of the several states on the qualifications of jurors. Wilson proceeded to emphasize that the bill was limited to securing fundamental rights without depriving the states of their governing authority.[15] The congressional debates show little apprehension about a latitudinarian construction of the last discussed portion of the statute, probably because the reference was to the rights of life, liberty, and property, matters that were generally of greatest concern during that period and therefore better understood.

A comparable episode occurred in the joint reconstruction committee during the final drafting of section 1 of the amendment. As previously discussed, the committee originally accepted Representative Stevens's provision specifically securing civil rights but finally eliminated it in favor of the one authored by Bingham.[16] The civil rights terminology was not only unacceptable to the committee but also would have probably failed on the floor for the same reasons that caused the elimination of comparable wording in the Civil Rights Act. Additionally, the language might have made ratification of the amendment more difficult, if not impossible, for much legally imposed segregation existed in the Northern and border states.

Sentiment in the Senate on the matter may be gauged from that body's 9 March 1866 proceedings, when it voted decisively against two proposals to remove all legal distinctions based on race. The subject under discussion was apportionment of representation among the former rebel states. By a 39-8 vote the Senate rejected a proposed provision by Massachusetts Senator Charles Sumner of Massachusetts requiring equality in all civil and political rights in those states "whether in the courtroom or at the ballot box." Senator Richard Yates of Illinois offered similar legislation applicable to all the states, and it was defeated by a 38-7 margin.[17]

In his explanation of section 1, Senator Howard commented on the fundamental and natural rights/political rights distinction. A state could neither abridge fundamental liberties nor qualify them unequally, but the amendment did not affect rights established by the political process.

> The right of suffrage is not, in law, one of the privileges or immunities thus secured by the Constitution. It is merely the creature of law. It has always been regarded in this country as the result of positive local law, not regarded as one of those fundamental rights lying at the basis of all society and without which a people cannot exist, except as slaves, subject to a de[s]potism.[18]

Although Representative Stevens's remarks on section 1 were perhaps less precise, they indicate his belief that it was confined to the enforcement of fundamental rights. Consistent with Bingham's position he noted that the provisions of section 1 were already "asserted" in the Declaration or Constitution. His opening comments also reveal disappointment at the failure to obtain a more comprehensive coverage. The proposed amendment, he observed,

> falls far short of my wishes, but it fulfills my hopes. I believe it is all that can be obtained in the present state of public opinion. . . . I will take all I can get in the cause of humanity, and leave it to be perfected by better men in better times. It may be that that time will not come while I am here to enjoy the glorious triumph; but that it will come is as certain as that there is a just God.[19]

Stevens's remarks were directed primarily at the failure to make any provision for Negro suffrage and probably also reflected regrets that his civil rights provision could not carry. In theory, Stevens was strongly against segregation despite the fact that he did not publicly reject separation of the races in the schools.[20] Although he supported Bingham's drafts at various stages, they were likely second best for him. Stevens's comments also suggest that he did not believe that section 1 was sufficiently open-ended to allow a future broad, antisegregation interpretation—a goal that some commentators believe that he and other "radicals" intended.[21] In September 1866, Stevens advised voters that the proposed amendment "does not touch social or political rights."[22]

The evidence is quite plain that in protecting against racial discrimination, Congress went as far as it could in the Civil Rights Act. Little reason exists to believe that its members deliberately expanded these guaranties when they adopted section 1 of the fourteenth amendment.

Section 1 and School Segregation

With this background in mind, I shall proceed to discuss the amendment's meaning in relation to public schooling. For this writer, the case is strong that the Thirty-ninth Congress did not seek to adopt an amendment that would affect racial segregation in the schools.

1. The Congress sought to maintain state authority except when it denied or deprived a person of fundamental or natural rights. No evidence exists that in the post-Civil War period, public schooling was considered a fundamental or natural right. Interestingly, to the present time, our

Supreme Court, even in its most socially activist periods, has never elevated education to this status.[23]

Conceptual considerations discourage such a holding. When a state refuses to provide education, it does not directly limit anyone's liberty. By contrast, providing education requires a state to establish and support certain facilities and programs. Both the Civil Rights Act and section 1 contain only prohibitory (negative), not mandatory (positive) language.

2. Was an exception to the general proposition intended for public schooling? None is evident in the debates. The only suggestion that it was even contemplated came from opponents of the statute or amendment, and this suggestion was denied by supporters. A congressman seeking guidance on the meaning of section 1 would surely never have concluded from the explanations given by the proponents that segregated schooling was affected. The evidence supports Alexander Bickel, who as law clerk to Justice Felix Frankfurter, advised the latter that "[it] is impossible to conclude that the 39th Congress intended that segregation be abolished." He thought it "impossible also to conclude [that Congress] foresaw [that segregation] might be, [abolished] under the language they were adopting."

> It was preposterous to worry about unsegregated schools, . . . when hardly a beginning had been made at educating Negroes at all and when obviously special efforts, suitable only for the Negroes, would have to be made.[24]

In the former slaveholding states, no system of public education existed. White children obtained their schooling from private groups, while such efforts for blacks were minimal. In some Northern states, Negroes were not allowed to attend public schools. "Even comparatively enlightened leaders then accepted segregation in the schools."[25] Under these circumstances, "an argument that the Fourteenth Amendment prohibits school racial segregation would have seemed fanciful in 1868."[26] Moreover, that the Thirty-ninth Congress was willing to accept school segregation is apparent from its support of such a program in the District of Columbia.

The argument that section 1 forbade school segregation has to be premised on its broad and imprecise language. Because no one could be certain about the reach of privileges and immunities, due process, and equal protection, the possibility existed that the Supreme Court would give any of or all these terms very expansive definitions. During the Civil War period many people were familiar with the *Dred Scott*[27] decision, which, among other things, illustrated the enormity of the Supreme Court's discretion in construing the Constitution. Students of the Court could not totally reject the Democrats' charges that the language in section 1 was sufficiently ambiguous to eliminate either at that time or in the future any state statute with racial impact. This, however, does not seem to be the majority perception in either House. Not many congressmen were constitutional lawyers, and most seemed willing to accept their leaders' assurances about the limitations of the language. (To be sure, the *Dred Scott* decision also suggested that a Court bent upon achieving a particular outcome could somehow find support in the Constitution, regardless of language.)

Contemporary proponents of constitutionally imposed desegregation cannot find much support for their position in the debates. Instead they must argue that the phraseology was deliberately left ambiguous. Contrary to his initial conclusion, Bickel later found that the language was receptive to subsequent latitudinarian construction for it was part of a living "Constitution."[28] Other scholars have offered comparable explanations.[29] Imaginative and creative as some of these commentators are, they still must rely on a constitutional construction oriented to a day far removed from the time when the language was written.

From the reception it has received in the Supreme Court, the fourteenth amendment seems tailored for judges inclined to making, instead of interpreting, the law. The background of section 1 is complex and involved; authors have consumed reams of paper analyzing it. By contrast, our highest tribunal has delivered important interpretations with very limited historical analysis. For example, after a minimal historical inquiry, Justice Miller for the *Slaughter-House Cases* majority found that the evil to be remedied by the equal protecton clause was: "The existence of laws in the states where the newly emancipated negroes resided, which discriminated with gross injustice and hardship against them as a class."[30] He doubted "very much" that state action for any other purpose would ever be held to come within the purview of this provision.[31] He similarly minimized the impact of the other two clauses. Miller thus confined section 1 mainly to race.

In *Strauder v. West Virginia*,[32] the first post-Civil War racial classification case to reach it, the High Court, per Justice Strong, followed suit and reversed by a 7-2 vote the murder conviction of a black because the state law under which he had been tried forbade blacks from serving on grand or petit juries.

The majority opinion provided two important interpretations of the equal protection clause. First, the amendment was designed "to assure the colored race the enjoyment of all the civil rights that under the laws are enjoyed by white persons." More than natural or fundamental rights were safeguarded, however. The Court included within the amendment's protection all laws and proceedings that affect blacks differently.

> The words of the Amendment, it is true, are prohibitory, but they contain a necessary implication of a positive immunity, or right, most valuable to the colored race—the right to exemption from unfriendly legislation against them distinctively as colored; exemption from legal discriminations, implying inferiority in civil society, lessening the security of their enjoyment of the rights which others enjoy, and discriminations which are steps toward reducing them to the condition of a subject race.[33]

Second, the amendment did not touch state classifications unrelated to race.

> We do not say that, within the limits from which it is not excluded by the Amendment, a State may not prescribe the qualifications of its jurors, and in so doing make discriminations. It may confine the selection to males, to freeholders, to citizens, to persons within certain ages, or to persons having educational qualifications. We do not believe the [Fourteenth] Amendment was ever intended to prohibit this. Looking at its history, it is clear it had no such purpose. Its aim was against discrimination because of race or color.[34]

Thus, while acknowledging the right of the states to make and enforce criminal laws, the Court held that this authority is subject to overriding federal powers when race is implicated.

However, no such purpose or distinction is evident in the debates of the Thirty-ninth Congress and a dissenting Justice Stephen Field assumed the responsibility of representing this perspective. Although in *Strauder* Justices Clifford and Field dissented without filing an opinion, the latter delivered one for both in a companion case.[35] According to the Justice, equality of protection secured under the equal protection clause extended only to "civil rights," as distinguished from political rights, which arise from the form of government and its mode of administration. As his dissent in the *Slaughter-House* cases showed, Field viewed the scope of section 1 much differently than did the majority. For him, although not at all unlimited, the reach and influence of the amendment's section 1 were nevertheless immense.

> It opens the courts of the country to everyone, on the same terms, for the security of his person and property, the prevention and redress of wrongs, and enforcement of contracts; it assures to everyone the same rules of evidence and modes of procedure; it allows no impediments to the acquisition of property and the pursuit of happiness, to which all are not subjected; it suffers no other or greater burdens or charges to be laid upon one than such as are equally borne by others; and in the administration of criminal justice it permits no different or greater punishment to be imposed upon one than such as is prescribed to all for like offenses.[36]

However, section 1 did not affect political rights. The equal protection clause had no more reference to them than it had to social rights and duties. Consistent with the distinctions accepted by Trumbull, Wilson, and Bingham, Field explained that unlike civil rights, which are absolute and personal, political rights are

> conditioned and dependent upon the discretion of the elective or appointing power, whether that be the People acting through the ballot, or one of the departments of their government. . . . The political rights which [an individual] may enjoy, such as holding office and discharging a public trust, are qualified because their possession depends on his fitness, to be adjudged by those whom society has clothed with the elective authority. The 13th and 14th Amendments were designed to secure the civil rights of all persons, of every race, color and condition; but they left to the States to determine to whom the possession of political powers should be intrusted [sic].[37]

Field viewed the selection of jurors as part of the political process to be administered by elected or appointed officials of the state. The case in which Field filed his dissent concerned the indictment of a Virginia county judge under the Civil Rights Act of 1875 for failing to select blacks as grand or petit jurors. The Justice regarded the judge as engaged in state administrative processes and therefore not constitutionally subject to oversight by federal authority. (The majority upheld the indictment.) The Justice's exposition was directed at state criminal processes, but it also bears upon the administration of local schools, a matter to be discussed subsequently.

To be sure, an argument can be made that criminal processes are always related to the protection of life, liberty, and property. However, as Field appraised it, the law that was stricken involved the administration and appointment powers of state government. There was no natural or fundamental right to be a juror. Nor did an accused have a right to be tried by jurors or judges of a certain racial mixture. In Field's view, these matters were to be determined by the states under their sovereign powers and were not affected by the equal protection clause.[38]

Field's view was similar to that espoused by Congressman Wilson when he represented that the Civil Rights Bill did not touch jury selection. No evidence exists that the Thirty-ninth Congress would have desired to or actually did assume a different position in section 1 of the fourteenth amendment.

The congressional debates make it apparent that the three rights clauses of section 1, while broad in scope, did not limit the plenary powers of the states to tax and spend and to administer and manage their governments. The congressional leaders considered this authority as involving state functions outside the reach of the fourteenth amendment. Application of the

Bill of Rights or other enumerated rights to the states would not generally affect these responsibilities. While movement and growth in the scope of the due process and equal protection clauses were not foreclosed, applying either to limit traditional state functions would obliterate the separation of federal and state powers, among the most recognized constitutional doctrines at the time of the adoption of the amendment.

The *Strauder* majority did not probe legislative intent and consequently did not even allude to this problem of construction. Substituting hypothesis for fact, it imposed a latitudinarian construction on the equal protection clause that was inconsistent with the intent of the Thirty-ninth Congress.

This interpretation affected a great many matters of local concern. In subsequent cases, the Justices continued to maintain it but they moderated its impact. In time, the Court confronted the problem of the separate but equal doctrine that prevailed in the Southern states. *Plessy v. Ferguson* involved an 1890 Louisiana law requiring that railway passenger cars have "equal but separate, accommodations for the white and colored races." The Court majority noted that the establishment of separate and equal schools had been upheld by courts "where the political rights of the colored race have been longest and most earnestly enforced," citing cases from Massachusetts, Ohio, Missouri, California, Louisiana, New York, Indiana, and Kentucky. In sustaining the Louisiana law, Justice Henry B. Brown wrote for the 8-1 majority that the laws separating the races were subject to review under a reasonableness standard.

> The object of the amendment was undoubtedly to enforce the absolute equality of the two races before the law, but in the nature of things it could not have been intended to abolish distinctions based upon color, or to enforce social, as distinguished from political equality, or a commingling of the two races upon terms unsatisfactory to either.[39]

The Court thus imposed a standard of equality that has no relation to that contemplated by leaders of the Thirty-ninth Congress, who rejected legal limitations based on race. As dissenting Justice Harlan explained this view, a legislative body or judicial tribunal must not "have regard to the race of citizens when the civil rights of those citizens are involved."

In 1954, the Court, in *Brown v. Board of Education* (*Brown I*),[40] unanimously reversed *Plessy*'s separate but equal interpretation. As discussed above, the background for the *Brown I* decision was as follows:

1. Section 1 was a broad but far from unlimited protection against discrimination on the basis of race. It was not intended to control matters within

the administrative authority of the states—those relating to the establishment, support, or mangement of government.

2. In *Slaughter-House* and *Strauder*, the Court overrode this distinction by subjecting to the equal protection clause state administrative processes affecting race.

3. In *Plessy*, the Court found that the clause was satisfied by laws requiring separate but equal arrangements, thereby enabling segregation to exist in schools and other public facilities.

4. In sum, the Court (incorrectly) applied the equal protection clause to state and local administrative matters but considerably modified the impact through its (incorrect) separate but equal interpretion.

Thus by 1954, the clause would hardly be recognizable to its authors. At the same time, many in the society found the clause as then interpreted totally inappropriate to contemporary circumstances. The condition of blacks had changed enormously over the years, and government sanctioned segregation harmed and demeaned them and the American society. In particular, school segregation denied many children an education their parents deemed essential to their well-being.

Reinterpreting the Constitution was not a simple task, however. For those committed to observing the designs of the Thirty-ninth Congress, constitutionally eliminating school segregation presented a most difficult problem. The debate over the years has covered a wide spectrum of thought. Thus, Professor Herbert Wechsler, a leading constitutional scholar, found it necessary to offer an alternative rationale. He asserted that "[a]ssuming equal facilities, the question posed by state-enforced segregation is not one of discrimination at all. Its human and constitutional dimensions lie . . . in the denial by the state of freedom to associate."[41] For strict constructionists the moral authority preferred in justification for the change did not overcome the immorality of constitutional abuse. The United States Supreme Court along with many commentators viewed the situation much differently.

Brown I adjudicated the complaints of black children in four states that the separate but equal requirements denied them educational opportunities in violation of the equal protection clause. At that time, seventeen states and the District of Columbia required separate schooling according to race, and four others permitted it. The opinion is not based on original understanding. It found the historical background of the fourteenth amendment at best "inconclusive" on the subject of school segregation and the *Plessy* interpretation inappropriate to contemporary conditions. Notwithstanding its "inconclusive" finding, the Court had to assume that history permitted both an interpretation of the issue involved in *Plessy* and a reinterpretation with respect to public schooling; otherwise, no foundation existed for either ruling. In eliminating *Plessy*, the Court let stand the *Strauder* decision with its broad and questionable interpretation of the equal protection clause. Thus, more than twenty state statutes were invalidated on the basis of a historical background found to be inconclusive.

The Court held *Plessy* incorrect when applied to contemporary public education because modern psychological understanding had determined that segregation "has a tendency to [retard] the education and mental development of Negro children and deprive them of the benefits they would receive in a racial[ly] integrated school system." Consequently, "separate educational facilities are inherently unequal."

Not being a state, the District of Columbia was not affected by *Brown* (and its interpretation of the equal protection clause). Again, this situation created little trouble for a Court disposed to achieve a particular result. In *Bolling v. Sharpe*,[42] decided the same day as *Brown*, the Court unanimously held that public segregation in the nation's capitol "constitutes an arbitrary deprivation [of] liberty in violation of the due process clause" of the fifth amendment. "[D]iscrimination may be so unjustifiable as to be violative of due process." One wonders, then, what the *Brown* contretemps was all about, for according to *Bolling*, the Thirty- ninth Congress's intent for the equal protection clause really did not matter.

The difficulty with *Bolling* is that the Court was not applying due process simply to remove discriminatory restraints on the liberties of black children; rather it reached much further into the administrative and management prerogatives of government. The problem was comparable to that presented by *Strauder*, as explained in Justice Field's dissent. *Bolling* applied the due process clause, not directly to secure a liberty, but in effect to determine how the federal government should establish and operate schools in the District of Columbia. To be sure, due process is an appropriate provision for the judiciary to use against oppressive legislation denying the exercise of a right; the concept does not, however, entitle justices to supervise the operations of the legislative and executive branches. The *Bowling* Court would have been on firmer ground had it found that the system's exclusionary policies violated a due process right—such as travel or access, which is discussed subsequently. The Thirty-ninth Congress, to be sure, would not consider the District of Columbia's segregated school system which it countenanced as violative of due process. In that period, the limited nature of public school facilities in the South together with prevailing experience and attitudes made such a position not very plausible. By 1954, however, the situation had changed greatly.

We shall return to this discussion after considering the remedy adopted by the Court to implement *Brown I*, which was essentially a negative decision invalidating existing laws. The Court had interpreted the Constitution and was under no obligation for further substantive action. Ordinarily, its jurisdiction should have terminated. Upon a finding of invalidity by the judiciary, the remaining problems shift for resolution to the other governmental branches, which then customarily proceed with their constitutional responsibilities consistent with the judicial interpretation. However, because of the unique character of the issue, the Court retained jurisdiction to consider whether and what additional process was required to effectuate the ruling.

After *Brown I*, the following scenario began to evolve. The opinion was delivered in May 1954. By the opening of the 1955 fall school term, only eight states retained completely segregated public schools. More than a quarter million black children were attending integrated schools in states that just one year earlier had mandated segregation.[43] Implementation was not left to the judiciary. In keeping with *Brown*, Congress passed the Civil Rights Act of 1964, providing relief for persons required to submit to segregation laws and practices.[44]

In May 1955, in *Brown II,* the Court decreed a program of school desegregation, premising enforcement jurisdiction on its equity powers. "Courts of equity may properly take into account the public interest in the elimination of [obstacles to banning school segregation] in a systematic and effective manner." Local federal courts were to invoke their equity powers "to achieve a system of determining admission to the public schools on a nonracial basis, and [consider] revision of local laws and regulations which may be necessary in solving" problems related to desegregating schools. These programs were to be instituted "as soon as practicable" and "with all deliberate speed."[45] These formulations gave the federal judiciary substantial authority over the operation of schools and school districts.

In applying its equity powers, the Court was charting a new course—a fact evident from its failure to cite supporting precedent in constitutional law.[46] Equitable principles are an integral part of American jurisprudence when applied to private and public disputes enabling judges to achieve a just result notwithstanding existing judicial rules. They do not entitle the judiciary to override the constitutional authority of the states or other branches of government. Nor does equitable enforcement seem necessarily required when the Constitution specifically authorizes a mode of political implementation, as it does in section 5 of the fourteenth amendment.

Vast as they are, considerable limits exist on the equitable powers of the judiciary. Blackstone commented on this issue, warning that the power of considering cases in an equitable light must not be indulged too far, lest all law be destroyed, leaving the decision of every question entirely to an individual judge's conscience. Blackstone believed that law without equity, though hard and disagreeable, is more to the public good than is equity without law, a situation that would allow every judge to be a legislator.[47] The great commentator's remarks are relevant to the situation under discussion.

Despite the affirmative language of *Brown II*, the *Brown* decisions were construed for some years and by some courts as requiring only state neutrality, allowing "freedom of choice" on school selection so long as the state itself assured that the choice was genuinely free of official restraint. Thus, in 1965, a federal circuit court asserted that a "state or a school district offends no constitutional requirement when it grants to all students uniformly an unrestricted freedom of choice as to schools attended, so that each pupil, in effect, assigns himself to the school he wishes to attend."[48] Another federal court earlier explained that the Constitution does not require intergration; it merely forbids discrimination.[49]

The Court did not accept these interpretations; from a position outlawing segregation, it moved to one requiring integration.

Decided in 1968, *Green v. New Kent County School Board*[50] concerned a freedom-of-choice plan adopted by a rural Virginia county, with a population that was about half black. Until 1964 its two combined elementary and high schools, previously segregated by law, remained wholly segregated in fact. The following year the Board adopted a freedom-of-choice program. During the next three years, no white child chose to go to the black school, but 115 black children were admitted to the white school containing 550 whites. For a unanimous Court, Justice Brennan contended that this system was tokenism and thus was not consistent with *Brown I* and *II*. "The transition to a unitary, nonracial system of public education was and is the ultimate end to be brought about." The school board's plan "fails to provide meaningful assurance of prompt and effective disestablishment of a dual system." *Brown II* was a "call for the dismantling of well-entrenched dual systems" within the earliest practical period. "School boards such as the respondent then operating state-compelled dual systems were . . . charged with the affirmative duty to take whatever steps might be necessary to convert to a unitary system in which racial discrimination would be eliminated root and branch."[51]

The most careful reading of *Brown I* and *Brown II* does not reveal such purpose. The Court had taken a giant step in ordering disestablishment of a system of white and black schools created under its authority (*Plessy*), and this goal could be accomplished only by transferring students from one school to another on a racial basis. Thus, maintaining that no change in principle had occurred, the Court invoked remedies that would have encountered much stiffer resistance 14 years earlier when it declared school segregation unlawful. The *Brown* decisions did not explain the extent to which disestablishment was required. In presenting interpretation, *Green* also provided the essential meaning of those opinions. Under the Constitution, all children possess the same right of access to the public schools and the services they provide. Consequently, black children are entitled to an education not controlled or influenced by practices adopted to create or maintain segregation. (See subsequent discussion of right of access.)

Three years later the Court continued on the same course with *Swann v. Charlotte-Mecklenburg Board of Education*,[52] allowing district courts vast discretion to compel school integration in the formerly segregationist states. Chief Justice Warren Burger, for a unanimous Court, held that district courts may exercise broad equitable powers in formulating "remedial desegregation plans" where segregation had once been mandated. Burger asserted that all elements bearing on racial composition in the schools were within the remedial discretion of the district court until such time as they become "unitary," the term used to denote fully integrated. Mathematical ratios ("a useful starting point in shaping a remedy"), altering attendance zones, and employing bus transportation, among other things, could be used as "tool[s] of school desegregation."

Swann limited relief to removing conditions brought about by legally imposed school segregation with the Court's jurisdiction to terminate upon achievement of a unitary school system:

> Our objective in dealing with the issues presented by these cases is to see that school authorities exclude no pupil of a racial minority, directly or indirectly, on account of race; it does not and cannot embrace all problems of racial prejudice, even when these problems contribute to disproportionate racial concentration in some schools.

The Court was not about to confine its integration program to the South. *Keyes v. School District No. 1, Denver, Colo.*,[53] was the first case to consider school segregation in a metropolitan area that had never been subject to a separate but equal policy. Applying the rationale that it had developed for the Southern schools, the Court held that a constitutional violation existed whenever there was "segregative purpose or intent" in school board actions. If it can be proven that government designed segregation affects a substantial portion of minority students, the presumption arises that segregation exists in the entire district. The district then carries the difficult burden of proving that the illicit intent did not cause or increase separation of the races in the schools. Failure to succeed in this regard places the district in the same constitutional status as were the Southern districts that had actually mandated segregation. In his dissent Justice William H. Rehnquist objected that "it certainly would not reflect normal English usage to describe the entire district as 'segregated' on such a state of facts."

Dayton Board of Education v. Brinkman[54] proceeded to apply *Brown I* to northern districts that never required separate but equal facilities. In that case, the High Court accepted the trial judge's findings that as of 1954 (the date of *Brown I*) the school board had engaged in acts intended to increase segregation of the schools. This being the situation, the "Board was thereafter under a continuing duty to eradicate the effects of that system." It had the "heavy burden" of showing that actions "that increased or continued the effects of the dual system serve important and legitimate ends." Although the *Brown* decisions did not relate to the Dayton school system, that city was bound by them and subsequent opinions that also concerned separate but equal systems.

Combining the *Keyes* and *Dayton* rulings means that a great many northern cities have engaged in some segregationist practices after 1954 to make them candidates for that which Justice Rehnquist described "is in practice a federal receivership."[55] The result would be, as he and Justice Lewis F. Powell noted, that parents who could not possibly be considered either as having violated any law or as having benefitted from a violation, would have their children bused, even against their wishes, to attend schools outside their neighborhoods. Their only alternative would be to enroll them in private schools, an option available only to the more affluent. In many instances, school officials who instituted the condemned policies would have long departed their posts when remedial action was ordered.

Such judicial policies reflect adversely on due process and equal protection concepts as a vehicle for combating government oppression. The application of equity jurisdiction is likewise adverse to this idea. There would seem nothing equitable about principles that impact harmfully on many law-abiding persons who did not institute or benefit from any illicit conduct. These observations are not inconsistent with Supreme Court doctrine in the school segregation cases. The problem is that judicial practice has gone beyond judicial theory which confines relief to conditions produced by constitutional violation.

These cases also raise issues about the powers of the judiciary over local taxation and expenditures. Busing and other integration programs, which are supervised by the courts, are quite expensive, and the funds have to come from the taxpayers, or at the expense of other established programs. For example, in *Swann*, for a district containing about 85,000 students, the school board proposed a busing plan that would cost $864,700 in the first year. A consultant appointed by the district judge submitted a plan costing $3,406,700 for that period.[56] The difference may be attributed to identifying the effects of intentionally segregated school practices, indicating the importance of this concern. Expenditures for matters outside the area of fault raise questions about the separation of powers. Of the various concerns of government, little would seem more political in character than the taxing and spending powers.

Preferential Treatment

Brown I and *II* and *Bolling* were directed at removing officially mandated school segregation, while in *Green, Swann,* and *Keyes,* the goal was to eliminate from the public schools all vestiges of official segregation. In combination, these decisions held that in order to eliminate dual and create unitary school systems, (1) courts may enter orders that assign students and faculty by reference to race, and (2) local school boards may adopt plans establishing fixed ratios of black and white students in each school. According to Justices Powell and Brennan, writing separately, this program was required to redress past constitutional violations "for the vindication of constitutional entitlement," according to the former, and for eliminating root and branch the "effects of past discrimination," according to the latter, who also wrote that this "was recognized [by the Court] as a compelling social goal justifying the overt use of race."[57]

The intensity of these concerns brings into focus the issue of preferential treatment. Integration policies intended to benefit blacks but not related to curing legal violations are not compatable with legal equality; they constitute legal preference. As previously noted, the line limiting judicial action to overcoming fault has not been diligently observed in the school cases. Consider Justice Powell's comments in *Keyes:*

> In imposing on metropolitan southern school districts an affirmative duty, entailing large-scale transportation of pupils, to eliminate segregation in the schools, the Court required these districts to alleviate conditions which in large part did *not* result from historic, state-imposed de jure segregation. Rather, the familiar root cause of segregated schools in *all* the biracial metropolitan areas of our country is essentially the same: one of segregated residential and migratory patterns the impact of which on the racial composition of the schools was often perpetuated and rarely ameliorated by action of public school authorities.[58]

Preferential treatment is inconsistent with the principle of equality, which Bingham and other leaders of the Thirty-ninth Congress espoused and incorporated in section 1 of the fourteenth amendment. However, this principle is not absolute and may be accommodated when conditions or situations demand. Pursuant to this understanding, the Supreme Court has frequently asserted that any differential treatment on the basis of race must be strictly scrutinized and will be annulled unless it is necessary to achieve compelling governmental interests. Federal and state law reports are filled with statements that race is a suspect classification subject to the trictest judicial review. Even if one assumes ground exists for the claim that in the school cases the Court is mostly remedying past constitutional violations, much of that which the Court has mandated falls outside this area. In fact, close scrutiny of the Court's own purpose and result would seem appropriate under its principles. Clearly if a legislative body was to enact the preferential treatment implemented by the Court, that institution would most carefully review the resulting statute.

The foregoing account reveals that original understanding provides little authority for the construction that the Court has accorded in the school segregation cases. Although such segregation is totally repugnant in modern society, it does not follow that the Constitution necessarily provides relief in this area. The original Constitution accepted slavery and the fourteenth amendment accepted segregation in contemporary public educational facilities. The framers of these documents were limited by their knowledge and understanding and could not possibly foresee the future changes and demands of society. However, provisions in the Constitution—the privileges and immunities, due process, and equal protection clauses—enable courts to provide protections not conceived of or contemplated in the original drafting. As previously explained, each of these provisions was intended to safeguard the exercise of natural and fundamental liberties. They do not, however, affect political rights created in the administration, financing, support, or management of state governments.

Accordingly, the fourteenth amendment can be applied to strike down school segregation laws if they curtail natural or fundamental rights of black school children. A persuasive argument can be made that these laws have this impact. Black children seeking to attend white schools were endeavoring to obtain access to public institutions which provided benefits of great importance to them—specifically the opportunity to share the learning experience with white children. The right of access is a component of the right to travel, a right long secured by the federal courts. While the United States Supreme Court has not determined whether to draw a constitutional distinction between interstate and intrastate travel, lower federal courts protect both. Freedom of travel has been variously described as a basic right under the Constitution, an element of the "liberty" secured by the due process clauses, and as among those natural rights "which of right belong to the citizens of all free governments."[59] This right protects a person's opportunity to pursue happiness and well being through free access to places and areas throughout the nation.

The school segregation laws were passed to prevent access by blacks to white schools, and at the demand of those who opposed it. As in any case concerning denial of liberty, the issue resolves into deciding whether the state has sufficient justification for imposing the restraint. Framing the issue in this manner readily gives rise to the answer: In the contemporary world, it is exceedingly difficult to justify laws adversely impinging upon the freedom of others on the basis of prejudicial attitudes and feelings. By protecting free access, the Court would have reached the result in *Brown I*; *Brown II* would not have been effected. Such construction would safeguard natural or fundamental rights without limiting the traditional and inherent responsibililties of the states. The same rationale would authorize Congress under the fourteenth amendment's section 5 to enact legislation to achieve access to public schools.

Because the Court accepted preferential racial treatment as consistent with the equal protection clause in one area, it should not be surprising that a number of justices are amenable to it elsewhere. This fact is especially evident from two recent cases. *University of California Regents v. Bakke*[60] involved the special admissions program of the medical school at Davis, designed to assure the admission of a fixed percentage (16 percent) of students from certain minority groups. At issue, in addition to the constitutional question, was the validity of the program under title VI of the Civil Rights Act of 1964. A majority struck down the Davis plan as violative of this statute. Only five justices spoke to the constitutional question, which was not relevant to the outcome. Justice Powell, writing solely for himself, treated the Davis program as a racial classification requiring strict scrutiny under the Constitution. Applying this standard of review, he found no compelling state interest that justified the program. Justice Brennan, writing for himself and Justices Thurgood Marshall, Harry Blackmun, and Byron White, rejected imposition of strict scrutiny to a racial classification designed to promote remedial purposes. In such situations, he asserted, the review should be at an intermediate level: The classification must serve important governmental objectives and be substantially related to the achievement of those objectives. Strict scrutiny was appropriate only when the classification was not intended for benign purposes. However, Justice Brennan was hardly presenting an equal standard by which to determine equal protection of the laws. Under his interpretation the clause would become a tool to foster preferential treatment for minorities.

These dissenting justices had a novel reply for the disadvantaged white persons. In the absence of past discriminatory practices, the minorities would have been able to score much higher on the exams, and people like Allan Bakke would not have been able to achieve admission.

> If it were reasonable to conclude—as we hold that it was—that the failure of minorities to qualify for admission at Davis under regular procedures was

due principally to the effects of past discrimination, than there is a reasonable likelihood that, but for the pervasive racial discrimination, respondent would have failed to qualify for admission even in the absence of Davis' special admissions program.[61]

Because the record discloses no facts to support such a conclusion, the justices obviously were relying on their own views, which, in this regard, are scarcely more worthy than those of any intelligent layperson. The American legal system is in large part based on pursuit of objectivity, removing opinion and relying on facts to support decisions and verdicts. The above quoted passage is hardly consistent with this purpose and reveals rather dramatically the ideological and political character of much decisionmaking at the High Court.

By a vote of 6-3, *Fullilove v. Klutznick*[62] upheld a federal statute requiring 10 percent of certain federal public works project funds to be allocated to businesses owned by members of designated minority groups. This approach was obviously constitutional for Justices Brennan, Marshall, and Blackmun under the test that they had advanced in *Bakke*. Justice Powell once again applied strict scrutiny, but this time he found that the government had met his standard of review. Chief Justice Burger, for himself and Justice White, adopted a third position. They found the statute a justifiable use of federal power to eliminate or overcome discrimination in past and existing construction practices. Dissenting Justices Potter Stewart and Rehnquist concluded that nearly all race classifications are unconstitutional. Although Justice John Paul Stevens was much less absolute in his approach, he indicated unwillingness to sanction most racial classifications. The equal protection clause has become a potpourri of standards, with the outcome in these cases often depending on a chance combination of the various justices' positions.

The fundamental law of the country should not depend on such reasoning and circumstances. The Justices would be more in keeping with their responsibilities were they concentrating on original meaning. Instead the opinions read as if they emanate from legislators. Thus, although countless opinions have discussed the meaning of the religion clauses in the first amendment, Justice Rehnquist recently devoted almost an entire opinion to the history of those clauses.[63] In my view, Rehnquist was strictly fulfilling the judicial function, clearly more so than would be the case were his discussion confined to pragmatic and utilitarian considerations.[64]

Application of original meaning might yield different outcomes in the *Bakke* and *Fullilove* cases. The constitutional interpretation that public schooling is not within reach of the due process and equal protection clauses is relevant to the medical school minorities program involved in *Bakke*. The right of access to a public institution would likewise be a consideration although possibly not as persuasive for banning exclusion as in *Brown.*

Inasmuch as *Fullilove* concerns the spending of public monies, an inherently legislative power, the separation of powers should be a major issue in that case. Assuming for purposes of the argument that constitutional authority for the proposed spending exists, the amount and allocation thereof is within the discretion of Congress and the executive.[65] Indeed, article I, section 9, clause 7 provides "No money should be drawn from the Treasury, but in consequence of appropriations made by law."

Interestingly, these examples suggest that an emphasis on original meaning is not necessarily beneficial to any particular position in current affirmative action controversies.

Notes

1. CONG. GLOBE, 39th Cong., 1st Sess. 599 (1866).
2. *Id.* at 474.
3. *Id.* at 474 and 599.
4. *Id.* at 1117-18.
5. *Id.* at 1117.
6. *Id.* at 1294.
7. *See* Chapter 3 *supra* text accompanying notes 27, 28, 82 and 83.
8. CONG. GLOBE, 39th Cong., 1st Sess. 1291 (1866).
9. *Id.* at 1292.
10. *Id.* at 1292-93.
11. *Id.* at 2542.
12. CONG. GLOBE, 35th Cong., 2d Sess. 985 (1859); *See* Chapter 3 *supra*, text accompanying notes 73 and 74.
13. Cong. Globe, 39th Cong., 1st Sess. 1367 (1866).
14. *Id* at App. 156-57.
15. *Id.*
16. *See* Chapter 3. *supra* text accompanying notes 81 and 82.
17. CONG. GLOBE, 39th Cong., 1st Sess. App. 98 and 1287 (1866).
18. *Id.* at 2766.
19. *Id.* at 2459. Stevens believed that nineteen of the loyal states would not ratify an amendment mandating Negro suffrage. *Id.*
20. FAWN BRODIE, THADDEUS STEVENS: SCOURGE OF THE SOUTH 320 (New York: Norton, 1959).
21. *See* discussion in RAOUL BERGER, GOVERNMENT BY JUDICIARY, 99-116 (Cambridge: Harvard University Press, 1977) in which the author discusses "The 'Open-Ended' Phraseology Theory."
22. JOSEPH B. JAMES, THE FRAMING OF THE FOURTEENTH AMENDMENT 201 (Urbana, Ill: University of Illinois Press, 1965).
23. *See* Brown v. Board of Education, 347 U.S. 483 (1954) and 349 U.S. 294 (1955); San Antonio Independent School District v. Rodriguez 411 U.S. 1 (1973).
24. RICHARD KLUGER, SIMPLE JUSTICE 654 (New York: Knopf, 1976).

25. HOWARD JAY GRAHAM, EVERYMAN'S CONSTITUTION 290 n.70 (New York: Norton, 1968) A leading authority on the fourteenth amendment, Graham was also a strong supporter of desegregation.
26. LINO A. GRAGLIA, DISASTER BY DECREE 21 (Ithaca, N.Y.: Cornell University Press, 1976).
27. Dred Scott v. Sanford, 60 U.S. (19 How.) 393 (1857).
28. Bickel, *The Original Understanding and the Segregation Decision*, 69 HARV. L. REV. 1 56-65 (1955). However, "[i]f the fourteenth amendment were a statute, a court might very well hold, . . . that it was foreclosed from applying it to segregation in public schools." *Id.* at 59.
29. See Berger *supra* note 21. The U.S. Supreme Court was not persuaded, however. It found the historical background "inconclusive." Brown v. Board of Education, 347 U.S. 483 (1954) discussed later in this chapter.
30. 83 U.S. (16 Wall.) 36, at 81 (1872).
31. 83 U.S. at 81.
32. 100 U.S. 303 (1879).
33. 100 U.S. at 307-8.
34. 100 U.S. at 310.
35. In the Matter of the Commonwealth of Virginia, 100 U.S. 339, 349 (1879) (Field, J., dissenting).
36. 100 U.S. at 367.
37. 100 U.S. at 368. Bingham considered civil rights as including political rights and distinguished between natural and political rights. *See* text accompanying note 12 *supra*.
38. Criminal processes are not absolute guarantees. For example, in recent years, the Court has limited them to accommodate freedom of the press. Nebraska Press Assn. v. Stuart, 427 U.S. 539 (1976); Richmond Newspapers, Inc. v. Virginia, 488 U.S. 555 (1980).
39. Plessy v. Ferguson, 163 U.S. 537, 544 (1896).
40. 347 U.S. 483 (1954).
41. Wechsler, *Toward Neutral Principles of Constitutional Law*, 73 HARV. L. REV. 1, 34 (1959).
42. 347 U.S. 497 (1954).
43. McKay, *"With All Deliberate Speed": A Study of School Disegregation*, 31 NEW YORK UNIV. L. REV. 991 (1956). It is estimated that as of 1955, 2,744,860 black children were enrolled in these schools. *Id.* at 992, n. 7.
44. 42 U.S.C., sects. 1971, 2000g-h (1970); Public Law No. 88-352, 78 Stat. 241.
45. Brown v. Board of Education, 349 U.S. 294 at 300-301 (1955).
46. The opinion cites two cases, neither of which bears significantly on the issue involved. 349 U.S. at 300 nn. 4 & 5.
47. 1 W. BLACKSTONE, COMMENTARIES* 62.
48. Bradley v. School Board, 345 F.2d 310, 316 (CA4 1965) (en banc). (Case later vacated without reviewing desegregation plans, 382 U.S. 103 (1965).
49. Briggs v. Elliott, 132 F. Supp. 776, 777 (E.D.S.C. 1955).
50. 391 U.S. 430 (1968).
51. 391 U.S. at 437-39.
52. 402 U.S. 1 (1971).
53. 413 U.S. 189 (1973).
54. 443 U.S. 526 (1979).
55. Keyes v. School District No. 1, Denver Colo., 413 U.S. 189 (1973) (Rehnquist, J., dissenting).

56. GRAGLIA *supra* note 26, at 110.
57. University of California Regents v. Bakke, 438 U.S. 265, 300, 324, 363 (1978).
58. *Id.* at 324, 363; Keyes at 222-23.
59. United States v. Guest, 383 U.S. 745, 757-58 (1966); Kent v. Dulles, 357 U.S. 116, 125-26 (1958); Slaughter-House Cases, 83 U.S. 36, 96-98 (Field, J., dissenting). *See* LAWRENCE TRIBE, AMERICAN CONSTITUTIONAL LAW, 953-58 (Mineola, N.Y.: Foundation Press, 1978). See also Richmond Newspapers Inc., v. Virginia, 448 U.S. 555 (1980) in which the Supreme Court held the constitution implicitly protects a right of access to attend criminal trials.
60. 438 U.S. 265 (1978).
61. 438 U.S. at 365-66.
62. 448 U.S. 448 (1980).
63. Wallace v. Jaffree, 105 S.Ct. 2479, 2508 (1985) (Rehnquist, J., dissenting).
64. Original understanding is a major but not decisive concern in reconsidering prior constitutional rulings. Courts should be most cautious in overruling precedents on which society has substantially relied.
65. See discussion of the spending power *infra* chapter 6.

5

The Establishment of Religion Clause

The United States Supreme Court controls church/state relations in this nation. It determines the extent to which government may limit the exercise of religion as well as the degree to which government may advance religion. However, religion is not mentioned in the original Constitution, ratified in 1788, except in article VI, clause 3, which states that "no religious Test shall ever be required as a Qualification to any Office or public Trust under the United States." The clause is important not only for the protection it provides but also as an indication of the Framers' concern for religious liberty.

The most important reference appears in the first amendment, adopted in 1791: "Congress shall make no law respecting an establishment of religion, or prohibiting the free exercise thereof." The first part of this provision is known as the establishment clause; the second as the free exercise clause. Both are now secured under the fourteenth amendment. In 1940 the Supreme Court ruled that the fourteenth amendment's due process clause incorporates free exercise and thus applied it to the states, and seven years later the Justices made the same ruling with respect to the establishment clause.[1]

That which is now the first amendment was framed by the First Congress in 1789 as the third in a series of twelve amendments submitted to the states. By 1791, the states had ratified the last ten amendments but not the first two, making the next in line the first amendment. The Framers considered the two clauses as distinct and serving different purposes, as will presently be explained. This chapter concerns mostly the establishment clause, which has received a much more controversial and questionable interpretation.

No doubt exists that the Constitution protects religious freedom. The first amendment is clear on the subject with respect to the federal government. Although not mentioned therein, the fourteenth amendment's protection of liberty would necessarily comprehend this fundamental freedom. Given the application of the latter amendment's due process clause over the years to securing various interests, ranging from economics to expression, its extension to protecting religious freedom in the states was inevitable.

The establishment clause is another matter, however. Its meaning is far less plain than that of the free exercise clause. Unlike most other provisions of the Bill of Rights, it does not safeguard an individual liberty. Instead the clause has to do with the welfare and spending powers of the national government—to what extent, if any, it may promote or advance religion. The original Constitution contains no specific authorization to Congress for the enactment of legislation regarding religion. In the absence of such a power, Congress could nevertheless promote religion if doing so was pursuant either to an enumerated power (such as maintaining the armed forces, coining money, conducting congressional proceedings)[2] or to the necessary and proper clause.

The Framers' thinking in this regard is evident from James Madison's motion made during the Constitutional Convention "to establish an University." Madison included the qualification "in which no preferences or distinctions should be allowed on account of religion." Without this reservation Congress might use its discretion to determine a religious orientation for the institution and Madison wanted to limit the legislature in this respect. (The motion lost, on a vote of 6-4.)[3]

In the ratification debates, Federalists represented that the central government had no power to limit freedom of religion. Madison told the Virginia ratification convention that "this subject [religion], is for the honor of America, perfectly free and unshackled. The government has no jurisdiction over it; the least reflection will convince us there is no danger to be feared on this ground."[4] Edmund Randolph agreed: "No part of the Constitution, even if strictly construed, will justify a conclusion that the general government can take away or impair the freedom of religion."[5]

As we all know, the Federalist position that a Bill of Rights was unnecessary did not prevail. The main purpose of the first ten amendments was to restrict the powers of the national government—or more accurately, to ensure that the restraints on it were maintained as represented. Clearly the Bill of Rights was not meant to provide more authority to the federal government than it already possessed. Inasmuch as the Constitution does not specifically provide the federal government authority over religion, the only purpose that the first amendment could serve in this regard is to restrain application of the necessary and proper clause. However, this federalist theory of constitutional construction has not been followed in interpreting the religion clauses.

Of the seven states that requested amendments to the Constitution in their ratification resolutions, five recommended changes affecting federal powers over religion. All five demanded protection for the free exercise of religion. In addition, they sought certain restraints on establishment. New Hampshire called for a provision that "Congress shall make no laws touching Religion." Virginia preferred a clause "that no particular religious sect or society ought to be favored or established by Law in preference to others." New York, North Carolina, and Rhode Island used either identical or almost identical language in their recommendations. The concern of these four states was religious favoritism; unlike New Hampshire, they did not seek to bar the federal government from *any* advancement of religion. Except for New Hampshire's, no resolution demanded complete or substantial separation of church and state.[6]

At that time separation was not observed in Georgia, South Carolina, Connecticut, Massachusetts, or New Hampshire, all of which had established churches. It can be assumed that although these states did not favor separation in principle, they viewed a national religious preference as a threat to their own. That the primary concern of the states at that time was free exercise is evident from the Northwest Ordinance of 1787 which was first adopted by the Congress of the Confederacy on 13 July 1787 and reenacted by the first Congress in 1789 to govern the territory northwest of the Ohio River. It contained a bill of rights to be observed by all the states from that territory later admitted to the Union. Article I proclaims: "No person, demeaning himself in a peaceable and orderly manner, shall ever be molested on account of his mode of worship, or religious sentiments, in the said territory."

No provision prohibited establishment of religion or otherwise required church-state separation for the states that were to be admitted. The inference is to the contrary in article III, which states that "religion, morality, and knowledge being necessary to good government and the happiness of mankind, schools and the means of education shall forever be encouraged." Casting great doubt on the idea that that body was otherwise motivated, the same Congress that framed the first amendment thus encouraged the advancement of religion by voicing governmental support for the then mostly church-sponsored schools.

In practice, the religion clauses have rarely been applied to overrule the federal government. They have, however, been invoked repeatedly against state legislation pursuant to the fourteenth amendment's due process provision. The contemporary importance of these clauses lies in determining what due process incorporates. We start from the fact that the two religion clauses had different meanings for their Framers.

The Original Understanding

On 8 June 1789 in response to demands for the inclusion of a Bill of Rights, James Madison introduced in the House a series of amendments to the Constitution, some of which concerned religion. He proposed the following limitation on the federal government, to be inserted in article I, section 9, between clauses 3 and 4: "The civil rights of none shall be abridged on account of religious belief or worship, nor shall any national religion be established, nor shall the full and equal rights of conscience be in any manner, or on any pretext, infringed."[7]

He further proposed a religious freedom limitation on the states but none with respect to establishment. The insertion intended for article I, section 10, between clauses 1 and 2, read: "No state shall violate the equal rights of conscience."

These proposed amendments were referred to a select House committee of eleven consisting of Madison and one member from each of the other states then represented. The committee altered his first proposal to read as follows: "No religion shall be established by law, nor shall the equal rights of conscience be infringed." It also modified slightly the restraint on the states: "No state shall infringe the equal rights of conscience."

Madison explained the first provision to mean "that Congress should not establish a religion, and enforce the legal observations of it by law, nor compel men to worship God in any manner contrary to their conscience." It did not otherwise demand separation. Although the words may not have been the best, he asserted they did respond to the demands of the states.

> [The language] had been required by some of the State Conventions, who seemed to entertain an opinion that under the clause of the Constitution, which gave power to Congress to make all laws necessary and proper to carry into execution the Constitution, and the laws made under it, enabled them to make laws of such a nature as might infringe the rights of conscience, and establish a national religion; to prevent these effects he presumed the Amendment was intended, and he thought it as well expressed as the nature of the language would admit.[8]

In reply to criticisms by other speakers, Madison sought to insert the word *national* before the word *religion* as he had done in his original proposal. He believed that

> if the word "national" was inserted before religion, it would satisfy the minds of honorable gentlemen. He believed that the people feared one sect might obtain a preeminence, or two combined together, and establish a religion to which they would compel others to conform. He thought if the word "national" was introduced, it would point the amendment directly to the object it was intended to prevent.

Madison withdrew this motion when Elbridge Gerry objected that *national* did not necessarily relate to the newly formed government,[9] which during the ratification debates many Federalists identified as only a federal government.

Thereafter, the House voted for complete separation by amending the provision to read as follows: "Congress shall make no law touching religion, or infringing the rights of conscience." This change was subsequently eliminated. The House altered the form of the committee's proposals, adopting them instead as additions to the Constitution, as follows:

> Article the Third: Congress shall make no law establishing religion, or prohibiting the free exercise thereof, nor shall the rights of conscience be infringed.
>
> Article the Fourteenth: No state shall infringe . . . the rights of conscience.

The Senate rejected any restriction on the states and adopted the national limitation in this language:

> Article the Third: Congress shall make no law establishing articles of faith, or a mode of worship, or prohibiting the free exercise of religion.

This provision appears to allow national support of religion except with respect to theology or ceremony. A conference committee of the two Houses subsequently changed the language to that which presently appears.

The foregoing account leads to certain observations:

1. Madison and the House sought to protect the free exercise of religion from interference by both the federal and state governments, but they chose to restrain only the national government from an establishment of religion. Understandably, no such limitation was directed at the states, for at that time one-fourth of them officially sanctioned certain religions and would thus have defeated such a restriction. The establishment limitation prevented the federal government from interfering with the religious programs of the states by sanctioning or preferring a particular religion for the country. Judging from their proposed restraint on the states, Madison and other members of the House voting with him believed that a state could both establish a religion and maintain freedom of conscience.
2. The House committee altered Madison's proposed establishment provision to read: "No religion shall be established by law." This mandate was in turn changed by the House to "Congress shall make no law establishing religion." Madison explained the reference was to a national religion and urged insertion of the word *national*. However, he subsequently abandoned the idea because some members raised semantic problems.

(During the ratification debates the word evoked fears of an all-powerful government.) The Senate's interest was that "Congress shall make no law establishing articles of faith, or a mode of worship." Both the House and Senate versions were consistent with those sought by Virginia, New York, North Carolina, and Rhode Island in their ratification resolutions. *Establish* at that time related to official sponsorship. The first American dictionary defined the word *establishment* as "the act of establishing, founding, ratifying or ordainin[(g,) [such as in] [t]he episcopal form of religion, so called, in England."[10] Accordingly, so long as no particular religion was officially sponsored or preferred, this language would not prohibit the central government from subsidizing or otherwise advancing religious practices, exercises, or instruction (each of which has been a major source of controversy in contemporary times). In the words of Justice Story, "the object of the Amendment was . . . to prevent any national ecclesiastical establishment, which should give to an hierarchy the exclusive patronage of the *national* government."[11]

3. Those who believe that the fourteenth amendment's due process clause is a general limitation on state government power to deprive people of their liberties will find little difficulty in including protection of religious freedom. As discussed in chapters 3 and 4, denying religious freedom to any person or group also violates the privileges and immunities and equal protection clauses as they were intended by their framers.

The establishment provision does not fit this analysis for it is not consistent with the general purpose of the fourteenth amendment to safeguard personal freedoms. In contrast the clause is a limitation on those powers of government authorizing the financing and supporting of programs and interests—in this case, religion. It deals with the administration and management of government; the free exercise provision secures liberty. The former is a restraint on the welfare and spending powers enumerated in article I, section 8, and elsewhere; the latter is a limitation on the authority of government over the freedom of its constituents. The issue is likewise one of state powers, as contemplated in the tenth amendment. By placing a limitation on the authority of the central government to advance a national religion, the establishment clause, as originally drafted, safeguards the powers of the states to sponsor or further religions of their own choosing.

This explanation is important in determining whether the fourteenth amendment incorporates the establishment clause. Chapter 3 provides evidence that the framers of the fourteenth amendment intended to apply to the states the liberties safeguarded in the first eight amendments. In introducing the fourteenth amendment to the Senate, Senator Howard included within his definition of privileges and immunities the "personal rights guaranteed and secured by the first eight amendments of the Constitution."

In providing examples of these personal rights, the senator made no reference to the religion clauses, although free exercise fitted fully within the context of his explanation. He mentioned rights

> such as the freedom of speech and of the press; the right of the people peacefully to assemble and petition the Government for a redress of grievances, a right appertaining to each and all of the people; the right to keep and to bear arms; the right to be exempted from the quartering of soldiers in a house without the consent of the owner; the right to be exempt from unreasonable searches and seizures, and from any search or seizure except by virtue of a warrant issued upon a formal oath or affidavit; the right of an accused person to be informed of the nature of the accusation against him, and his right to be tried by an impartial jury of the vicinage; and also the right to be secure against excessive bail and against cruel and unusual punishments.[12]

The emphasis was on safeguarding individual rights. The rationale behind both the due process and the equal protection clauses was similarly directed; each was a guarantee against government oppression. Representative John Bingham explained, as the reader will recall, that section 1 of the fourteenth amendment protects "the privileges and immunities of all of the citizens of the Republic and the inborn rights of every person within its jurisdiction." He and most other civil rights activists insisted that they never sought federal supervision over the spending and welfare policies of the states.[13] Consequently, section 1 was not a bar to the establishment of religion by the states unless the program in question was a deprivation of liberty. In particular, due process would be implicated only if liberty was being curtailed.[14]

The language of the due process clause reveals its inapplicability to an establishment of religion. It bars the states from depriving "any person of life, liberty or property without due process of law"—a prohibition that normally has little relevance to a state's decision to support or advance religion.

For the framers of the fourteenth amendment, due process and equal protection were restraints against laws that treated individuals or groups unequally. Consequently, both would also protect against discriminatory laws that either gave preference to or imposed restraints on members of particular religious sects or societies. Interestingly, the desires of Madison and others of his day to prevent establishment of a national religion are thus consistent with the due process and equal protection objectives of the Thirty-ninth Congress. The intention was not to inhibit religion, for according to Justice Joseph Story:

> Probably at the time of the adoption of the Constitution, and of [the first amendment], the general if not universal sentiment in America was, that

Christianity ought to receive encouragement from the state so far as was not incompatible with the private rights of conscience and the freedom of religious worship. An attempt to level all religions, and to make it a matter of state policy to hold in utter indifference, would have created universal disapprobation, if not universal indignation.[15]

The U.S. Supreme Court has never authored a majority opinion that provides a reasoned explanation for why the fourteenth amendment's due process clause incorporates the establishment provision. In *Everson v. Board of Education*,[16] Justice Hugo Black extended this restraint simply by explaining there is "every reason to give the same application and broad interpretation to the 'establishment of religion' clause" as to the one on free exercise. He did not discuss history or original meaning, and he did not cite cases to sustain this assertion. He did, however, quote a pre–civil war case about the separation of church and state to support the assumption that this concept requires enforcement of both clauses of the first amendment. Thus *Everson* is another illustration of the enormity of the Court's review power and the cavalier manner in which members at times exercise it.

The *Everson* decision is also noted for its acceptance of the "wall of separation" that supposedly exists between church and state in this country. The phrase first appeared in an 1802 letter that Thomas Jefferson wrote to the Danbury, Connecticut Baptist Association, stating that "I contemplate with sovereign reverence that act of the whole American People which declared that their legislature should 'make no law respecting an establishment of religion, or prohibiting the free exercise thereof,' thus building a wall of separation between church and State."[17]

Jefferson was not a member of the first Congress, which framed the amendment, nor do Jefferson's actions reveal that he subscribed to strict separation. In the same year that he wrote this letter, then President Jefferson signed legislation providing tax exemption for churches in Alexandria County. The following year he made a treaty with the Kaskaskia Indians pledging federal money to erect for them a Roman Catholic Church and to support their priest. Subsequently, he sought congressional funding to implement the treaty.[18]

The expression (wall of separation) was not employed, as far as I am aware, during framing or ratification of the amendment. Although quoted extensively in cases, it has been recognized more in the breach than in the observance. Justice Black contended that in pursuit of this objective, the "scope of the First Amendment . . . was designed forever to suppress" the establishment or prohibition of religion. The wall between church and state "must be kept high and impregnable." Nevertheless, Black upheld New Jersey's statute authorizing reimbursement to parents for money spent on transporting their children to parochial (as well as to public and private nonsectarian) schools. His conclusion that the statute advanced education and not religion was sharply rejected by four other members of the Court who contended that strict separation meant exactly that.[19] In recent cases some majority opinions have regarded the wall-of-separation concept as without more than literary significance.

Black's view that the establishment clause creates strict separation is based on the theory that the Framers sought to obtain the same complete protection against governmental involvement as had been secured in Virginia prior to the framing of the U.S. Constitution. He claimed in particular that a Virginia statute that Thomas Jefferson and James Madison helped write and enact was embodied in the first amendment. This statute mandates:

> That no man shall be compelled to frequent or support any religious worship, place, or ministry whatsoever, nor shall be enforced, restrained, molested, or burthened in his body or goods, nor shall otherwise suffer on account of his religious opinions or belief. . . .[20]

The flaw in Black's theory is that Madison, as previously reported, never proposed complete separation for the national government. His draft amendment to the Constitution went no further vis-a-vis establishment than prohibiting a national religion, and he did not demand greater separation in his remarks on the floor of the House. In any event, both the House and Senate changed Madison's proposed religion clauses. Neither body sought to eliminate all federal sponsorship of religious activity. The House rejected a provision that it had initially adopted requiring that Congress shall make no law "touching religion." In the very week that it approved the establishment clause, Congress enacted legislation providing for paid chaplains for the House and Senate.[21] Madison was a member of the committee urging appointment of the chaplains, hardly a position for a strict separationist.[22] Nor, as previously discussed, did Virginia in its ratification resolution demand complete separation. It also sought a ban only against preferential treatment for any religious sect or society.

Black's position was essentially that for separation to exist, it had to relate to both establishment and free exercise. Therefore, when the framers of the fourteenth amendment protected free exercise, they necessarily also comprehended establishment. The difficulty with this analysis is evident again from proposals of, among others, James Madison. Madison and the House sought to restrict the states' power only over free exercise and not over establishment. The language of each of the House drafts of the Amendment, as previously quoted, shows that the authors separated establishment and free exercise. Black neither mentions nor considers the fore-going information, which is critical to comprehending the meaning of the amendment.

In a concurring opinion in 1963, Justice Brennan presents the most extensive defense of the Court's ruling that the fourteenth amendment's due process clause absorbs the establishment provision.[23] He regards the latter as a co-guarantor of religious freedom and therefore as within the meaning of liberty contained in the due process clause. The problem with this view is that not every establishment of religion is a violation of free-dom. It is difficult to understand how the *Everson* statute violated anyone's religious freedom. On the contrary, it enabled some parents to obtain religious instruction for their children that they could not otherwise afford, enlarging their freedom to practice religion. The statute may have taken tax money from A to support B, but that situation is hardly noteworthy any longer as a compromise of freedom. State financial support for students in religious schools does little to deny anyone else the opportunity to practice freely and fully, a religion of choice.

Brennan's position implies a belief that any government support of re-ligion curtails free exercise for the nonbeneficiaries. To the extent that this implication is true, it is amply provided for in the due process clause. There would seem to be no need for the establishment ban in this respect, es-pecially since it may at times be interpreted to inhibit activities that ad-vance and do not violate religious freedom. A further difficulty is that Brennan's interpretation disregards the original purpose of the establish-ment clause to limit the federal government's intrusion into state religion programs. It was a provision fashioned to secure the autonomy of the states in establishment matters, not to curtail it.[24] If the concern is religious freedom alone, the normal guarantees of due process are adequate for the task.

Considerable controversy remains over whether the framers intended to incorporate protection of religious freedom within the fourteenth amend-ment. Among the doubts on this score are those raised by the fact that in 1875 Senator James Blaine of Maine, upon President Grant's recommen-dation, introduced a resolution proposing a constitutional amendment that "[n]o state shall make any law respecting an establishment of religion or prohibiting the free exercise thereof." The language is the same as that in the first amendment, except that it limits the states and not the Congress. Twenty-three members of the Congress that had authored the fourteenth amendment remained in the body when the Blaine resolution was consid-ered. No member of Congress who spoke on it suggested that its provisions were embodied in the amendment. If there is doubt about the incorporation of the free exercise clause, even more question would exist about the establishment clause.

Contemporary Interpretation of the Establishment Clause

As in so many other areas of the law, consistency does not abound in the establishment cases. The scope of the limitation is largely a matter of degree for the Justices, enabling them to exercise considerable discretion in the cases that they decide. Justice Robert H. Jackson explained the situation quite candidly in a concurring opinion.

> It is idle to pretend that this task is one for which we can find in the Constitution one word to help us as judges to decide where the secular ends and the sectarian begins in education. Nor can we find guidance in any other legal source. It is a matter on which we can find no law but our own prepossessions.[25]

The contemporary Court has applied a three-part test for determining whether a violation of the establishment clause has occurred. A legislative enactment will be upheld if it has a secular purpose, if its principal or primary effect neither advances nor inhibits religion, and if it does not foster excessive government entanglement.[26] This effort at objectivity is so broad and imprecise that it has probably changed few positions. Maintaining a steady course is difficult for two reasons.

First, as *Everson* illustrates, in seeking to further particular public interests, the states may also benefit religion. In this case the Justices were reluctant to curtail spending for education that also favorably affected religion. They found the state was advancing a public and not a private interest. Utilizing the same analysis, they sustained a New York statute authorizing the lending of secular textbooks to parochial school students. They have also approved publicly funded diagnostic and therapeutic services for parochial schools.[27] The line of validity is not clear, however. The Court has struck down state funding for transportation of parochial students on field trips and state aid in the form of instructional materials such as projectors, tape recorders, record players, maps, and globes.[28] The distinctions involved are very subjective—a fact revealed in the sharply divided opinions.

Second, as many opinions have observed, complete separation of church and state has never existed in this nation. From inception, state and federal systems have extended aid to religion. As previously noted, the first Congress provided for paid chaplains in both houses and in the armed forces.

Over the years Congress has provided considerable tax exemptions and benefits for religious bodies. Only a few of the original states accepted a complete separation of church and state in principle. In 1962, Justice Douglas observed that "[o]ur system . . . is presently honeycombed with [religious] financing" and proceeded to give numerous examples.[29] Nearly every new case is similar to an existing or judicially approved practice, allowing the exercise of considerable discretion.

Recent cases indicate that the establishment clause is less of a restriction on state government than it once was. Two decisions delivered during the 1983 and 1984 terms even suggest serious limitations on the clause, although later decisions have not confirmed a trend.

The 1983 case of *Mueller v. Allen*[30] involved a Minnesota law permitting state taxpayers to claim a deduction from gross income for actual expenses incurred for tuition, textbooks, and transportation of dependents attending elementary or secondary schools, with a ceiling of $500 or $700 per child. This law benefits mainly parents whose children attend religious schools. The state contended that the law advances education generally by promoting pluralism and diversity, while the plaintiff said that it primarily advances religion. Writing for the 5-4 majority, Justice Rehnquist interpreted the prevailing three-part test to uphold the statute. Indicating a changing approach, the opinion raises serious questions about the continuing validity of the 1973 *Nyquist* decision that struck down a tuition reimbursement plan for lower income parents of children attending nonpublic elementary or secondary schools.[31] The reimbursement was $50 per grade-school and $100 per high-school student, so long as these amounts did not exceed 50 percent of actual tuition paid. *Nyquist* also annulled another part of the state program giving tax relief to parents failing to qualify for tuition reimbursement. This provision had permitted qualifying parents to deduct a stipulated sum from their adjusted gross income for each child attending a nonpublic school. Unlike the Minnesota statute, the *Nyquist* law provided relief only for parents of children attending private schools, a difference more of form than of substance. The importance of *Mueller* is that it upholds financial support for religious schools without any qualification that the monies be used solely for nonreligious instruction.

Lynch v. Donnelly[32] is another serious limitation on the separation doctrine. As part of the observance of the Christmas holiday season, Pawtucket, Rhode Island annually erects a display showing various figures and decorations, including in one portion a creche containing the traditional figures associated with the religious observance of the holiday, the infant Jesus, Mary and Joseph, angels, shepherds, kings, and animals, all ranging in height from five inches to five feet. Some Christians found the representation of the Nativity appropriate to the religious nature of the holiday; some non-Christians found it objectionable and offensive to their beliefs and four Justices found that it amounted to a governmental endorsement of a particular faith. Although the city insisted that the creche merely helped celebrate a public holiday season, no one could deny that it presented the beliefs of certain religious groups and not of others. Nevertheless, after dutifully considering the three-part test, the High Court, on a 5-4 vote, upheld city sponsorship of the display.

Considerably less deference was given localities in two 1985 cases involving publicly supported instruction in secular schools. The Court invalidated two Grand Rapids programs that had provided classes for nonpublic school students at public expense in classrooms located in and leased from the nonpublic schools.[33] One program offered classes during the regular school day that were intended to supplement the "core curriculum" courses required by the state. The other offered elective courses at the conclusion of the regular school day, some of which were not offered at the public schools. The students attending both programs were the same students who otherwise attended the particular school in which the classes were held.

The Court also struck down a New York City program in which the city used federal funds to pay for and provide remedial instruction and clinical guidance in both religious and public schools.[34] To avoid inculcation of sectarian beliefs in the religious schools, the city adopted a system for monitoring the religious content of the instruction. The federal program authorized financial assistance to local educational institutions to meet the needs of educationally deprived children from low-income families. A major constitutional fault for both the Grand Rapids and New York City programs was that the instruction was afforded on the premises of the religious schools.

As these cases demonstrate, the quest for certainty is quite difficult in the establishment rulings.

Establishment and Free Exercise Conflicts

The foregoing cases concern only state-church separation and not free exercise. In them, no one's right to worship has been affected. However, some other establishment cases are not so straightforward. They may also affect freedom of worship. Two of the most controversial establishment cases are of this character—*McCullom v. Board of Education*,[35] concerning religious education on public school premises, and *Engel v. Vitale*,[36] the famous school prayer case, probably the most controversial of all the religion decisions.

In *McCullom*, the Champagne, Illinois school system allowed teachers employed by religious groups to provide, with parental approval, religious instruction for students during regular school hours and in public school buildings. Students who did not participate pursued secular studies in other parts of the school building. These teachers received no compensation from the school system. To avoid truancy, attendance was taken, and reported to the school authorities.

Citing *Everson* as standing for the proposition that the Constitution requires a wall of separation between church and state, Justice Black, for an 8-1 majority, held that the Champagne program was invalid because it "is beyond all question a utilization of the tax-established and tax-supported public school system to aid religious groups to spread their faith."

At issue in the *Vitale* case was the requirement of the New York Board of Regents that a "non-demominational" prayer be recited in all public schools at the beginning of each school day. The prayer read as follows: "Almighty God, we acknowledge our dependence upon Thee, and we beg Thy blessings upon us, our parents, our teachers and our Country." Pupils did not have to participate; they could remain silent or be excused from the classroom while the prayer was being recited. Black found that the state had gone further than the establishment clause allows but made no ruling with respect to free exercise.

Both of the latter cases do raise the issue of liberty. The argument is that peer pressures and general community attitudes operate to coerce parents to enroll their children in the religious programs. Official sponsorship of the programs, it is said, encourages this conformity and makes deviation very uncomfortable. The legal difficulty with these arguments is that the alleged compulsion does not emanate from government. The state has not forced parent or child to engage in these programs but instead has made every effort to make participation voluntary. Whatever problem in this regard exists is not created by government mandate but rather by conditions outside its control. The same conditions might at times function against religious observances.

"Constitutional concerns are greatest when the State attempts to impose its will by force of law; the State's power to encourage actions deemed to be in the public interest is necessarily far broader."[37] Moreover, when the effects are entirely consequential, the matter is one for resolution by the legislature and not by the courts. The complaints about the prayer relate to private attitudes that in the racial area the Court has held cannot constitutionally justify government decisions. Thus, in a 1984 case, the Court rejected a child custody award based on race although the trial court had made it to accommodate racial prejudices and thereby prevent harm to the child.[38]

Interestingly, Justice Douglas presented an analysis along the foregoing lines in the *Zorach* case[39] which concerned a New York law that also permitted religious instruction during the school day except that the students were released from school to attend religious centers for this purpose (an insignificant difference from *McCullom*, according to the minority Justices). Douglas, who generally took a strong separation stand during his tenure on the Court, voted with the majority in both *McCullom* and *Vitale* on the ground that the establishment clause had been violated. However, he also wrote the opinion upholding the *Zorach* statute. In it he presented a perspective very supportive to the kind of government involvement at issue there, one that seems highly relevant to the *McCullom* and *Vitale* situations. Rejecting the contention that the *Zorach* program was coercive, his opinion is devoid of any reference to peer or community pressures, suggesting that for him, they are not material to determining whether an abridgment of freedom has occurred.

> It takes obtuse reasoning to inject any issue of the "free exercise" of religion into the present case. No one is forced to go to the religious classroom and no religious exercise or instruction is brought to the classrooms of the public schools. A student need not take religious instruction. He is left to his own desires as to the manner or time of his religious devotions, if any.[40]

The Justice thus rejected objections that the system was inherently coercive for many parents. Douglas found the program fully consistent with the Constitution. To rule otherwise would be to read into the Bill of Rights "a philosophy of hostility to religion."

> We are a religious people whose institutions presuppose a Supreme Being. We guarantee the freedom to worship as one chooses. We make room for as wide a variety of beliefs and creeds as the spiritual needs of man deem necessary. We sponsor an attitude on the part of government that shows no partiality to any one group and that lets each flourish according to the zeal of its adherents and the appeal of its dogma. When the state encourages religious instruction or cooperates with religous authorities by adjusting the schedule of public events to sectarian needs, it follows the best of our traditions. For it then respects the religious nature of our people and accommodates the public service to their spiritual needs. To hold that it may not would be to find in the Constitution a requirement that the government show a callous indifference to religious groups. That would be preferring those who believe in no religion over those who do believe. . . . We find no constitutional requirement which makes it necessary for government to be hostile to religion and to throw its weight against efforts to widen the effective scope of religious influence. . . . It may not coerce anyone to attend church, to observe a religious holiday, or to take religious instruction. But it can close its doors or suspend its operations as to those who want to repair to their religious sanctuary for worship or instruction.[41]

Justice Douglas' comments reflect the tension between separation and free exercise. Consider again the *Vitale* situation. Parents supporting the prayer believe that its invocation at the beginning of the school day is morally and spiritually inspiring. They insist that their children should not be deprived of a moral environment that would attend the learning process were it in their own homes. Those opposed to the prayer believe that it injects a religious flavor into the classroom. They object that peer and community pressures might force their children to accept it, and that even if that situation does not result, a doctrine that many reject will be advanced among the students.[42]

This latter contention is based on an inaccurate assessment of contemporary American schools, that they are neutral—antiseptic—centers of learning without partisanship toward any dogma or doctrine. In fact, whether by accident or design, teachers and textbooks are not always sterile disseminators of information, nor can they be expected to be. Schools are subject to a wide variety of opinion, but, due to the Court's rulings, not that of a traditional religious nature. The free exercise of religion frequently may be at a competitive disadvantage in the classrooms.

There are, for example, proponents of the New Humanism who urge that teachers be proselytizers of "this faith." Consider this comment in an article in *The Humanist*, organ of the American Humanist Association.

> I am convinced that the battle for humankind's future must be waged and won in the public school classroom by teachers who correctly perceive their role as proselytizers of a new faith: a religion of humanity that recognizes and respects the spark of what theologians call divinity in every human being. These teachers must embody the same selfless dedication as the most rabid fundamentalist preachers, for they will be ministers of another sort, utilizing a classroom instead of a pulpit to convey humanist values in whatever subject they teach, regardless of the educational level—preschool day care or large state university. The classroom must and will become an arena of conflict between the old and the new—the rotting corpse of Christianity, together with all its adjacent evils and misery, and the new faith of humanism, resplendent in its promise of a world in which the never-realized Christian ideal of 'love thy neighbor' will finally be achieved.
>
> Then, perhaps, we will be able to say with Tom Paine that "the world is my country, all [h]umankind are my brethren, and to do good is my religion." It will undoubtedly be a long, arduous, painful struggle replete with much sorrow and many tears, but humanism will emerge triumphant. It must if the family of humankind is to survive."[43]

No law prevents teachers from furthering this prospective or other general tenets of Humanism, which rejects most major traditional religious concepts. Thus, when teachers proclaim people's competency to shape their own lives, as so often occurs, they deny the idea held by many religious persons that people are dependent for their existence and future on a Supreme Being. Textbooks may espouse "relativism" in areas of moral concern to religious people. These books tend to de-emphasize personal integrity, patriotism, and family loyalty, each of the highest priority to those who practice traditional religion. Nevertheless, religious persons are forbidden to invoke modest prayer to assert their beliefs.

Religious doctrine is not the sole subject of controversy. Various moral and ethical concerns are considered in an atmosphere devoid of and sometimes even hostile to traditional religious doctrines. Many teachers belong to the National Education Association (NEA), the nation's largest teacher organization, whose Western States Regional staff prepared a "Participant's Manual" on "Combatting the New Right," which views with alarm and paints an extremist label on organizations that it identifies as the New Right.[44]

Teachers are advised to counter ideas advanced by these groups. Included in the condemned list are certain religious or religiously oriented groups: Moral Majority, Christian Voice, Religious Roundtable, James Robison Evangelistic Association, Christian Voters Victory Fund, Californians for Biblical Morality, and Church League of America. Also named are Citizens for the Republic, Young Americans for Freedom, National Taxpayers Union, Institute for Educational Affairs, and the Hoover Institution ("The Brookings of the Right"). Now lest it not be immediately apparent to all teachers that such groups as those listed above and at least another fifty cited of similar persuasion damage the minds of young America, the manual spells out the threat:

> Following the recession of 1974, in the wake of the Civil Rights Movement of the 1960s and the anti-war activism of the early 1970s, organizations of the radical right began to proliferate and to move in from the fringes toward the vital centers of power in America. Leaders of these organizations began to work together with new sophistication and pragmatism, coordinating their efforts toward the goal of putting into place their own economic and political agenda for the nation—an agenda that would escalate military expenditures and erase most of the social and educational advances of the past generation. . . .

> What is emerging today is a powerful convergence of forces on the right— militant cold warriors, anti-education would-be censors, anti-union, anti-regulatory free enterprise boosters, so called pro-life; pro-family and pro-flag superpatriots, and fundamentalist preacher politicians.

Included are groups that many proponents of the New Humanism also seek to overcome. Other NEA publications have frequently stressed humanist ethical values to replace those of traditional religion.[45] Teachers can exert a powerful influence on young minds, surely comparable to that emanating from modest voluntary prayer. Thus, the classroom is already a battleground of ideas on cultural, social, and moral values in which it seems all but traditional religion is permitted to participate.[46]

Given this state of affairs, religious prayer provides a perspective that augments pluralism and diversity. It offers moral and ethical values that might not otherwise be disseminated in the public schools or that may even be partisanly condemned. "Neutrality" in the classroom, it seems, requires, rather than rejects, some traditional religious input. I doubt the classroom ever has been, or ever will be, a neutral source of ideas.[47]

In the absence of constitutional controls, it might be feared that schools will be inundated with religious prayers and learning. It is doubtful that the religious groups have the will, political power or unity to achieve this result. Equally important, the dissemination in the classroom of other and counter messages is inevitable, as contemporary experience reveals, moreover, due process limits input harmful to religious liberty.

Conclusion

Little basis exists for the Supreme Court's conclusion that the fourteenth amendment's due process provision applies the establishment clause to the states. Were the Court to reverse position on this issue, religious liberty would not be affected. Due process would continue to protect freedom of conscience, and it would prohibit religious discrimination. No evidence comes to light that either Madison or the first Congress intended to erect a "wall of separation" between church and state. The extent of nonpreferential aid to religious institutions was left to the political process.

Despite its rhetoric, the Supreme Court has never required strict separation between church and state, for some government support of religion has always been upheld. The decisions have shown that line-drawing between the legal and illegal, in these cases, is highly subjective. They involve spending of the people's monies, a concern constitutionally appropriate for the political process rather than for the judiciary.

Notes

1. Cantwell v. Connecticut, 310 U.S. 296 (1940) and Everson v. Board of Education, 330 U.S. 1 (1947).
2. The first Congress provided for paid chaplains in the armed services and in both Houses of Congress and the Treasury Department has stamped "In God We Trust" on coins that it has minted. These actions seem part of the discretion necessarily associated with enumerated powers.

3. 2 MAX FARRAND, THE RECORDS OF THE FEDERAL CONVENTION OF 1787, at 616 (rev. ed. 1937)(New Haven, Conn. and London: Yale University Press, 1966).

4. 3 JONATHAN ELLIOT, ELLIOT'S DEBATES 93 (Philadelphia: J.B. Lippincott Company, 1836).

5. *Id.* at 469.

6. THE MAKING OF THE AMERICAN REPUBLIC, THE GREAT DOCUMENTS 1774-1789 at 1009-59 (Charles Callan Tansill, ed.) (New Rochelle, N.Y.: Arlington House, 1972).

7. This account of the framing of the religion clauses is from *The Story of the Bill of Rights* published by The National Archives in 1966 and 1 ANNALS OF CONG. (Gales and Seaton, ed., 1789).
   Representative Roger Sherman of Connecticut, who had been a delegate to the Constitutional Convention, opposed the amendment applicable to the central government because "Congress had no authority whatsoever . . . to make religious establishments." 1 ANNALS OF CONG. 730 (Gales and Seaton, ed., 1789).

8. 1 ANNALS OF CONG. 730 (Gales and Seaton, ed., 1789).

9. *Id.* at 731.

10. 1 N. WEBSTER, AMERICAN DICTIONARY OF THE ENGLISH LANGUAGE (1st ed. 1828). Cited by Rehnquist, J., dissenting in Wallace v. Jaffree, 105 S.Ct. 2479, 2516 (1985). "By establishment of religion is meant the setting up or recognition of a state church, or at least the conferring upon one church of special favors and advantages which are denied to others." THOMAS COOLEY, PRINCIPLES OF CONSTITUTIONAL LAW, 224-25, 3d ed. (1898).

11. 2 JOSEPH STORY, COMMENTARIES ON THE CONSTITUTION OF THE UNITED STATES 728 (New York: DaCapo Press, 1970). [Emphasis added.]

12. CONG. GLOBE, 39th Cong., 1st sess. 2765 (1866).

13. John Bingham and Thaddeus Stevens insisted that they had no intention of controlling the state's administrative and management powers. Supporters did not regard the amendment's protections as intruding on the normal operations of the states. *See generally* Chapters 3 and 4 *supra.*

14. "*So far as the Fourteenth Amendment is concerned, states are entirely free to establish religions, provided they do not deprive anyone of religious liberty.* It is only *liberty* that the Fourteenth Amendment protects." Corwin, *The Supreme Court as National School Board.* 14 LAW AND CONTEMP. PROB. 3, 19 (1949).

15. STORY, *supra* note 11, at 630-32.

16. 330 U.S. 1 (1947).

17. 8 WRITINGS OF THOMAS JEFFERSON 113 (H. Washington, ed. 1861).

18. ROBERT L. CORD, SEPARATION OF CHURCH AND STATE 115-16, 226, 262 (New York: Lambeth Press, 1982).

19. Note should also be taken of Justice Rutledge's strong and lengthly dissent (joined by three other Justices) in which he contended that the *Everson* statute violated the establishment clause. Like Black, he thought that the Virginia experience explained the meaning of the clause—that is, that it required complete separation. I agree with historian Kelly that Rutledge's opinion is "extreme and didactic." Kelly, *Clio and the Court : An Illicit Love Affair,* 1965. SUP. CT. REV. 119, 141 n. 93.

20. 330 U.S. at 13. The statute referred to is the "Virginia Bill for Religious Liberty."

21. *See* discussion in Lynch v. Donnelly, 465 U.S. 668 (1984) and Marsh v. Chambers, 463 U.S. 783 (1983).

22. Cord, *supra* note 18, at 46.
23. School District v. Schempp, 374 U.S. 203, (1963) (Brennan, J., concurring).
24. "Thus the whole power over the subject of religion is left exclusively [by the first amendment] to the State governments, to be acted upon according to their own sense of justice, and the State Constitutions; and the Catholic and Protestant, the Calvinist, the Armenian, the Jew and the Infidel, may sit down at the common table of the national councils without any inquisition into their faith or mode of worship." Story, *supra* note 11 at 596-97.
25. McCollum v. Board of Education of Champaign, Illinois, 333 U.S. 203, 237-38 (Jackson, J., concurring).
26. Lemon v. Kurtzman, 403 U.S. 602, (1971). The test is not always decisive. It assumes that the three main evils against which the establishment clause was intended to afford protection were sponsorship, financial support, and active involvement of the sovereign in religious activity. Walz v. Tax Commission, 397 U.S. 664, 668 (1970). This test is quite distant from Madison's and the first Congress's purpose merely to prevent establishment of a national religion.
27. Board of Education v. Allen, 392 U.S. 236 (1968); Wolman v. Walter, 433 U.S. 229 (1977).
28. Wolman v. Walter, 433 U.S. 229 (1977).
29. Engel v. Vitale, 370 U.S. 421, 437 fn.1 (1962) (Douglas, J., concurring). Interestingly, Douglas even found that the first congress violated the amendment that it authored by providing for chaplains in Congress and the armed services.
30. 463 U.S. 388 (1983).
31. Committee for Public Education v. Nyquist, 413 U.S. 756 (1973).
32. 465 U.S. 668 (1984).
33. Grand Rapids School Dist. v. Ball, 105 S.Ct. 3216 (1985).
34. Aguilar v. Felton, 105 S.Ct. 3232 (1985).
35. 333 U.S. 203 (1948).
36. 370 U.S. 421 (1962).
37. Maher v. Roe, 432 U.S. 464, at 476 (1977).
38. Palmore v. Sidoti, 104 S.Ct. 1879 (1984). "[C]onstitutional rights may not be denied simply because of hostility to their assertion or exercise." Watson v. City of Memphis, 373 U.S. 526, 535 (1963).
39. Zorach v. Clausen, 343 U.S. 306 (1952).
40. *Id.* at 311.
41. *Id.* at 313-14. Religion was a strong force at the time the fourteenth amendment was adopted. "The culture of nineteenth century America was impregnated by religion. For most people religion was an essential part of the social fabric, and even those without strong attachments to Christian faith believed in the existence of a moral order to which the Bible was the best—if not the only—guide." W. R. BROCK, THE UNITED STATES: 1789-1890, at 287 (Ithaca, N.Y.: Cornell University Press (1975). " [U]ntil at least World War II and longer in some places, the public schools frequently had a strongly religious character. Clergymen often served as teachers. The Bible was read. Prayers were recited every day. When the first Catholic schools were established in the mid-nineteenth century, it was not because the public schools were secular but because they were too Protestant." JAMES HITCHCOCK, WHAT IS SECULAR HUMANISM? (Ann Arbor, MI: Servant Publications, 1985), p. 99.
42. The *Vitale* result was recently affirmed in Wallace v. Jaffree, 105 S.Ct. 2479 (1985), which struck down an Alabama statute authorizing a one minute period

of silence in all public schools "for meditation or voluntary prayer." A 6-3 majority determined that the statute was not neutrally motivated but was solely an "effort to return voluntary prayer" to the public schools. For the Court, Justice Stevens held that the legislation endorsed prayer activities contrary to the governmental responsibility to pursue a course of complete neutrality toward religion.

43. Dunphy, *A Religion for a New Age, Humanist Magazine* (Jan.-Feb., 1983). Interestingly, in Torcaso v. Watkins, 367 U.S. 488 (1961) the Supreme Court referred to "Secular Humanism" as a religion (at 495, n. 11). United States v. Seeger, 380 U.S. 163 (1965) held that for purposes of qualifying young men for the statutory exemption from military services, religion embraces belief that denies existence of a traditional God.

44. *Western States Regional Staff, National Educational Association, Combatting the New Right* (undated).

45. BLUMENFELD, NEA: TROJAN HORSE IN AMERICAN EDUCATION (Boise, Idaho: The Paradigm Company, 1984).

46. *See* HITCHCOCK, *supra* note 41, pp. 105-6.

47. Some groups have long sought to use the classroom to advance their thinking. Samuel Blumenfeld observes that the forces that generated the public school movement were religious and philosophically disposed. "The Unitarians wanted public schools in order to secularize education and perfect humanity, the Owenite Socialists wanted them to create a communist society, the Hegelians wanted them to glorify the state, and the Protestants wanted them to preserve Protestant culture seemingly threatened by large-scale Catholic immigration." BLUMENFELD *supra* note 45, at 214. *See* HITCHCOCK, *supra* note 41.

6

Gender

In 1948, Justice Felix Frankfurter wrote the majority opinion in *Goesaert v. Cleary*,[1] upholding a provision in Michigan's bartender licensing law prohibiting licensing for any female unless she was "the wife or daughter of the male owner" of a licensed liquor establishment. He rejected the complaint that the law violated the equal protection clause.

Contrary to that which the contemporary reader may think, the statute was not challenged primarily as being discriminatory on the basis of gender. In that period, this argument was not the most persuasive. Instead, the plaintiff contended that Michigan could not forbid females generally from being barmaids and at the same time make an exception in favor of the wives and daughters of the owners of liquor establishments.

For Frankfurter, the case was not very troubling. To ask whether the equal protection clause barred the law "is in effect, to answer it." The fourteenth amendment did not "tear history up by the roots" and ban regulation of liquor traffic, "one of the oldest and most untrammeled of legislative powers." Michigan could forbid all women from working behind a bar.

> This is so despite the vast changes in the social and legal position of women. The fact that women may now have achieved the virtues that men have long claimed as their prerogatives and now indulge in vices that men have long practiced, does not preclude the States from drawing a sharp line between the sexes, certainly in such matters as the regulation of the liquor traffic. . . . The Constitution does not require legislatures to reflect sociological insight, or shifting social standards, any more than it requires them to keep abreast of the latest scientific standards.

Still, Michigan must have a "basis in reason," which could not include merely an "unchivalrous desire of male bartenders to try to monopolize the calling." Applying this minimal standard of review, the majority found it sufficient that the state "evidently believes that the oversight assured [by a husband's or father's ownership] minimizes hazards that may confront a barmaid without such protecting oversight."

Justice Wiley B. Rutledge dissented for himself and Justices William O. Douglas and Frank Murphy on the ground that the statute arbitrarily discriminated between male and female owners.

While the words are different, the Court had not deviated much from its earliest gender decision under the equal protection clause. In *Bradwell v. Illinois*, decided in 1873, the Court sustained a ruling of the Illinois Supreme Court denying women, on the ground of their sex, licenses to practice law.[2] This case is also known for Justice Joseph P. Bradley's concurring remarks that contemporary justices quote as indicative of prior discrimination against women.

> Man is, or should be, woman's protector and defender. The natural and proper timidity and delicacy which belongs to the female sex evidently unfits it for many of the occupations of civil life. The constitution of the family organization, which is founded in the divine ordinance, as well as in the nature of things, indicates the domestic sphere as that which properly belongs to the domain and functions of womanhood. The harmony, not to say identity, of interests and views which belong, or should belong, to the family institution is repugnant to the idea of a woman adopting a distinct and independent career from that of her husband. . . . The paramount destiny and mission of woman are to fulfill the noble and benign offices of wife and mother. This is the law of the Creator.

Times do change. Neither Frankfurter's nor Bradley's words and reasoning would be very kindly received in the 1980s. To be sure, the constitutional language remains the same, but the interpretation is drastically different. Michigan's erstwhile law would have no chance of survival before the present Court, which very carefully scrutinizes any law affecting gender. The Supreme Court has adopted its own version of the Equal Rights Amendment, which provides for a standard of review that is only minimally less strict than that which would obtain under the amendment.

In *Frontiero v. Richardson*,[3] decided in 1973 while the Equal Rights Amendment was pending, four Justices sought to abolish this variance by voting to impose strict judicial scrutiny on gender classifications. *U.S. Law Week* concluded: "The Court came within a vote of rendering state ratification of the Equal Rights Amendment superfluous."[4] Such a vote would also have been possibly the most dramatic illustration of the Supreme Court's affect on the Constitution, for it would have accomplished that which the constitutionally directed political process failed to do over a period of many years. Three of the Justices, per Justice Powell, mildly rebuked their brethren for considering such judicial action.

> There are times when this Court, under our system, cannot avoid a constitutional decision on issues which normally should be resolved by the elected

representatives of the people. But democratic institutions are weakened, and confidence in the restraint of the Court is impaired, when we appear unnecessarily to decide sensitive issues of broad social and political importance at the very time they are under consideration within the prescribed constitutional processes.

This chapter will set forth the Supreme Court's record in achieving that which supporters of the Equal Rights Amendment assume requires a constitutional amendment. Ruth Bader Ginsburg advises that the proposed amendment "would eliminate the historical impediment to judicial recognition of the legal equality of men and women: the absence of any intention by eighteenth and nineteenth-century Constitution-makers to deal with gender-based discrimination."[5] This description is accurate except for the implication about discrimination; the respective framers wrote their provisions for a society that accepted a very limited public role for women. With the passage of time, changes in that role occurred and the nineteenth amendment was adopted in 1920, giving women the right to vote.[6] Because they account for about 50 percent of the eligible vote, suffrage gave women a potentially powerful political weapon against legalized discrimination. Changes in the woman's role can also be recognized in interpreting the due process and equal protection clauses to determine if different treatment for the sexes is justified in a particular situation. However, the reach of each of the clauses is far from coterminous with the scope of the proposed amendment or with the one that the judiciary has affected, as we shall see.

Change in the Gender Standard

Until 1971, the *Goesaert* and *Bradwell* decisions generally reflected the constitutional law on gender—the period that Judge Ginsburg refers to as "Anything Goes."[7] In that year, without any acknowledgement that a reversal in the law was occurring, a unanimous Court in *Reed v. Reed*[8] elevated the existing minimal standard of scrutiny in gender cases to a much higher one. Indeed, Justice Brennan in *Frontiero* construed *Reed* as implicitly supporting the imposition of the highest standard.[9]

Chief Justice Burger's opinion in *Reed* gives no clue about the great change it effected in the law. At issue was an Idaho statute providing that when a male and female who are otherwise equally entitled compete for appointment as administrator of an estate, the male applicant must be preferred. Under the then existing minimal standard, the Idaho Supreme Court had accepted the state's explanation (1) that the measure was designed to reduce the work load on probate courts by eliminating one class of contests, and (2) that the Idaho legislature might have reasonably concluded that in general men are better qualified to act as administrators than are women.

In reversing the Idaho Court, Burger chose to ignore the long existing standard and instead invoked an intermediate scrutiny entirely on the basis of a holding in a 1920 state tax case, *Royster Guano Co. v. Virginia.*[10] Quoting from that case, Burger asserted that the equal protection clause required that a classification "must be reasonable, not arbitrary, and must rest upon some ground of difference having a fair and substantial relation to the object of the legislation, so that all persons similarly circumstanced shall be treated alike."

The opinion avoided any explanation about why and under which reasoning the gender standard was being elevated. As future decisions reveal, the Court had decided as a matter of policy to impose the higher standard. In keeping with age-old legal practice, *Royster* was trotted out in support of a proposition advanced for other reasons. The holding in that case had long been ignored in the gender area and for good reason.

1. The equal protection clause was not intended to alter or abolish the gender distinctions that permeated state laws in the 1860s. To a great extent, American law treated men and women differently. Among other things, women could not hold office, serve on juries, file lawsuits in their own names, hold or convey property, or serve as legal guardians of their own children. The fourteenth amendment would never have passed Congress or been ratified had it been interpreted as eliminating these restraints. The reader will recall that the Civil Rights Act of 1866 did not apply generally to women.[11]
2. Until *Reed*, *Royster* would not be thought of as applicable to gender classifications, which, as *Goesaert* shows, were regarded as being on a separate track under the equal protection clause.
3. Beginning with the advent of the Roosevelt-appointed Justices and until 1971, the equal protection clause was interpreted on a two tier basis— strict and minimal scrutiny—without any intermediate level.[12] During this time, *Royster*'s intermediate scrutiny did not fit within the prevailing judicial thinking that only two levels of review existed.
4. While *Royster* involved property rights which were protected under the amendment, *Reed* concerned political rights, which were not. (See discussion in Chapter 4). The plaintiff in the earlier case complained that Virginia's taxation statute arbitrarily deprived it of its earnings—essentially an issue of civil liberty. Mrs. Reed sought to obtain a position created by and having no independent existence outside the political process. As explained in Chapter 4, this distinction was important for the fourteenth amendment's framers who, differentiating between natural and political liberty, denied intention to limit the political and administrative processes of the states except when their governments

deprived constituents of natural or fundamental rights. On the one hand, there is no natural right to be a probate administrator, a position that does not exist in the absence of the political process. On the other, there is a natural right to follow a calling of one's own choosing that exists in the private marketplace—for example, bartending.

Interestingly enough, the language from *Royster* quoted above was actually a dictum, for a minimal standard of review was therein applied. The Virginia statute taxed all income of local corporations while exempting income derived from outside the state by local corporations doing no local business. Acknowledging that the state has "notably wide" discretion in classifying for purposes of taxation, the Court stated that nevertheless "a discriminatory tax law cannot be sustained if the classifications appear to be altogether illusory"—a standard that reads much like Frankfurter's in *Goesaert*. *Royster* was thus a ruling about the extent of legislative discretion in property taxation, a subject far removed from gender discrimination. The *Reed* opinion does not discuss these difficulties.

Frontiero, next in the contemporary gender cases, also involved administrative processes and alleged a violation of the fifth amendment's due process clause. Under federal statutes governing the Armed Forces, a serviceman could claim his wife as a "dependent" without regard to whether she was, in fact, dependent on him for any part of her support. A servicewoman, however, could not claim her husband as a "dependent" unless he was in fact dependent on her for over one-half of his support. No one seriously contended the statutory intent was to disadvantage either of the sexes; nor did the Court so find. According to the government, the differential treatment served no other purpose than administrative convenience. Congress might reasonably have concluded that it would be cheaper and easier to presume conclusively that wives are financially dependent on their husbands, whereas the reverse was much less likely to be the case.

The Court struck down these provisions on a 8-1 vote, with seven members relying on *Reed*, a technically questionable interpretation of a constitutional provision that does not affect the federal government. The Court has found that the fifth amendment's due process clause contains an equal protection component, but it has also held "that the two protections are not always coextensive" when special national interests are involved.[13] None of the majority opinions dealt with this issue, ignoring several enumerated congressional powers relating to the armed forces and spending. Article I, section 8 provides that Congress shall have the powers "to raise and support armies, but no appropriation of money for that use shall be for a longer term than two years," "[t]o provide and maintain a Navy," and "to make rules for the government and regulation of the land and naval forces." Section 9 states that "no money shall be drawn from the Treasury, but in consequence of appropriations made by law."

Under these provisions, Congress has the authority to appropriate money for the support of the armed forces as it deems best suited to those purposes. The Constitution does not grant the judiciary any authority in this regard. If any role for the judiciary exists, it must be highly deferential to these legislative powers—a word that does not describe the standard established in *Reed*. Numerous cases have recognized the limited role of the judiciary in supervising the military.[14] Moreover, under the Court's own rules, the existence of congressional authority limits the applicability of *Reed*'s equal protection criteria in interpreting the fifth amendment's due process clause. Nevertheless, *Frontiero* opened to judicial supervision all governmental spending programs treating the sexes differently.

The Justices' silence on the separation of powers in *Frontiero* parallels their failure to discuss a constitutional foundation for the *Reed* ruling. The Justices do, however, command recognition of their boldness in having established on a questionable basis rules of law that much of the nation believes requires constitutional amendment.

The fact situation in *Frontiero* does not present a strong case that women generally were being disadvantaged. In point of fact, wives of many servicemen likely received preferential treatment. If as some of the justices insist, the traditional family is disappearing, and increasing numbers of wives are working outside the home, many women benefitted from the extra income their husbands received that would not have been obtained under a dependency test. Working husbands of servicewomen were denied this option unless they were over 50 percent dependent.

Nor was Congress at that time indifferent to gender discrimination. By a two-thirds vote of both the House and Senate, Congress in 1972 submitted the Equal Rights Amendment for ratification by the States. Moreover, in title VII of the Civil Rights Act of 1964, it decreed protection against sex discrimination. The Equal Pay Act of 1963 provides that no employer covered by the Act "shall discriminate . . . between employees on the basis of sex." These factors diminish the contention that the cause of sexual equality demanded Supreme Court intervention.

The Court as a Legislator in the Gender Cases

Congress is the branch of government charged with taxing the people and spending the receipts. These are peculiarly legislative powers, stemming from the idea that only the people, acting on their own or through their representatives, are entitled to decide how they will utilize their own funds. Our government rests on the historical foundation of no taxation without representation. Implicit in this understanding is that the spending that necessitates collecting of taxes will also be with representation.

It cannot be otherwise in our system of government. The demands on government for taxing and spending are beyond precise description. Some are well and others badly motivated; some are commendable and others selfish or arbitrary. In a representative society, the test of value must rest with a political process that is geared to effecting the solutions most acceptable to the people. While many determinations will by themselves surely be regarded as arbitrary or even tyrannical, they may tend to be less offensive when considered in light of the needs, demands, and pressures to which the political process must respond. The judiciary is not similarly situated.

Apparently the *Frontiero* decision did not result in increased budget requirements. However, in *Weinberger v. Wisenfeld*, concerning a challenge on the basis of gender to certain social security provisions, the solicitor general advised the Court that the annual cost of providing the relief sought would be at least $20 million and over $300 million if other closely analogous provisions were similarly altered.[15] When figures of this magnitude are revealed, the case can no longer be regarded as confined to the settling of gender equities. If additional funds are not appropriated, the program will suffer; or if they are, other programs or the taxpayers will suffer. A great many of those harmed will be women. Like the other gender decisions, *Wisenfeld* gave little recognition to these factors; it is instead based on one facet of a problem that has other important dimensions. A definitional equality in gender is being protected at a price—possibly a very significant one. Making this outcome even harder to justify is the dubious authority of the Court in the matter. As has frequently occurred in other areas, the Court's projected moral position is compromised by the harm it imposes on those who trace their rights to original understanding. Change in interpretation results in both benefits and costs and when improperly effected is morally as well as legally objectionable.

The Supreme Court's penchant for legislating is even more evident in *Califano v. Westcott*.[16] A section of the Social Security Act relating to the Aid to Families with Dependent Children program provided help to families whose dependent children were deprived of parental support because of the father's unemployment, but it did not require such benefits when the mother was unemployed. In defending the statute, the secretary of health, education, and welfare denied that it was gender biased, contending that Congress regarded the gender of the parent only as a guide for the most efficient dispensation of the funds. The impact of the rule would be on the family; the denial or grant of aid based on a father's unemployment necessarily affects to an equal degree one man, one woman, and one or more children. Moreover, even if considered a gender classification, argued the secretary, it is substantially related to achievement of an important governmental objective—a requisite of the current constitutional standard in this area. The secretary submitted that reducing the father's incentive to desert was an important objective. "Solid statistical evidence" was available that fathers are more likely to desert than mothers. In addition, Congress sought to allocate the funding more fairly: Certain states were making assistance available to families in which the mother was out of work but the father remained fully employed and able to support the family.

Writing for the Court, Justice Blackmun rejected both explanations as either being predicated on outmoded notions of the "traditional family" or not supported by the evidence, a conclusion he did not elaborate on. Legislation that presumes that the father has the primary responsiblity to provide a home and its essentials, with the mother serving as center of home and family life, is not founded on reason but on sexual stereotypes and therefore violates the fifth amendment's due process clause. To a weak legal base, Blackmun thus added a defective factual assumption—that the differences in the traditional sexual roles had virtually disappeared. At the time of the decision, fewer than 50 percent of women over age sixteen were in the labor force.

Blackmun went on to approve the district court's remedial order in the case that benefits be paid to families deprived of support because of the unemployment of the mother to the same extent they are paid to families deprived of support because of the unemployment of the father. Although up to this point, Blackmun's opinion received approval or concurrence from all the other justices, four defected with respect to the remedy. Writing for these dissenters, Justice Powell complained that the relief decreed by the majority would "compel exactly the extension of benefits Congress wished to prevent." Moreover, leaving the "resolution to Congress is especially desirable in cases such as this one, where the allocation and distribution of welfare funds is peculiarly in the province of the Legislative Branch." Powell concluded that the program should be enjoined to allow Congress to act. In reply to Blackmun's contention that hardships may result from such an injunction, Powell wrote that other hardships may be occasioned in the allocating of the limited funds available for the program, and that restricting further payments would "conserve the funds appropriated until Congress determined which group, if any, it does want to assist. The relief ordered by the Court today, in contrast, ensures the irretrievable payment of funds to a class of recipients Congress did not wish to benefit."

These gender cases contrast sharply with the many in which the Supreme Court has acknowledged the financial responsibilities of the legislative and executive branches under the Constitution and refused to interfere with them. Thus, in sustaining a Maryland regulation mandating a monthly welfare limit of $250.00 for each family, regardless of the family's size or need, the Court explained:

> The intractable economic, social, and even philosophical problems presented by public welfare assistance programs are not the business of this Court. . . . The Constitution does not empower this Court to second-guess state officials charged with the difficult responsibility of allocating limited public welfare funds among the myriad of potential recipients.[17]

Under a similar rationale, the Court has refused to mandate changes in state tax programs to increase funding for schools in lower income areas[18] or to require funding for the procurement of abortions.[19] In the latter cases, the Court denied that the constitutional right to an abortion requires that the government pay for it. "It simply does not follow that a woman's freedom of choice carries with it a constitutional entitlement to the financial resources to avail herself of the full range of protective choices." A decision requiring the funding of abortions would inject the Supreme Court into the policy question of how public welfare money should be spent. The Court reasoned similarly in the tax case in which the plaintiffs demanded that the Court annul property tax programs that yielded less funds for lower than for higher income area schools.

In many gender cases, the Court has involved itself in resolving the "intractable" issues whose dispensation require neither the skill nor the knowledge of judges. Consider *Califano v. Goldfarb*,[20] in which a widower applied for federal old-age, survivors, and disability insurance benefits after the death of his wife but was denied on the basis that he had not been receiving at least one-half support from her when she died, as required by the social security law. Widows' benefits, under that law, are payable regardless of dependency. Justice Brennan's plurality opinion found the discrimination to be directed against female workers whose social security taxes produced less protection for their spouses than was produced by the efforts of a man. On the other hand, Justice Stevens contended that "the relevant discrimination . . . is against surviving male spouses, rather than against deceased female wage earners." Citing *Frontiero v. Richardson*, the Court held that the statutory scheme was a denial of equal protection.

The decision is also troubling in that the Court ignored the idea of "remediation" for past inequality of sexes that it had accepted in a quite comparable situation in *Kahn v. Shevin*.[21] In the latter case, the Court upheld a Florida regulation granting widows a $500 property tax exemption and completely denying such an exemption to widowers. The major rationale, which the Court accepted to justify this differential practice, was that women had a lesser earning power in the past and hence deserved remediation. The same rationale—lesser earning power of women in the past due to gender discrimination—could have been used to uphold the provisions involved in *Goldfarb*, which at least allowed widowers to prove dependency on the deceased spouse.

A similar quandary is presented by *Wengler v. Druggists Mutual Insurance Co.*[22] A provision of the Missouri worker's compensation law denied a widower benefits as a result of his wife's work-related death unless he was either physically or mentally incapacitated or proved dependence on his wife's earnings. However, the law granted a widow death benefits without her having to prove dependence on her husband's earnings. The Court invalidated the law as violating equal protection.

The state's only rationale was administrative convenience. It was presumed that women were numerically much more financially dependent than men, and would be more in need of speedy payment of death benefits. The Court gave the state a choice of two remedies: either force everyone to prove dependency or simply give unconditional benefits to both sexes. Neither option seems much of an improvement over the existing program. Forcing everyone to prove dependency would increase individual costs, although it would reduce government payouts. Granting unconditional benefits to everyone would operate in reverse manner, eliminating legal costs while increasing payouts. To be sure, as more women enter the workforce, the sexual difference on which the statute was based will lessen. Yet, so long as this difference remains, ground exists for solutions reflecting it. In any event, decisions of this nature are highly subjective and essentially involve matters of fairness and efficiency, not of constitutional proscription.

There seem to be few limits to the reach of the gender rulings. In *Mississippi University for Women v. Hogan*,[23] two of the four dissenters complained that gender has taken on a life of its own above and beyond constitutional boundaries. This 1982 case presented the issue of whether a regulation that excludes males from enrolling in a state-supported professional nursing school violates equal protection. The state operated two other schools that granted baccalaureate degrees in nursing to males, one located 130 and the other 160 miles from the city that was the site of the controversy. The Court applied a test difficult to distinguish in practice from strict scrutiny—that the party seeking to uphold a statute classifying on the basis of gender must carry the burden of showing an "exceedingly persuasive justification." In a 5-4 vote, it struck down the regulation excluding the plaintiff. This was too much for Justice Blackmun:

> I have come to suspect that it is easy to go too far with rigid rules in this area of claimed sex discrimination, and to lose—indeed destroy—values that

mean much to some people by forbidding the State to offer them a choice while not depriving others of an alternative choice. . . .

I hope we will not lose all values that some think are worthwhile (and are not based on differences of race and religion) and relegate ourselves to needless conformity. The ringing words of the equal protection clause of the Fourteenth Amendment . . . do not demand that price.

Justice Powell elaborated on the theme that the equal protection clause was never intended to deny the states the opportunity to provide both single-sex and coeducational institutions of higher learning.

The Court's opinion bows deeply to conformity. Left without honor—indeed, held unconstitutional—is an element of diversity that has characterized much of American education and enriched much of American life. The Court in effect holds today that no State now may even provide a single institution of higher learning open only to women students. It gives no heed to the efforts of the State of Mississippi to provide abundant opportunities for young men and young women . . . who over the years have evidenced their approval of an all-women's college by choosing Mississippi University for Women (MUW) over seven coeducational universities within the State. The Court decides today that the Equal Protection Clause makes it unlawful for the State to provide women with a traditionally popular and respected choice of educational environment. It does so in a case instituted by one man, who represents no class, and whose primary concern is personal convenience.

For Powell, imposition of a strict scrutiny standard was not warranted under sex or education discrimination decisions, for nondiscriminating alternatives existed in all of Mississippi's other colleges and universities, none of which were confined to a single sex. Instead of being coercive, the Mississippi system provided for considerable choice. Indeed, observed the Justice, it is difficult to consider the equal protection clause as directed to eliminating single sex schools; The imposition of high scrutiny "frustrates the liberating spirit of the Equal Protection Clause."

More correctly, as explained in Chapter 4, because it is part of the administration and management of state government, education was not to be affected by the fourteenth amendment. No natural right to education exists, for it is a service provided by government. However, the credibility of the dissenting Justices in objecting to the *Hogan* expansion is considerably flawed in view of their prior record on gender. How does a Court, which in this area has continually disregarded original meaning, suddenly observe it? As interpreted by the Court since 1971, equality in gender depends on the normative designs of the justices. *Hogan* reveals that a majority is prepared in the name of eliminating gender discrimination to affect vast educational and cultural changes on the country. This, notwithstanding that the national ERA debate over the past years is predicated on the assumption that gender equality is a matter requiring constitutional amendment.

Protecting Against Gender Discrimination Under Due Process and Equal Protection

In the gender cases, the Court has for the most part not exhibited the restraint that it has maintained in the racial area, although its constitutional responsibility is much clearer in the latter. In *Washington v. Davis*,[24] the Court rejected an impact test for determining the validity of laws affecting the races differently. It held that official action is not unconstitutional solely because it results in a racially disproportionate impact. Instead, proof of racially discriminatory intent or purpose is required to show a violation of the equal protection clause. Writing for the majority, Justice White explained that an impact test "would raise serious questions about, and perhaps invalidate, a whole range of tax, welfare, public service, regulatory, and licensing statutes" that, for reasons having nothing to do with purposeful discrimination, may burden the races differently. The Court has not applied this wisdom in the gender cases where it would seem to be likewise appropriate.

Section 1 of the fourteenth amendment was intended to secure the exercise of natural liberties. Recall John Bingham's explanation that it protected "the inborn rights of every person within [a state's] jurisdiction"[25] and his assertion that due process applies the highest reaches of justice to all, including the poor, the friendless, and the ignorant.[26] These views are consistent with the historic role of due process reasoning to overcome governmental injustice or oppression.[27] Bingham and colleagues intended a similar role for equal protection through the elimination of unequal laws. It is most doubtful that they cabined either of these provisions to the conditions and attitudes of their day.

While the pre-1971 record of the Supreme Court on gender was generally one of minimal scrutiny, there was an important exception. In the 1923 case of *Adkins v. Children's Hospital*,[28] the court invalidated a classification based on gender as inconsistent with the substantive due process requirements of the fifth amendment. At issue was congressional legislation providing for the fixing of minimum wages for women and minors in the District of Columbia. One of the plaintiffs was a woman elevator operator, who in effect complained that the act deprived her of her natural liberty to obtain employment in competition with men and that as a result of the statute, she had lost her job to a male. In its 5-3 decision, the Court refused to uphold the law on the ground that it safeguarded women. Rejecting the government's contention that the difference in sexes justifies a separate rule respecting hours of labor, Justice Sutherland, for the majority, wrote that the ancient inequality of the sexes has continued "with diminishing intensity."

> While the physical differences must be recognized in appropriate cases, and legislation fixing hours or conditions of work may properly take them into account, we cannot accept the doctrine that women of mature age, *sui juris*, require or may be subjected to restrictions upon their liberty of contract which could not lawfully be imposed in the case of men under similar circumstances. To do so would be to ignore all of the implications to be drawn from the present day trend of legislation, as well as that of common thought and usage, by which woman is accorded emancipation from the old doctrine that she must be given special protection or be subjected to special restraint in her contractual and civil relationships.

The case presented an appropriate issue for resolution under the due process clause. Whereas, at an earlier period in history, conditions may have provided justification for substantial employment differentiation between the sexes, circumstances and understandings had changed over the years. In recent times, courts considering special wages and working conditions for women have gone along with such thinking.[29] These opinions have struck down restraints on a woman's freedom of contract. In the 1980s, Justice Frankfurter's resolution of the controversy in *Goesaert* would have to give way to the wide acceptance of women as bartenders, based on many years of actual experience. Unlike then, it now appears almost senseless to limit women's opportunities in that occupation.

Another illustration that the application of due process or equal protection is appropriate is *Craig v. Boren*,[30] concerning an Oklahoma law that prohibited the sale of 3.2 percent beer to males under the age of 21 and to females under the age of 18. Involved was the natural liberty to purchase and sell goods and services. The Court, on the basis of an intermediate standard of review, struck down the statute as in violation of the equal protection rights of males.

Due process and equal protection are concepts intended by the fourteenth amendment's Framers to preserve natural and fundamental liberties and are consequently appropriate to scrutinizing state restraints on such liberty, including those based on gender. An intermediate standard of scrutiny is required to make these concepts meaningful, while at the same time maintaining the vitality of the political processes. Accordingly, constitutional authority exists to safeguard against gender discrimination.

Notes

1. 335 U.S. 464 (1948).

2. Bradwell v. Illinois, 83 U.S. 130 (1873).
3. 411 U.S. 677 (1973).
4. 42 U.S. L. Week 3057 (17 July 1973).
5. Ginsburg, *Gender in the Supreme Court: The 1973 and 1974 Terms*, 1975 SUP. CT. REV. 1 at 23.
6. U.S. Const. amend. XIX.
7. Ginsburg *supra* note 5 at 2.
8. 404 U.S. 71 (1971).
9. 411 U.S. at 682.
10. 253 U.S. 412 (1919).
11. *See* Chapter 3 *supra* text accompanying note 57.
12. Gunther, *In Search of Evolving Doctrine on a Changing Court: A Model for Newer Equal Protection*, 86 HARV. L. REV. 1 (1972).
13. Hampton v. Mow Sun Wong, 426 U.S. 88, 100 (1976).
14. Rostker v. Goldberg, 101 S. Ct. 2646, 2651-55 (1981).
15. Ginsburg *supra* note 5 at 18.
16. 443 U.S. 76 (1979).
17. Dandridge v. Williams, 397 U.S. 471, 487 (1970).
18. San Antonio Independent School District v. Rodriguez, 411 U.S. 1 (1973).
19. Maher v. Roe, 432 U.S. 464 (1977) and Harris v. McRae, 448 U.S. 297 (1980).
20. 430 U.S. 199 (1977).
21. 416 U.S. 351 (1974).
22. 446 U.S. 142 (1980).
23. 458 U.S. 718 (1982).
24. 426 U.S. 229 (1976).
25. *See* Chapter 3 *supra* text accompanying note 109.
26. *See* Chapter 3 *supra* text accompanying note 78.
27. BERNARD H. SIEGAN, ECONOMIC LIBERTIES AND THE CONSTITUTION, 24-27 (Chicago and London: University of Chicago Press, 1980).
28. 261 U.S. 525 (1923).
29. *See* Mengelkoch v. Industrial Welfare Comm'n, 442 F.2d 1119 (9th Cir. 1971); Rosenfeld v. Southern Pacific Co., 293 F. Supp. (C.D. Cal.) 1219 (1968); *aff'd* 444 F.2d 1219 (9th Cir. 1971).
30. 429 U.S. 190 (1976).

7

Abortion and Sexual Privacy

According to accounts contained in THE BRETHREN, the Justices decided the abortion issue in accordance with their personal views about the subject.[1] From the information that has come to my attention, I have no doubt that this story is essentially correct. A major problem confronted by the majority Justices was how best to rationalize constitutionally this enormously important decision, destined to strike down, in whole or in part, the statutes of every state in the Union and of the District of Columbia. Instead of interpreting a particular provision of the Constitution as requiring invalidation of a statute, the Justices sought to find a constitutional basis for that which they had already determined. Justice White referred to the decision as "an exercise of raw judicial power."[2]

To be sure, the approach was not unusual for the Justices; normative determinations in constitutional law may be more the rule than the exception. However, whether typical or not, this process is incompatible with a society dedicated to majority rule. Majorities are supposed to govern, except when they violate rights protected by the Constitution, notwithstanding offense to the Justices' perceptions of the social good. The abortion statutes were struck down because by chance a majority of the Court, appointed by various presidents who probably gave no thought to the constitutional questions involved, believed that this action would advance or improve society. The outcome might well have been different had it been possible for the appointment and confirmation processes to consider this issue when the Justices were nominated for office. Constitutional checks and balances do not operate in these situations, although they are intended to be a major force underlying our constitutional system.

Logically, one comments on a decision arrived at for normative values by examining and considering those concerns. But that is not the way of legal commentary. For whatever reasons, the Court has delivered an opinion, which must be the basis for the analysis. We are advised that Justice Blackmun, who wrote it, spent a considerable period in preparing the best legal exposition for the predetermined result.[3] In essence, therefore, the analysis relates to how well the Justice performed this assignment.

Because the Constitution provides little guidance on abortion, the personal feelings of the Justices may have been more decisive in this decision than might otherwise be expected. Blackmun's opinion in *Roe v. Wade*, which was approved by a 7-2 margin, held that the fourteenth amendment's due process clause protects a woman's liberty to obtain an abortion.[4] The Justice cited no historical basis for this interpretation; nor is there any, for it is quite clear that neither the framers nor ratifiers of that amendment ever contemplated the amendment's application to the subject matter. It was a right, Justice Rehnquist observes, "that was apparently completely unknown to the drafters of the Amendment."

> As early as 1821, the first state law dealing directly with abortion was enacted by the Connecticut Legislature. . . . By the time of the adoption of the Fourteenth Amendment in 1868, there were at least 36 laws enacted by state or territorial legislatures limiting abortion. While many States have amended or updated their laws, 21 of the laws on the books in 1868 remain in effect today. Indeed, the Texas statute struck down today was, as the majority notes, first enacted in 1857 and "has remained substantially unchanged to the present time."[5]

However, as previously noted, the due process concept in English and American law is very broad, not limited to any set of specific objectives contemplated by those responsible for its insertion in the Constitution.[6] The fourteenth amendment's framers regarded due process as an extensive guarantee of life, liberty, and property, leaving specific applications to future interpreters. In the absence of historical directive, the Court's responsibility in interpreting due process is exceedingly delicate. It must determine which liberties are entitled to protection and accord appropriate deference to the political process that seeks to secure other or competing interests and values. The indistinct contours of the Due Process concept do not leave judges at large, since it "is primarily a guarantee of legality itself."[7] The history of the provision teaches caution and restraint, advises Justice Powell.[8] As we shall see, the vigor of the Court's rulings on abortion is not in keeping with these admonitions.

Roe v. Wade

We begin the abortion discussion with *Roe v. Wade*, decided in 1973, the earliest and still leading case. The majority, per Justice Blackmun, ruled that a woman has a fundamental right under the due process clauses to decide whether or not to terminate her pregnancy; therefore, only a compelling interest of the state may justify limitation of that right. As the pregnancy proceeds from the moment of conception, the state acquires increasingly greater interest in regulating it in order to accomplish two purposes: first, to protect the health of the woman, and second, to preserve a fetus after it becomes viable.

For the stage prior to approximately the end of the first trimester, the state may require little more than that the abortion be performed by a licensed physician, for an abortion during that period is less hazardous to a woman's life than is carrying the pregnancy to term. For the stage subsequent to approximately the end of the first trimester, legitimate concerns exist for protecting the woman's health, and the state may therefore regulate the abortion procedure to the extent that the regulation reasonably relates to these purposes. For the stage subsequent to the time the fetus becomes "viable"—that is, potentially able of living outside the womb, albeit with artificial aid—the state may regulate and even proscribe abortion except when it is necessary in appropriate medical judgment for preserving the woman's life or health. The opinion dates viability generally between 24 to 28 weeks after conception.

Scientific advances occurring subsequent to the decision have changed the time frame for the occurrence of these critical events. Justice Sandra Day O'Connor has observed that as medical science becomes better able to provide for the separate existence of the fetus, the point of viability comes closer to conception, while the point at which the state may protect the woman's health recedes further toward actual childbirth as the medical risks of abortion lessen.[9] In 1983, the Court found that certain abortion procedures could be safely performed in a nonhospital setting up to the sixteenth week of pregnancy, well into the second trimester.[10] Thus, as O'Connor concludes, the "*Roe* framework is inherently tied to the state of medical technology that exists whenever particular litigation ensues . . . . [causing] legislatures . . . to speculate about what constitutes 'accepted medical practice' at any given time."

The *Roe* Court rejected the major argument of the state that the fetus is a person within the language and meaning of the due process clause of the fourteenth amendment. Acknowledging that if this contention of personhood is established, the woman's case collapses, Blackmun concluded, however, that the unborn had never been recognized in the law as a person "in the whole sense." However, the state could protect the fetus from and after the point of viability since it presumably has the "capability of meaningful life outside the mother's womb." "State regulation protective of fetal life after viability thus has both logical and biological justifications." Assuming continued technological advances to preserve the life of the fetus outside the woman's body, this formula makes inevitable substantial shrinkage in the time of the abortion option.

To arrive at his holding, Blackmun had to resolve a number of legal issues in a supportive manner. Failure in any one of them would destroy the decision. A discussion of these issues follows.

Due Process

Although the original objectives are not decisive in interpreting the due process clause, the question remains about how free the Court is to make an interpretation contrary to them. Had the Thirty-ninth Congress or the ratifying conventions believed that the due process clause was applicable to state abortion statutes, considerable doubt exists that the fourteenth amendment would have been framed or adopted in its present form. Blackmun failed to consider this historical difficulty. The due process concept is indeed broad in scope: But should it be used to countenance an interpretation inconsistent with the intent of its framers? This subject is surely worthy of discussion, especially when the statutes of fifty-one jurisdictions are in question. Nevertheless, Blackmun went no further than to explain that existing precedent warranted the abortion ruling. He asserted that the Court had long recognized that a right of personal privacy, or a guarantee of certain areas or zones of privacy, exists under the Constitution (which does not mention any right of privacy), citing cases interpreting a number of specific amendments. Only personal rights that are deemed "fundamental" or "implicit in the concept of ordered liberty" were included in this guarantee of personal privacy. The right has some extension to activities relating to marriage (citing cases on procreation, contraception, family relationships) and to child rearing and education. Although considerable distance exists between these cases and one that involves the destruction of a fetus, the Justice asserted that this right of privacy "is broad enough to encompass a woman's decision whether or not to terminate her pregnancy."

The application of due process of law in the sense of protecting natural or fundamental liberties from the oppression of the state might seem appropriate in these other situations. Imposing it to allow extermination of life destined to become a human being would seem to be an entirely different matter, particularly because a major premise of due process is to preserve life. While the other opinions Blackmun cited could be viewed as enhancing life, abortion, which likewise may enhance as much or even more the woman's life, simultaneously destroys the unborn's life. The difference is thus one of kind, not of degree. Terminating a pregnancy is not the same sort of social action as eliminating oppressive limitations on one's right to privacy. A fetus, arguably, may not be a person under the Constitution, but its survival is not on the same order as maintaining the public comfort, convenience, morals, and tranquility.

Blackmun ignored this aspect of the problem. He viewed the antiabortion statute as mainly a limitation on a woman's desire to exercise a personal liberty.

> The detriment that the State would impose upon the pregnant woman by denying this choice altogether is apparent. Specific and direct harm medically diagnosable even in early pregnancy may be involved. Maternity, or additional offspring, may force upon the woman a distressful life and future. Psychological harm may be imminent. Mental and physical health may be taxed by child care. There is also the distress, for all concerned, associated with the unwanted child, and there is the problem of bringing a child into a family already unable, psychologically and otherwise, to care for it. In other cases, as in this one, the additional difficulties and continuing stigma of unwed motherhood may be involved.[11]

As envisioned in the writings of Coke and Blackstone, among others, and in the debates of the Thirty-ninth Congress, due process or its equivalent law of the land, secured the exercise of natural liberty to enable people to engage in ordinary activity. A woman desiring an abortion cannot be deemed to be seeking to exercise a natural liberty. The activity cannot be separated from the impact on life. The exercise of natural liberty does not comprehend the destruction of future or existing human life.[12]

Fundamental Rights, Strict Scrutiny, and Compelling State Interests.

The Court not only established a constitutional right to an abortion but also elevated it to the position of a fundamental liberty. Any restraint on a right accorded this status is subject to the highest level of judicial review, which is to say that it will be strictly scrutinized to determine if it is necessary to achieve a compelling governmental interest—the contemporary constitutional test when a fundamental right is restricted. Not all rights are equal before the contemporary Court. The Supreme Court has its own hierarchy of liberties that cannot be explained by reference to constitutional language and purpose.

This hierarchy is the most important element in deciding whether a constitutional transgression has occurred. When a law is challenged as violating a personal liberty, the Court will impose different standards of review—such as, strict, high-intermediate, low-intermediate, and minimal scrutiny—depending on the liberty involved. Thus restrictions on abortion call for strict scrutiny, while those on economic freedom require only minimal scrutiny, allowing virtually any reason advanced by the government to suffice.[13] Yet a much greater similarity in impact exists than the difference in the level of scrutiny suggests. Governmental restraints on entering a particular livelihood or engaging freely in that undertaking once entry has occurred frequently are highly injurious to people, their families, and their careers. Moreover, there is far more historic basis for protecting economic freedom than there is for protecting sexual freedom.[14]

Were a fundamental interest not involved, the Court would accord the legislatures much greater deference in protecting the fetus against intentional destruction. The result in *Roe* would not be possible under a low level of scrutiny. We learn this from subsequent decisions, in which the Court imposed low levels of scrutiny in certain abortion cases. *Maher v. Roe* adjudicated Connecticut's program to fund the costs associated with childbirth, but not those associated with nontherapeutic abortions.[15] The Court held, 6-3, that the state's decision was a rational means for advancing legitimate interests in protecting human life by encouraging childbirth. *Harris v. McRae* concerned the Hyde amendment to the federal Medicaid program. This amendment denied the states use of federal funds for abortion, except in the most urgent circumstances.[16] No such ban was imposed on the funding of childbirth. By a 5-4 margin, the Court, per Justice Stewart, sustained the constitutionality of the amendment on the ground that it is "rationally related to the legitimate governmental objective of protecting potential life." Stewart continued: "Congress has established incentives that make childbirth a more attractive alternative than abortion for persons eligible for Medicaid. These incentives bear a direct relationship to the legitimate congressional interest in protecting potential life." To the contention that it was irrational for Congress to authorize federal reimbursement for medically necessary services generally, but not for certain medically necessary abortions, Stewart replied: "Abortion is inherently different from other medical procedures, because no other procedure involves the purposeful termination of a potential life."

In both cases, a majority denied any retreat from *Roe*, contending that the fundamental right declared in that case was unlimited in application. However, *Roe* protected solely against unwarranted government interferences and did not comprehend any entitlement to obtain "such funds as may be necessary to realize all the advantages of that freedom." Strict scrutiny analysis was consequently not relevant to the funding aspect of the problem.

The strict scrutiny/compelling interest standard is a creation of the contemporary Court. "I must reiterate," said Justice Harlan in 1969, "I know of nothing which entitles this Court to pick out particular human activities, characterize them as 'fundamental,' and give them added protection under an unusually stringent equal protection test."[17] Imposition of the rule removes nearly all legislative power over the area affected, compromising the separation of powers and the federal-state balance. To be sure, whenever the judiciary protects rights, it limits legislative authority. But the degree of judicial preemption is very large under strict scrutiny. In applying such a severe test, the Court is effectively acting as a super-legislature, according only minimal deference to the political process. Prior to the advent of the strict scrutiny standard in the 1960s, the Court generally probed social and economic legislation with that which would now be deemed either an intermediate or a lesser standard. It thus accorded considerably greater recognition to majority rule.

Consider the application of strict scrutiny in *Roe v. Wade*. The majority opinion mandates severe limitations on government regulation of a pregnancy. Over the years, courts have generally allowed the states considerable latitude in health and safety matters on the theory that the Constitution grants the states primary responsibility in this area. Absent merely arbitrary fiat, the Court has long held that a state must have considerable power to pass measures safeguarding the physical well-being of its people. The abortion cases have rejected this principle based on the premise that a fundamental liberty is involved. As we shall observe in the cases to be discussed subsequently, the Court has carefully examined all and struck down most significant medical curtailments on early abortions enacted by legislatures, including those that would have survived under the more traditional approach. All three branches of government are supposed to be equal; the difficulty with strict scrutiny is that it reflects not a sharing but rather a supremacy of power by the judiciary.

The strict scrutiny test exists as part of a hierarchy of liberties established by the Court, and this fact, in itself, raises serious inquiry about the judicial role. Establishing a priority of liberties is more in the nature of a political rather than a judicial judgment. It relates to major concerns of a free society and is an issue that follows ideological lines. Thus, the democratic left emphatically rejects most governmental controls over conceptual, social, and political liberties and often approves regulation in the economic area. The center and right have much different preferences. Judging by performance, the contemporary Court sides mainly with the left in this area, and in doing so, allocates powers accordingly among various ideological and interest groups. To be sure, in protecting individual liberties, the Court will always affect the political process. While inevitable, this result should go no further than necessary to accommodate legitimate implementation of the judicial power of veto. An even-handed judicial approach to safeguarding freedoms would be more in keeping with this objective.

Furthermore, because rights are highly personal matters, no person can determine objectively their importance to another. I doubt that anyone can prove that from the position of the individual, one's right to speak, write, vote or obtain an abortion deserves more societal recognition than does one's right to earn a living, enter business, produce and distribute products, or offer services. For people who do not engage in certain activities, protection for them may not be important except insofar as the entire society gains. History is replete with examples of some people willing to die for a cause that others totally repudiate.

In virtually eliminating legislative power in the abortion area, the Court has gone beyond judicial authority. It has virtually terminated instead of curtailed the political process. The Constitutional Convention never intended to grant political authority to the branch considered "least dangerous to political rights of the Constitution." Reflecting the predominant sentiments of his day, Hamilton considered the judicial review power to be limited to the negative veto, for the judiciary would "have neither *FORCE* nor *WILL*, but merely judgment." "The courts of justice," declared Hamilton, "were to be no more than bulwarks of a limited Constitution against legislative encroachments."[18]

The Meaning of Viability and of Person

The onset of viability is an event that can be used for purposes of defining legislative powers and limitations. The Court could hardly have ignored it and maintained a respect for human life. That viability is the most important, logical, or appropriate point of distinction is another matter; many would argue that it is subordinate in this respect to the actual commencement of fetal existence. Thus the United States Supreme Court's position contrasts sharply with the German high court's determination of this issue. Interpreting West Germany's constitutional guarantee of the "right to life," the court concluded it was an affirmation of the fundamental value of all human life:

> The process of development [from the 14th day after conception] is a continuing process which exhibits no sharp demarcation and does not allow a precise division of the various steps of development of the human life. The process does not end even with birth; the phenomena of consciousness . . . for example, appear for the first time a rather long time after birth. . . . The right to life is guaranteed to everyone who "lives"; . . . "Everyone" . . . is "every one living"; . . . every life possessing human individuality; . . . the yet unborn human being.[19]

The court explained the guarantee as a reaction against the Nazi regime's measures for the "destruction of life unworthy of life" and as consistent with a concept of state emphasizing the fundamental worth of human life.

The attainment of viability does not confer personhood on the fetus in the view of the American Court. The Constitution uses the word *person* in a number of places, and, Blackmun's opinion asserts, "in nearly all of these instances, the use of the word is such that it has application only post-natally. None indicates, with any assurance, that it has any possible pre-natal application." His opinion then concludes that all this, "together with our [prior] observation . . . that throughout the major portion of the 19th century prevailing legal abortion practices were far freer than they are today, persuades us that the word 'person,' as used in the Fourteenth Amendment, does not include the unborn. This is in accord with the results reached in those few cases where the issue has been squarely presented."

Critics of the opinion have noted an important omission in this discussion of person, and it is that the word as used in the fourteenth amendment includes corporations. The Court so ruled in the late nineteenth century.[20] This definition reveals that the Court has not confined the word *person* to a living human being. Inasmuch as corporations are invested with guarantees of personhood under the fourteenth amendment, extension of the definition to include the fetus cannot be regarded as a breach of an existing pre- and postnatal line of distinction.

Family Relations

The paucity of its constitutional analysis did not inhibit the Court from further extending the *Roe* ruling. In *Planned Parenthood of Missouri v. Danforth*,[21] the Court invalidated a number of antiabortion requirements imposed by Missouri relating to minors. A 5-4 majority annulled a provision requiring that any single woman under eighteen obtain written consent of one parent as a prerequisite for obtaining an abortion. A district court majority had found "a compelling basis" in the state's interest "in safeguarding the authority of the family relationship." However, writing for a plurality of the Justices, Justice Blackmun maintained that the state was without authority "to give a third party an absolute, and possibly arbitrary, veto over the decision of the physician and his patient to terminate the patient's pregnancy." The Justice seemed to have sided with those who regard pregnancy as akin to a medical problem and therefore outside the competency of the family relationship. Justice Stevens objected that the most significant consequences of the abortion decision affect personal welfare and are not medical in character.

Missouri also prohibited a married woman from obtaining an abortion without her husband's written consent. Again, the court upheld the woman's right: Since the state had none, it could not delegate authority to the spouse to prevent abortion during the first trimester.

A majority did, however, sustain a Utah statute requiring a physician to notify the parents of a minor whenever possible before performing an abortion on her.[22] Chief Justice Burger reasoned that the law "furthers a constitutionally permissible end by encouraging an unmarried pregnant minor to seek the help and advice of her parents in making the very important decision whether or not to bear a child." Even though the statute did not provide for a parental veto, it still reached excessively for Justices Marshall, Brennan, and Blackmun, who dissented.

Bellotti v. Baird[23] concerned a Massachusetts statute that required an unmarried minor desiring an abortion to obtain the consent of both parents or the authorization of a state judge if parental consent was not obtained. Eight members of the Court agreed that the statute was unconstitutional under existing precedent, but they split evenly on how much discretion the minor had to obtain an abortion. Four Justices asserted that *Danforth* rejected all third party interference in the minor's decision to obtain an abortion, including parents and courts. The judicial role was objectionable because it both involved public scrutiny of the minor's decision and enabled existing community attitudes to influence the minor. The other four Justices, with whom Justice White (a dissenter in *Roe*) joined because they sought greater restriction on the abortion decision, favored judicial intervention to determine if the minor was competent to make the decision independently or, in the absence of such finding, to determine if the decision was in her best interest.

One would never gauge from these opinions the importance that American society attaches to the family relationship, its intimacy and self-resolution of problems. In *Bellotti*, four Justices had in effect concluded that when abortion is involved, judges are better able to discern a child's best interest and maturity than are her parents. Four others voted to eliminate all adult oversight in the matter. It is hard to believe that the "Constitution" requires such governmental intrusion into the parent/child relationship. In other contexts, the Court has found the Constitution highly supportive of the family. Consider Justice Powell's remarks in another situation: "Our decisions establish that the Constitution protects the sanctity of the family precisely because the institution of the family is deeply rooted in this Nation's history and tradition. It is through the family that we inculcate and pass down many of our most cherished values, moral and cultural."[24] It is even harder to square Justice Brennan's views in that case with those he has espoused in the abortion area. He there lauded "family associational rights that historically have been central, and today remain central, to a large proportion of our population."[25] Justice Powell and he spoke of a "private realm of family life which the state cannot enter."[26] In one case, Chief Justice Burger rested his majority opinion on "Western civilization concepts of the family as a unit with broad parental authority over minor children."[27] This is hardly the tenor of the abortion decisions.

American and English law have never treated minors and adults alike. Minors are entitled to rights, but it has long been acknowledged that "the power of the state to control the conduct of children reaches beyond the scope of its authority over adults."[28] Restraints on minors are intended for their protection as well as for maintaining the authority and tranquility of the family. The courts have accorded considerable deference to state regulations relating to minors, but that deference no longer holds in the area of sexual relations. In *Danforth*, the Court ruled that state restrictions inhibiting privacy rights of minors are valid if they serve "any significant state interest . . . that is not present in the case of an adult." The test is a very high one, as Justice Brennan suggests in his observation that it is "apparently less rigorous"[29] than the compelling state interest test. That the difference is not considerable is indicated by *Carey v. Population Services International*, which struck down a New York provision prohibiting the distribution of contraceptives to those under sixteen years of age.[30] The Justices subjected the law to an intensity of review that differs little from strict scrutiny.

It is difficult to view the Court's excursions into the sexual problems of minors as judicial rather than psychological or sociological exercises or no more than maybe just parenting. In many of the Justices' views, providing a parent with power to overrule a determination of a minor to terminate a pregnancy will not strengthen the family unit, a conclusion that many others with as much understanding of the matter might strongly dispute.

Regardless of these views, however, the more pressing question relates to the constitutional authority under which they are imposed. Little evidence exists that the fourteenth amendment was intended to monitor social and family relations. Thus, the Civil Rights Act of 1866 (the basis for the amendment) as previously explained in chapter 3, did not apply to minors. Domestic and family relations were then considered as exclusively within the control of the states, and not subject to the legislative and judicial controls established in sections 1 and 5 of the fourteenth amendment (as explained in Chapter 4). The 1866 debates evidence no serious intention to limit existing state authority as described by Chancellor Kent: "The principal rights and duties which flow from our civil and domestic relations, fall within the control, and we might also say, the exclusive cognizance of the state governments."[31]

Medical Procedures in Abortions

Unraveling the mysteries of the compelling interest standard requires the highest Court in the land to function, in Justice White's words, as the nation's "*ex officio* medical board with powers to approve or disapprove medical and operative practices and standards throughout the United States."[32] White made this observation in *Danforth*, and two recent cases further substantiate his conclusion. In *Akron v. Akron Center for Reproductive Health*,[33] the Justices, by a 6-3 vote, struck down Akron's ordinance that required, among other things, (1) that abortions after the first trimester be performed in an accredited hospital, (2) that an attending physician (and not anyone else) orally provide their patients pertinent medical and other designated information on the subject, and (3) that a twenty-four hour waiting period lapse between the signing of a consent form and the actual performance of an abortion. Both Justice Powell, for the majority, and Justice O'Connor, for the dissenters, relied on reports and recommendations of professional medical organizations to support their positions, interpreting these recommendations differently.

The subjectivity of the medical analysis was even more evident in *Planned Parenthood Association v. Ashcroft*,[34] in which the Justices separated into three groups to decide the validity of a Missouri statute mandating that a second physician attend an abortion of a viable fetus to safeguard its life and safety and that a certified pathologist examine a sample of tissue removed in any abortion. Blackmun, Brennan, Marshall, and Stevens voted to strike down these requirements, while Powell and Burger, who frequently side with them, voted to sustain. The abortion critics, O'Connor, White, and Rehnquist provided a majority in support of the statute. The Blackmun group subjected the legislation to a degree of scrutiny that very few statutes could satisfy—which is to say that for them the political process is almost not operative in this area.

These significant variations among the Justices greatly complicate the work of legislators dealing with abortion issues, because a foremost consideration of legislators should be to predict how the Justices will rule. It is hard to counter Justice O'Connor's assertion that

> the State must continuously and conscientiously study contemporary medical and scientific literature in order to determine whether the effect of a particular regulation is to "depart from accepted medical practice" insofar as particular procedures and particular periods within the trimester are concerned.[35]

She notes that one professional group on which the Court relied for its opinion changed its standards after the trial in the case.

As has occurred in other areas previously discussed, the Court has vested itself with vast responsibilities not usually associated with the judicial function. It has applied the due process clause beyond the issue of abortion to limit family and professional authority. Nine persons monitor many private activities. In the abortion area, no constitutional basis exists for the exercise of such power.

Notes

1. BOB WOODWARD AND SCOTT ARMSTRONG, THE BRETHREN (New York: Simon and Schuster, 1979). pp. 165-77, 182-89, 218, 229-40, 413-16.
2. Roe v. Wade, 410 U.S. 113, 222 (1973) (White, J., dissenting).
3. THE BRETHREN at 167-77, 182-89, 413-16.
4. 410 U.S. 113 (1973).
5. *Id.* at 174-77 (Rehnquist, J., dissenting).
6. *See* Chapter 3.
7. RODNEY L. MOTT, DUE PROCESS OF LAW (Indianapolis: The Bobbs-Merrill Co., 1926), p. 604.
8. Moore v. City of East Cleveland, 431 U.S. 494 (1977).
9. Akron v. Akron Center for Reproductive Health, Inc., 462 U.S. 416, 452 (1983) (O'Connor, J., dissenting).
10. Akron v. Akron Center for Reproductive Health, Inc., 462 U.S. 416 (1983).
11. 410 U.S. at 153. For Justice Rehnquist to find a violation of due process would apparently require at least a statutory prohibition on an abortion for a woman whose life is in danger. 410 U.S. at 173. (Rehnquist, J., dissenting.)
12. As a concept concerned with protecting and advancing human life, due process seems entirely at variance with the termination of life. Consider in this regard the reasoning of the German Federal Constitutional Court in deciding that the German state has an affirmative duty to protect and foster the unborn: "The degree of seriousness with which the state must take its obligation to protect increases as the rank of the legal value in question increases in importance within the order of values of the Basic Law. Human life represents, within the order of the Basic Law, an ultimate value . . . it is the living foundation of human dignity and the prerequisite for all other fundamental rights." Gorby, *Introduction to the Translation of the Abortion Decision of the Federal Constitutional Court of the Federal Republic of Germany*, 9 J. MAR. J. OF PRAC. AND PROC. 557, 587 (1976).
13. *See generally* BERNARD H. SIEGAN, ECONOMIC LIBERTIES AND THE CONSTITUTION (Chicago and London: University of Chicago Press, 1980).
14. *Id.*
15. 432 U.S. 464 (1977).
16. 448 U.S. 297 (1980).
17. Shapiro v. Thompson, 394 U.S. 618, 662 (1969) (Harlan, J. dissenting).
18. THE FEDERALIST NO. 78 (A. Hamilton).
19. Jonas and Gorby, *West Germany Abortion Decision: A Contrast to Roe v. Wade* 9 J. MAR. J. OF PRAC. AND PROC. 605, 638 (1976). Unlike the United States and German courts, constitutional courts in Austria, Canada, France and Italy indicate the regulation of abortion is a legislative matter except possibly when the life or health of the mother is involved. Gorby *supra* note 12 at 561 n. 15.
20. Santa Clara County v. Southern Pacific R.R., 118 U.S. 394 (1886).
21. 428 U.S. 52 (1976).
22. H.L. v. Matheson, 450 U.S. 398 (1981).

23. 443 U.S. 622 (1979).
24. Moore v. City of East Cleveland, 431 U.S. 494, 503-04 (1977).
25. 431 U.S. at 510 (Brennan, J., concurring).
26. Citing Prince v. Massachusetts, 321 U.S. 158 (1944).
27. Parham v. J.R., 442 U.S. 584 (1979).
28. *Id.* at 170.
29. Carey v. Population Services International, 431 U.S. 678, n. 15 (1977).
30. 431 U.S. 678 (1977).
31. 1 JAMES KENT, COMMENTARIES ON AMERICAN LAW 418 (New York: Da Capo Press, 1971) (reprint of original published in 1826). *See* Chapter 4, text accompanying nn. 1-22; Chapter 3, text accompanying n. 57.
32. Planned Parenthood v. Danforth, 428 U.S. 52, 99 (1976) (White, J., concurring in part and dissenting in part).
33. 462 U.S. 416 (1983).
34. 462 U.S. 476 (1983).
35. Akron v. Akron Center for Reproductive Health, 462 U.S. 416, 456 (1983) (O'Connor, J., dissenting).

8

The First Amendment and Libel

Contemporary Supreme Court reports abound with discourses and dissertations on freedom of expression. The Justices seem to have devoted more thinking to this liberty than to any other, and their decisions have been enormously favorable to the concept. Such great commitment to free expression exists that Justice Blackmun was once moved to admonish some of his colleagues that the "First Amendment, after all, is only one part of an entire Constitution."[1]

However, at the time the first amendment was written, the intellectual climate was far less supportive of free expression. In fact the right of free speech was not included as a fundamental liberty in any Bill of Rights adopted by any state prior to the adoption of the federal Constitution.[2] The reader will find no reference to free speech or free press in the first of Blackstone's four volumes which is devoted largely to "The Rights of Persons." Rather, his interest lies with reputation, which he designates as a right of personal security (one of his three "absolute rights" of life, liberty, and property),[3] thereby limiting the area of protected expression.

> The security of his reputation or good name from the arts of detraction and slander, are rights to which every man is entitled, by reason and natural justice; since without these it is impossible to have the perfect enjoyment of any other advantage or right.[4]

In his discussions of libel in Chapter 11, Volume 4, dealing with "Public Wrongs" and entitled "Of Offences Against the Public Peace," Blackstone considers liberty of the press and exhibits a greater interest in securing the rights of the private individual than in protecting those of the publisher.[5] For Blackstone, the law relating to press freedom was part of the law of libel, and this approach obtained in England and America.

Prior to the Revolution, the American colonies adopted the common law of libel, and the states have proceeded on this course ever since except as overruled by the federal judiciary in contemporary times. Consistent with Blackstone's analysis, free expression was subject to liability for libel.

Although by 1792 ten of the fourteen states that ratified the Constitution had provided constitutional guarantees for free expression, thirteen had also provided for the prosecution of libels.[6]

The federal constitutional protections accorded expression were, as we shall see, consistent with the common law and far less than James Madison desired. In the proposed amendments to the Constitution that he filed in the House on 8 June 1789 he sought two separate guarantees for expression. The first, which was to be inserted in article I, section 9, (containing limitations on the central government) between clauses 3 and 4, follows:

> The people shall not be deprived or abridged of their right to speak, to write, or to publish their sentiments; and the freedom of the press, as one of the great bulwarks of liberty, shall be inviolable.

The second, which was to be inserted in article I, section 10, between clauses 1 and 2, reads as follows: "No state shall violate . . . the freedom of the press."[7]

As evident from the result, these proposals did not fare well in the first Congress. Madison's suggestions were too far-reaching for the times, exceeding even Thomas Jefferson's recommendations.[8] The restriction on the states was rejected, and the limitation on the federal government was much confined. Congress eventually adopted a much narrower restraint, which it applied only to itself: "Congress shall make no law . . . abridging the freedom of speech, or of the press."

Although debates in the first Congress are silent as to the meaning of this guarantee, with respect to the press, no need exists for referring to them for this phrase was, at the time, legally definable. Blackstone enunciates the most commonly quoted meaning in his aforementioned discussion of libels. However, nowhere does he define freedom of speech—a fact suggesting that as late as the 1760s, this concept was not legally definable.

The great commentator viewed publishing similarly to other human actions. No restraint on publication should exist except when the publication actually harmed others.

> The liberty of the press is indeed essential to the nature of a free state: but this consists in laying no *previous* restraints upon publications, and not in freedom from censure for criminal matter when published. Every freeman has an undoubted right to lay what sentiments he pleases before the public: to forbid this, is to destroy the freedom of the press: but if he publishes what is improper, mischievious, or illegal, he must take the consequences of his own temerity.[9]

The United States Supreme Court has essentially maintained this meaning throughout the years except, of course, that it has reduced enormously the scope of that which is "improper, mischievious, or illegal." The Court currently emphasizes an "unhibited, robust, and wide-open" press and evidences far less interest in accuracy, reputation, state security and public order. The legal scene has turned radically from an emphasis on the interests of the state and private individual that had held steady on the High Court at least through 1907. At that time, with only one of his colleagues disagreeing, Justice Oliver Wendell Holmes asserted that the main purpose of the constitutional guarantees of speech and press was "to prevent all such *previous restraints* upon publications as had been practiced by other governments" and that these guarantees

> do not prevent the subsequent punishment of such as may be deemed contrary to the public welfare. [citations] The preliminary freedom extends as well to the false as to the true; the subsequent punishment may extend as well to the true as to the false. This was the law of criminal libel apart from statute in most cases, if not in all.[10]

Holmes cited Blackstone in support of his comment. According to the latter, the common law required writers to exercise considerable caution inasmuch as libels were "malicious defamations of any person, and especially a magistrate, . . . in order to provoke him to wrath, or expose him to public hatred, contempt, and ridicule."[11] In a civil action, the libel had to appear to be both false (for, if the charge was true, the plaintiff had received no private injury) and scandalous. However, in a criminal prosecution, the tendency that all libels have to create animosities and to disturb the public peace was the law's sole consideration. Neither criminal nor civil libels impinged on or violated "liberty of the press, properly understood." Similarly, blasphemous, immoral, treasonable, and schismatical libels were also not within its meaning.

> [T]o punish (as the law does at present) any dangerous or offensive writings, which, when published, shall on a fair and impartial trial be adjudged of a pernicious tendency, is necessary for the preservation of peace and good order, of government and religion, the only solid foundations of civil liberty. Thus the will of individuals is still left free; the abuse only of that free will is the object of legal punishment. Neither is any restraint hereby laid upon freedom of thought or enquiry: liberty of private sentiment is still left; the disseminating, or making public, of bad sentiments, destructive of the ends of society, is the crime which society corrects. . . . So true will it be found, that to censure the licentiousness, is to maintain the liberty, of the press.[12]

Justice Story and Chancellor Kent, the two other legal commentators from whom many early Americans sought guidance, were similarly inclined. For Story, the first amendment imports no more than that every man shall have a right to speak, write and print his opinions upon any subject whatsoever, without any prior restraint, so always that he does not injure any other person in his rights, person, property or reputation; and so always that he does not thereby disturb the public peace, or attempt to subvert the government. It is neither more or less than an expansion of the great doctrine recently brought into operation in the law of libel, that every man shall be at liberty to publish what is true, with good motives and for justifiable ends.[13]

Kent asserts that the right of personal security, which he regarded with the rights of personal liberty and property as an "absolute" human right, includes "the preservation of every person's good name from the vile arts of detraction. The law of the ancients, no less than those of modern nations made private reputation one of the aspects of their protection." While discussion of public issues and candidates is vital to representative government, this concern does not outweigh the interests of an individual to protection of his fair fame and character.[14]

Kent was a member of the Supreme Court of New York, which divided equally in *People v. Croswell* (1804)[15] on whether, in a trial for criminal libel, the defendant was entitled to present evidence regarding the truth of the charges. While Kent favored admission of such evidence, he considered it only indicative and not decisive of whether the publication had been made for malicious purposes—the essence of the offense. Kent supported Blackstone's position that in a private action for damages arising from printed defamation, the better opinion was that truth may in all cases be pleaded by way of justification. If the charge was true, he maintained, the law considers the plaintiff as not having any equitable title to relief.[16]

Blackstone, Story, and Kent thus analyzed freedom of the press in terms of libel law. American common law generally followed this approach. Government had little authority to forbid or censor a publication; freedom of expression was limited only when it collided with certain rights of the public. With private libels, the press was held to the normal standard of the common law that required compensation for the infliction of harm. Libelous expression was considered a form of personal assault for which vindication could come only through compensation for the injury sustained. The injured party was given the same legal protection as anyone else who was the victim of tortious conduct.

Because such suits were tried in the ordinary courts, governmental control over this area was limited to the same extent as it was in other matters. For a long period, the law governing publications in this country was essentially similar to that followed in England, even if the terminology was at times much different. For example, in 1885, Professor A.V. Dicey made this interesting comment:

The liberty of the press, then, is in England simply one result of the universal predominance of the law of the land. The terms "liberty of the press," "press offences," "censorship of the press," and the like, are all but unknown to English lawyers, simply because any offence which can be committed through the press is some form of libel, and is governed in substance by the ordinary law of defamation.[17]

Until 1964 in the United States the right of a person to recover for a defamatory publication was not regarded as affecting the federal Constitution; rather, it was a matter left to state courts and legislatures. Libelous publications were considered a form of speech entirely unprotected by the first amendment. Libel was a tort, subject to the penalties prescribed by the governmental agencies that dealt with such wrongful conduct—that is, the state legislatures and courts. The United States Supreme Court changed all this with two highly important decisions, *New York Times v. Sullivan*[18] in 1964, and *Gertz v. Welch*[19] ten years later. Together these cases overruled the prevailing law of libel in every state, and as a result, actionable libel is now a matter of first amendment interpretation. Because both cases involved state action, the first amendment was not directly implicated. However, the Court had long ago found that the fourteenth amendment incorporated, or absorbed, the first. As to what the fourteenth incorporated, see discussion hereafter on protecting reputation.[20]

State libel laws prior to the *Sullivan* case typically sought to balance the interests of the press and of the ordinary citizen by protecting both truthful publication and good reputation. These laws presumed that a publication defaming the plaintiff—that is, subjecting him to hatred, contempt, or ridicule—was false, and to be relieved of liability, the defendant had the burden of pleading and proving its truth. Upon a finding for the plaintiff, general damages to reputation were presumed, the amount to be determined by a jury, which could also award special damages for pecuniary loss and emotional distress. Proving malice would permit awarding of additional damages.

The existence of damage was conclusively assumed from the publication of the libel itself on the theory that pecuniary harm normally results from defamation. The effect of defamatory statements was considered so subtle and indirect as to make tracing the extent of the harm impossible. ("Truth never catches up with a lie.") The law thus placed the risk of falsehood on the persons who launched a publication that they knew could harm a reputation. In theory at least, libel did not effect appreciably the rights of publishers to disseminate accurate information nor did it involve censorship by the government, for juries, not officials, assessed damages. Moreover, excessive jury awards were subject to limitation by both trial and appellate judges.[21]

New York Times v. Sullivan

In *New York Times v. Sullivan*, a portion of libel law became part of the first and fourteenth amendments. The Court applied these amendments to strike down, in the instance of public officials, the prevailing common law rule that a defendant could escape liability for defamation only by proving the truth of the expression. The *New York Times* had printed an advertisement soliciting public contributions that was highly critical of Montgomery, Alabama police conduct during civil rights protests. The ad contained a number of falsehoods. Sullivan, a Montgomery city commissioner in charge of the police department, sued the *Times* and four clergymen whose names appeared on the ad for personal libel. A jury verdict awarding $500,000 in damages was upheld by the Alabama Supreme Court but was overruled by a unanimous United States Supreme Court.

Writing for the Court, Justice Brennan found portions of the Alabama libel laws unconstitutional and held that a public official could not recover damages for defamatory falsehood relating to his official conduct unless he proved that the statement was made with "actual malice"—that is, with knowledge that it was false or with reckless disregard for the truth. Brennan provided two explanations for the rule.

> [W]e consider this case against the background of a profound national commitment to the principle that debate of public issues should be uninhibited, robust, and wide-open, and that it may well include vehement, caustic, and sometimes unpleasantly sharp attacks on government and public officials.[22]
>
> Allowance of the defense of truth, with the burden of proving it on the defendant, does not mean that only false speech will be deterred. . . . Under such a rule, would-be critics of official conduct may be deterred from voicing their criticism, even though it is believed to be true and even though it is in fact true, because of doubt whether it can be proven in court or fear of the expense of having to do so. They tend to make only statements which "steer far wider of the unlawful zone."[23]

Sullivan is an illustration of those troubling cases in constitutional law that make application of precedent extremely difficult for some judges. The case arose in the emotion-laden days of the civil rights demonstrations in the South. The size of the award raised considerable concern that it was not compensation for the harm sustained and for the dereliction of the newspaper but that it instead represented a decision by the jury in favor of one side of the civil rights struggle. The Supreme Court's ruling may well have been influenced by such suspicions.

The Court viewed the case as one of constitutional dimension: expression on a public issue that undoubtedly merits constitutional protection contained false information defaming a public official. Brennan explained that falsehood by itself is never the basis for justifying repression of speech. However, that should not be the situation when defamation has also occurred. Then the issue is no longer limited to freedom of expression; it becomes instead a conflict between the interests of the publisher and the rights of the defamed citizen. The *Sullivan* rule severely limits the protection a public official has against press falsehoods. It enables the press to operate under standards that are contrary to generally prevailing tort rules, and it countenances ordinary negligence inasmuch as only "deliberate or reckless disregard for truth" is penalized. Thus, Brennan asserted that the evidence against the *Times* showed at most negligence and that this negligence was not sufficient under his interpretation of the Constitution to sustain a finding of libel in that case.

The Justice sought historical support for the position that truth was not required for the existence of a Constitutional shield by discussing a most questionable example, the Sedition Act of 1798. The statute made it a crime, punishable by a $5,000 fine and five years in prison,

> if any person shall write, print, utter or publish . . . any false, scandalous and malicious writing or writings against the government of the United States, or either house of the Congress . . . or the President . . . with intent to defame . . . or to bring them or either of them into contempt or disrepute; or to excite against them, or either or any of them the hatred of the good people of the United States.[24]

Departing from the common law, the Act recognized the defense of truth and provided for the jury to decide the criminality of the accused's words. As the *Sullivan* opinion notes, in spite of its protection of truth, the Act had been vigorously condemned as unconstitutional by Jeffersonians. Brennan agreed, and one hundred and sixty-six years after its passage, he declared the sedition law invalid "in the court of history," notwithstanding that every member of the Supreme Court, in rulings on circuit between 1798 and 1800, had regarded it as constitutional. All the justices of this period were Federalists, and no Federalist is known to have opposed the constitutionality of the law.[25] Indeed, the Federalists accepted Blackstone's position that under the common law government has authority to punish seditious libel. Brennan's explanation relied on certain views expressed by Madison, Jefferson, and several other opponents of the statute and ignored completely its consistency with contemporary common law rules.

Madison considered the law unconstitutional because Congress had no power to control the press under either the document itself or the common law in this country, which he believed differed on this issue from that in England. But Madison's broad perspective on free expression was unacceptable to both the first Congress (as previously reported) and many prominent lawyers of the time. He believed that the press enjoyed a special role in American government as a representative of the people, a view that I do not consider as being widely accepted during our early history. On the contrary the libertarian position on free expression that regards it as a marketplace for ideas did not emerge for a long time after the ratification of the first amendment.[26]

Brennan's reliance on Jefferson is similarly dubious. Jefferson thought that Madison's proposed amendment restraining the power of the federal government over speech was too broad. He recommended to Madison that "the following alterations and additions would have pleased me. Art. 4. 'The people shall not be deprived or abridged of their right to speak to write or otherwise to publish anything but false facts affecting injuriously the life, liberty, property, or reputation of others or affecting the peace of the confederacy with foreign nations.'"[27] This position is contrary to the *Sullivan* ruling, and its adoption would considerably hamper the press in reporting foreign affairs.

Jefferson was a strong opponent of the sedition law but not because he believed in unrestrained speech. The probable explanation is that, as he once stated in a letter to Abigail Adams, he regarded it as beyond the authorized powers of the federal government.

> Nor does the opinion of the unconstitutionality and consequent nullity of that law [the Sedition Act] remove all restraint from the overwhelming torrent of slander which is confounding all vice and virtue, all truth and falsehood in the U.S. The power to do that is fully possessed by the several state legislatures. It was reserved to them, and was denied to the general government, by the constitution according to our construction of it. While we deny that Congress have a right to controul the freedom of the press, we have ever asserted the right of the states, and their exclusive right to do so.[28]

After his election to the presidency, Jefferson wrote a letter condemning the "licentiousness" and "lying" that he perceived in the Federalist press, saying in part: "I have therefore long thought that a few prosecutions of the most eminent offenders would have a wholesome effect in restoring the integrity of the presses."[29] On the basis of the foregoing information, the conclusion that Jefferson opposed seditious libel in principle is not warranted.

In his opinion Brennan also did not address the fact that Jeffersonians, like their leader, opposed the law mostly because they thought Congress had no authority over speech or press; they did not reject the application of seditious libel in the states.[30] Their opposition also had a very pragmatic basis. They feared that the Adams administration might use the law to eliminate political criticism and thereby help ensure a Federalist victory in the elections of 1800. Also noticeably absent in the *Sullivan* opinion is any reference to Blackstone and numerous other early legal authorities who expounded a very narrow view of press freedom.

In his discussion of the Sedition Act, Brennan cites Professor Leonard Levy's classic examination of free speech during the early years of the nation but omits reference to the book's most important conclusion, which contradicts the justice's position on the law. Levy writes as follows:

> What is clear is that there exists no evidence to suggest an understanding that a constitutional guarantee of free speech or press meant the impossibility of future prosecutions of seditious utterances. The traditional libertarian interpretation of the original meaning of the First Amendment is surely subject to the Scottish verdict: not proven. Freedom of speech and press, as all the scattered evidence suggests, was not understood to include a right to broadcast sedition by words. The security of the state against libelous advocacy or attack was always regarded as outweighing any social interest in open expression, at least through the period of the adoption of the First Amendment. The thought and experience of a lifetime, indeed the taught traditions of law and politics extending back many generations, supplied an a priori belief that freedom of political discourse, however broadly conceived, stopped short of seditious libel. [31]

The *Sullivan* facts did not by themselves present a pressing need for legal change. The case involved a paid commercial advertisement soliciting funds for a civil rights cause. Brennan rejected the argument that such an ad was entitled to less protection than was an ordinary news story. Yet a distinction is quite plausible, and it is one that the Court has acknowledged in another context. In meeting publication deadlines, reporters and editors may encounter difficulty in assembling facts from incomplete and sometimes conflicting accounts. Justice Stewart thus distinguished news stories from commercial advertising, stating that "the commercial advertiser generally knows the product or services he seeks to sell and is in a position to verify the accuracy of his factual representations before he disseminates them." The Justice made these remarks to explain why false or deceptive price or product advertising should not obtain constitutional protection.[32] The High Court has accepted this distinction, which seems just as applicable to political advertising. In *Sullivan*, neither the newspaper nor advertiser was under time constraints; the ad would have been no less effective had it been delayed to assure accuracy. Safeguarding the falsehoods it contained was scarcely essential "in order to protect speech that matters."

Gertz v. Welch

Three years after *Sullivan*, the Supreme Court enlarged its holding to comprehend "public figures,"[33] which Chief Justice Warren defined as nonpublic persons who "are nevertheless intimately involved in the resolution of important public questions, or by reason of their fame, shape events in areas of concern to society at large."[34] In the two companion cases involved, the Court included within this definition football coach Wally Butts of the University of Georgia and former Major General Edwin Walker, well-known individuals, neither of whom was at the time employed by a public institution.[35] Nor did either have substantial responsibility for or control over the conduct of governmental affairs, one of the elements identified in *Sullivan* as necessitating its rule.

Subsequently, a plurality of the Court further extended *Sullivan* to defamatory falsehoods relating to private persons if the publication concerned matters of general or public interest.[36] Rejecting the distinction between public and private individuals in these situations, Justice Brennan, writing for the plurality, emphasized society's interest in learning about certain issues, notwithstanding the additional injury that may be sustained by a private citizen without access to the informational resources available to public officials and figures. Brennan's position was never adopted by a majority of the Justices, who subsequently in *Gertz v. Welch* reached an accommodation on how best to resolve the libel law as it relates to private persons.

The *Gertz* result further federalized major aspects of libel law that had not been affected by *Sullivan* and its supporting decisions. Under the rule that was adopted in *Gertz*, a plaintiff in a defamation action based on the publication of a falsehood must prove that the defendant was at fault—acting negligently or intentionally—and that as a result of the publication, he sustained actual damage to his reputation. Previously, the rule generally applicable in the states did not require either a finding of fault on the part of the defendant or actual damage to the plaintiff. Thus, *Gertz* shielded the press from both strict liability for defamatory falsehood and payment of presumed damages. The Court also changed the requirements for obtaining punitive damages. A showing of ill will had previously been sufficient for this purpose. Under the new rule, however, knowing falsehood or reckless disregard of the truth is required. Recently the Court confined the ruling in *Gertz* to matters where the subject is of public and not private concern.[37]

It is difficult to contest dissenting Justice White's objections to *Gertz* as encompassing "radical changes in the law and severe invasions of prerogatives of the States. They should at least be shown to be required by the First Amendment or necessitated by our present circumstances. Neither has been demonstrated." The Court, asserted White, "discards history and precedent in its rush to refashion defamation law in accordance with the inclinations of a perhaps evanescent majority of the Justices." In Chief

Justice Burger's view, the Court "abandon[ed] the traditional thread"; he preferred "to allow this area of law to continue to evolve as it [had] up to [then] with respect to private citizens rather than embark on a new doctrinal theory which [had] no jurisprudential ancestry."[38]

Costs and Consequences

The *Sullivan* and *Gertz* decisions greatly expanded freedom of the press, but not without cost to society. The right of individual reputation, long considered of the highest priority, was curtailed. The integrity of public communication as well as the quality of the national dialogue were diminished. Accordingly, the press freedom that the Court has advanced is far from an unqualified blessing. Whether the benefits exceed the costs is an issue so closely entwined with personal beliefs that the reliability of any such an examination is questionable. Under the authority of judicial review, the Court has taken upon itself to resolve a question that has been considered over the centuries by courts and legislatures throughout the Anglo-Saxon world. No reason exists to believe that state authorities are less competent in or sensitive to its resolution. According to Justice White: "At the very least, the issue is highly debatable, and the Court has not carried its heavy burden of proof to justify tampering with state libel laws."[39]

Libel laws once demanded accuracy, and the press nevertheless remained vibrant and strong. It would be relevant to know to what extent the former libel laws restrained the press. How typical was the jury verdict in *Sullivan*? How costly is it to maintain accuracy? The Supreme Court's opinion is replete with conclusions that might not bear up under statistical analysis. In Justice White's words: "I cannot assume that the press, as successful and powerful as it is, will be intimidated into withholding news that by decent journalistic standards it believes to be true."[40]

Lest there be any misunderstanding of how important the new rules are, consider the facts of the *Gertz* case. The publisher presented false information about Gertz that could seriously harm his reputation. The magazine that the defendant published inaccurately implied that Gertz had a criminal record. It also falsely stated that Gertz was a "Leninist," and that he had been an official of the "Marxist League for Industrial Democracy, originally known as the Intercollegiate Socialist Society, which advocated the violent seizure of our government." It was also false that Gertz was a central figure in a conspiracy that framed a policeman. Under the traditional law of libel, Gertz would likely have received compensation for some or all of the injury inflicted on him, and the jury that heard the case did award him $50,000. That result is far less probable under rules requiring the jury to determine if the publisher acted negligently in printing the falsehoods. The writer in *Gertz* was a contributor to the defendant's magazine, and the editor had sufficient confidence in him not to bother verifying the information. A finding of negligence in the matter is far from certain, for this practice is not uncommon. In the absence of such a finding, the lies could not be judicially refuted and at least to this extent would stand.

Protecting Reputation

Despite what one may conclude from the foregoing decisions, the Justices are cognizant of the importance of reputation in modern society. The *Gertz* Court acknowledged that the individual's right to the protection of his own good name is a fundamental consideration in our constitutional system, reflecting "our basic concept of the essential dignity and worth of every human being—a concept at the root of any decent system of ordered liberty."[41]

When so inclined, Justice Brennan is most eloquent on the subject of reputation. He is among a minority of the Justices that believes reputation is a liberty protected from government attack by procedural due process. However, unlike Brennan, the Court's majority requires that certain other deprivations occur as a result of injury to reputation ("reputation plus") in order to trigger such constitutional protection.[42] Objecting to the severity of this rule, Brennan asserted in a dissent joined by two other Justices that "the enjoyment of one's good name and reputation has been recognized repeatedly in our cases as being among the most cherished of rights enjoyed by a free people, and therefore as falling within the concept of personal liberty."[43] He went on to quote Justice Stewart's observation that the individual's right to the protection of his own good name

> reflects no more than our basic concept of the essential dignity and worth of every human being—a concept at the root of any decent system of ordered liberty. The protection of private personality, like the protection of life itself, is left primarily to the individual States under the Ninth and Tenth Amendments. But this does not mean that the right is entitled to any less recognition by this Court as a basic of our constitutional system.[44]

Such concern seems to evaporate for Justice Brennan and some of his colleagues in the libel cases. In the 1986 *Philadelphia Newspapers, Inc. v. Hepps* decision, a 5-4 majority further limited the amount of protection the states may accord the reputation of a private individual.[45] With respect to publications of public concern, it reversed the common law rule that the defendant must bear the burden of proving truth, and held that the plaintiff instead must satisfy it before recovering damages. *Gertz* required the plaintiff to prove fault—that the defendant acted negligently or deliberately— but left standing the requirement concerning proof of truth. *Hepps* has now removed this safeguard for reputation. Thus, in suits brought by either public or private figures, the law of libel has moved enormously from where it was prior to the *Sullivan* decision.

This outcome contradicts an often repeated observation that the Supreme Court has expanded liberties over the years. This may be true for the right of expression but it is surely not accurate for the right of reputation. A primary purpose of judicial review to preserve and protect liberty has not been effected with respect to the latter. To be sure, the enhancement of the publisher's liberty necessarily leads to the curtailment of the subject's. Regardless, a liberty has been substantially diminished, and such a result should always invite serious inquiry.

Accordingly, let us consider again a major issue with which this chapter is concerned: whether the judicial discretion that has been exercised in the libel area is authorized by the Constitution. In *Sullivan* and later supporting decisions, the court has in effect asserted authority to change the then prevailing balance between the federal and state governments with respect to the rights of expression and reputation.

The existence of a constitutional basis for such power is doubtful. Neither the original constitution ratified in 1788 nor the first amendment asserts any federal power over state expression laws. The former is silent in the matter, and the latter applies by its terms only to laws passed by Congress. Nor, as previously reported, is there significant evidence that the amendment was intended to affect libel laws. This leaves the fourteenth amendment's section 1 as the only source for the power in question. It (or more precisely its privileges and immunities clause) incorporated "the personal rights guaranteed and secured by the first eight amendments to the constitution" including the freedom of speech and of the press.[46] But section 1 also provided protection for other fundamental and natural liberties,[47] which would have included reputation. As previously noted, the foremost legal commentators for the thirty-ninth Congress were Blackstone and Kent, both of whom held the right of reputation to be of the highest order, at least equal to or greater in status than press rights. The importance of the right of reputation was well recognized in the libel laws of the 1860s.

In extending the expression guarantee to the states, it is most unlikely the thirty-ninth Congress meant to limit the protection the libel laws then afforded reputation. In all probability this Congress considered libel a matter for tort, not constitutional law, and consequently, one of state and not federal concern. Prevailing legal opinion viewed the marketplace of ideas as not comprehending libelous publications.[48] It is difficult to conceive this states-rights oriented Congress according federal authorities power to over-rule state libel laws.

Conclusion

Until 1964, state courts and legislatures generally accepted that defamatory falsehoods were not entitled to federal Constitutional protections. The right of expression was not thought to include any license to harm a private citizen. The interest of a person in an untarnished reputation was considered no less important than that of the press to disseminate truthful information. However, beginning with the *Sullivan* decision in 1964, the U.S. Supreme Court expanded the first and fourteenth amendments to comprehend false publications defaming private citizens. The Justices decided that the preservation of a free press demanded this outcome.

The background and history of the first and fourteenth amendments provide little support for the *Sullivan* or *Gertz* decisions. As I have observed so often in these pages, the justices again implemented their own concerns and values by changing the existing rules.

Notes

1. New York Times v. United States, 403 U.S. 713, at 761 (1971) (Blackmun, J., dissenting).
2. Charles Warren, *The New Liberty Under the 14th Amendment*, 39 HARV. L. REV. 431 (1925). However, Pennsylvania's Declaration of Rights adopted in 1776 protected free speech. LEONARD W. LEVY, EMERGENCE OF A FREE PRESS at 5 (New York: Oxford University Press, 1985). This work is a revised version of LEONARD W. LEVY, LEGACY OF SUPPRESSION (Cambridge, Mass.: Harvard University Press, 1960). The latter is hereinafter referred to as LEVY (1) and the former as LEVY (2).
3. 1 W. BLACKSTONE, COMMENTARIES *125. "The right of personal security consists in a person's legal and uninterrupted enjoyment of his life, his limbs, his body, his health, and his reputation." *See also* volume 3, 123-26. BLACKSTONE'S COMMENTARIES were highly authoritative during the Constitutional period and for much time thereafter. For a discussion of expression guarantees not related to defamation, see Bernard H. Siegan, ECONOMIC LIBERTIES AND THE CONSTITUTION 256-63 (Chicago and London: University of Chicago Press, 1980).
4. *Id.* at 130.
5. 4 W. BLACKSTONE, COMMENTARIES *150-53. He also discusses slander and libel in volume 3, 123-26.
6. Gertz v. Welch, 418 U.S. 323, 380-81 (1974) (White, J., dissenting).
7. 1 ANNALS OF CONGRESS 434-35 (Gales & Seaton, 1789).
8. *See* text accompanying footnote 27 *infra*.
9. 4 W. BLACKSTONE *151-152.

10. Patterson v. Colorado, 205 U.S. 454, 462 (1907). Holmes changed his view on seditious libel and other post publication restraints in cases arising subsequent to World War I. *See* Abrams v. United States, 250 U.S. 616, 630 (1919) (Holmes, J., dissenting).
11. 4 W. BLACKSTONE at 150.
12. *Id.* at 152-53.
13. 3 JOSEPH STORY, COMMENTARIES ON THE CONSTITUTION OF THE UNITED STATES 732-33 (New York: Da Capo Press, 1970).
14. 2 JAMES KENT, COMMENTARIES IN AMERICAN LAW 12-14 (New York: DaCapo Press, 1971).
15. 3 JOHNS. (N.Y.) CASES 336 (1804).
16. 2 KENT at 15.
17. A. V. DICEY, INTRODUCTION TO THE STUDY OF THE LAW OF THE CONSTITU-TION (Indianapolis, Ind.: Liberty Classics, 1982), p. 156.
18. New York Times Co. v. Sullivan, 376 U.S. 254 (1964).
19. Gertz v. Welch, 418 U.S. 323 (1974).
20. *See* text accompanying notes 46 and 47 *infra*.
21. *See generally* W. PROSSER, LAW OF TORTS (4th ed. 1971); RESTATEMENT OF TORTS (1938).
22. 376 U.S. at 270.
23. 376 U.S. at 279.
24. Act of Congress of July 14, 1798.
25. LEVY (2) at 280.
26. *See* Berns, *Freedom of the Press and the Alien and Sedition Laws: A Reappraisal*, 1970 SUP. CT. REV. 109.
27. LEVY (2) at 251 citing 15 PAPERS OF JEFFERSON 367.
28. 10 THE WRITINGS OF THOMAS JEFFERSON (Paul Leicester Ford ed. 1892-99) at 90 cited in LEVY (1) at 267.
29. *Quoted in* LEVY (2) at 341.
30. LEVY (2) at 307-08.
31. LEVY (1) at 237; Levy (2) at 269.
32. Virginia State Board of Pharmacy v. Virginia Citizens Consumer Council, 425 U.S. 748, 777, 778, (1976) (Stewart, J., concurring). *See also* Friedman v. Rogers 440 U.S. 1 (1979).
33. Curtis Publishing Co. v. Butts and Associated Press v. Walker, 388 U.S. 130 (1967).
34. 388 U.S. at 164 (Warren, C. J., concurring).
35. Warren reasoned that "public figures" unlike public officials are not subject to the restraints of the political process and that consequently "public opinion may be the only instrument by which society can attempt to influence their conduct." *Id.*
36. Rosenbloom v. Metromedia, 403 U.S. 29 (1971).
37. Dun and Bradstreet, Inc. v. Greenmoss Builders, Inc. 105 S.Ct. 2939 (1985).
38. 418 U.S. at 376-77, 380 (White, J., dissenting); 418 U.S. at 354 (Burger, C.J., dissenting).
39. Justice White dissenting in Gertz v. Welch 418 U.S. at 401.
40. Dun & Bradstreet, Inc. v. Greenmoss Builders, Inc. 105 S.Ct. 2939, 2953 (1985) (White, J., concurring).
41. Gertz, 418 U.S. at 341, quoting Rosenblatt v. Baer, 383 U.S. 75 (1966) (Stewart, J. concurring).

42. Paul v. Davis, 424 U.S. 693 (1976).
43. 424 U.S. at 722-23.
44. Rosenblatt v. Baer, 383 U.S. 75, 92 (1966) (concurring opinion).
45. 54 LW 4373 (1986). The case relates only to libels involving issues of public concern.
46. *See* text accompanying notes 92 and 93 in chapter 3 and 12 in chapter 5, *supra.*
47. *See* text accompanying note 92, 93, 94, 104, 106, 107, 109 and 111 in chapter 3.
48. *See* Patterson v. Colorado, cited in note 10, *supra.* The view expressed in this 1907 case prevailed prior thereto as well. See also discussion in chapter 4 *supra,* on the reach of the fourteenth amendment with respect to state laws.

9

Conclusion: An Emphasis on Original Understanding

The foregoing pages describe a serious problem for a representative society: the establishing of major national policies by the nonelected Supreme Court. In each of the eight areas discussed, the Court would find it most difficult if not impossible to prove that a majority of the persons responsible for framing the relevant sections of the Constitution provided authority for major rulings the Court has imposed. A great many in the society have been affected both favorably and unfavorably; rights and powers have been created for some and denied or withdrawn from others, depending on the composition of a majority of the Court at a particular time. Such practices erode the rule of law, at the root of constitutional government.

Remedies exist for constitutional transgressions. Impeachment might be one but would not be acceptable inasmuch as the public would regard these breaches as of relatively benign character. Another remedy may be provided in sections 1 and 2 of article III which state that

1. The judicial power of the United States, shall be vested in one Supreme Court, and in such inferior courts as the Congress may from time to time ordain and establish.
2. The judicial power shall extend to all cases in law and equity arising under the Constitution, the laws of the United States, etc.

In these cases, the Constitution provides that "the Supreme Court shall have appellate jurisdiction, both as to law and fact, with such exceptions, and under such regulations, as the Congress shall make."[1]

This latter clause gives Congress power to curb judicial opportunism but its exact scope and reach remain undefined. That it does have considerable potential in this respect is suggested by the decision in *Ex Parte McCardle* (1869).[2] In that case, the Supreme Court accepted the repeal by Congress of an act conferring jurisdiction on it to hear appeals in certain Habeas Corpus matters decided in the Circuit Court of the United States. Congress withdrew jurisdiction from the Court after the Justices had heard the arguments in *McCardle* and taken it under advisement preparatory to issuing an opinion. Chief Justice Chase for a unanimous Court held that it could no longer consider the case: "Without jurisdiction the Court cannot proceed at all in any cause."

In recent times congressional critics of the decisions in the abortion, mandated school busing, and school prayer cases have sought without success to pass legislation curtailing the Court's powers to rule in these areas, citing the said constitutional provisions as authority for the proposed legislation. To be sure, the validity of any such efforts would be subject to decision by the targeted institution, the Supreme Court of the United States, a fact which may not bode well for the proposals.

Notwithstanding *McCardle* and other cases, the meaning of the exceptions provision is far from clear. Consider the guarantees of the Bill of Rights. The latter was appended to the Constitution to accord greater power to the judiciary primarily to limit Congress' authority over individual rights. The exceptions provision seems to allow for the reverse. Thus, it might be thought that under this provision Congress would be able to remove the Supreme Court's power to protect certain rights, but this result might be considered contrary to the essential purpose of the Bill to protect liberty from oppressive legislation. Another concern about the provision is that if the Supreme Court's appellate power in certain areas were removed, judicial finality would rest with the various federal circuit and State Supreme courts. The basic constitutional structure would be altered. It is apparent the exceptions provision require considerable interpretation.

Another remedy is one always available in a representative society to curb legal transgressions: the power of public opinion. Although the Supreme Court's deliberations are by design insulated from the public, the Justices cannot totally ignore public credibility and image. This influence on the Court has not been sufficiently recognized or utilized; yet has potential of being a powerful force. For many, Supreme Court decisions are viewed like sports results that identify the winners and the losers. The concern instead should be to process, whether the Court has abided by its mandate. The question deserving the highest priority is whether the Constitution authorizes the Court's opinion. As the Bicentennial of the framing and ratification of the Constitution approaches (1987 and 1988), such resolve should form part of the celebration, a rededication to constitutionalism in its true sense, which means implementing the document's words and meanings unless strong justification exists to proceed otherwise. The public's emphasis should be on the legitimacy of the actions of this most powerful institution.

Notes

1. U.S. Const., art. III, § 2.
2. 74 U.S. (7 Wall.) 506 (1869). *See* United States v. Klein, 80 U.S. (13 Wall.) 128 (1872); Ex parte Yerger, 78 U.S. (8 Wall.) 85 (1869); Van Alstyne, *A Critical Guide to Ex parte McCardle*, 15 ARIZ. L. REV. 229 (1973).

Supplement
The Constitution of the United States of America

We the People of the United States, in Order to form a more perfect Union, establish Justice, insure domestic Tranquility, provide for the common defence, promote the general Welfare, and secure the Blessings of Liberty to ourselves and our Posterity, do ordain and establish this Constitution for the United States of America.

Article I

Section 1

All legislative Powers herein granted shall be vested in a Congress of the United States, which shall consist of a Senate and House of Repesentatives.

Section 2

The House of Representatives shall be composed of Members chosen every second Year by the People of the several States, and the Electors in each State shall have the Qualifications requisite for Electors of the most numerous Branch of the State Legislature.

No Person shall be a Representative who shall not have attained to the Age of twenty-five Years, and been seven Years a Citizen of the United States, and who shall not, when elected, be an Inhabitant of that State in which he shall be chosen.

Representatives and direct Taxes shall be apportioned among the several States which may be included within this Union, according to their respective Numbers, which shall be determined by adding to the whole Number of free Persons, including those bound to Service for a Term of Years, and excluding Indians not taxes, three fifths of all other Persons. The actual Enumeration shall be made within three Years after the first Meeting of the Congress of the United States, and within every subsequent Term of ten Years, in such Manner as they shall by Law direct. The Number of Representatives shall not exceed one for every thirty Thousand, but each State shall have at Least one Representative; and until such enumerations shall be made, the State of New Hampshire shall be entitled to chuse three, Massachusetts eight, Rhode-Island and Providence Plantations one, Connecticut five, New-York six, New Jersey four, Pennsylvania eight, Delaware one, Maryland six, Virginia ten, North Carolina five, South Carolina five, and Georgia three.

When vacancies happen in the Representation from any State, the Executive Authority thereof shall issue Writs of Election to fill such Vacancies.

The House of Representatives shall chuse their Speaker and other Officers; and shall have the sole Power of Impeachment.

Section 3

The Senate of the United States shall be composed of two Senators from each State, chosen by the Legislature thereof, for six Years; and each Senator shall have one Vote.

Immediately after they shall be assembled in Consequence of the first Election, they shall be divided as equally as may be into three Classes. The Seats of the Senators of the first Class shall be vacated at the Expiration of the second Year, of the second Class at the Expiration of the fourth Year, and of the third Class at the Expiration of the sixth Year, so that one-third may be chosen every second Year; and if Vacancies happen by Resignation, or otherwise, during the Recess of the Legislature of any State, the Executive thereof may make temporary Appointments until the next Meeting of the Legislature, which shall then fill such Vacancies.

No Person shall be a Senator who shall not have attained to the Age of thirty Years, and been nine Years a Citizen of the United States, and who shall not, when elected, be an Inhabitant of that State for which he shall be chosen.

The Vice President of the United States shall be President of the Senate, but shall have no Vote, unless they be equally divided.

The Senate shall chuse their other Officers, and also a President pro tempore, in the absence of the Vice President, or when he shall exercise the Office of President of the United States.

The Senate shall have the sole Power to try all Impeachments. When sitting for that Purpose, they shall be on Oath or Affirmation. When the President of the United States is tried, the Chief Justice shall preside: And no Person shall be convicted without the Concurrence of two thirds of the Members present.

Judgment in Cases of Impeachment shall not extend further than to removal from Office, and disqualification to hold and enjoy any Office of honor, Trust or Profit under the United States: but the Party convicted shall nevertheless be liable and subject to Indictment, Trial, Judgment and Punishment, according to Law.

Section 4

The Times, Places and Manner of holding Elections for Senators and Representatives, shall be prescribed in each State by the Legislature thereof; but the Congress may at any time by Law make or alter such Regulations, except as to the Place of Chusing Senators.

The Congress shall assemble at least once in every Year, and such Meeting shall be on the first Monday in December, unless they shall by Law appoint a different Day.

Section 5

Each House shall be the Judge of the Elections, Returns and Qualifications of its own Members, and a Majority of each shall constitute a Quorum to do Business; but a smaller number may adjourn from day to day, and may be authorized to compel the Attendance of absent Members, in such Manner, and under such Penalties as each House may provide.

Each House may determine the Rules of its Proceedings, punish its Members for disorderly Behavior, and, with the Concurrence of two thirds, expel a Member.

Each House shall keep a Journal of its Proceedings, and from time to time publish the same, excepting such Parts as may in their Judgment require Secrecy; and the Yeas and Nays of the Members of either House on any question shall, at the Desire of one fifth of those Present, be entered on the Journal.

Neither House, during the Session of Congress, shall, without the Consent of the other, adjourn for more than three days, nor to any other Place than that in which the two Houses shall be sitting.

Section 6

The Senators and Representatives shall receive a Compensation for their Services, to be ascertained by Law, and paid out of the Treasury of the United States. They shall in all Cases, except Treason, Felony and Breach of the Peace, be privileged from Arrest during their Attendance of the Session of their respective Houses, and in going to and returning from the same; and for any Speech or Debate in either House, they shall not be questioned in any other Place.

No Senator or Representative shall, during the Time for which he was elected, be appointed to any civil Office under the Authority of the United States, which shall have been created, or the Emoluments whereof shall have been encreased during such time; and no Person holding any Office under the United States, shall be a Member of either House during his Continuance in Office.

Section 7

All Bills for raising Revenue shall originate in the House of Representatives; but the Senate may propose or concur with Amendments as on other Bills.

Every Bill which shall have passed the House of Representatives and the Senate, shall, before it become a Law, be presented to the President of the United States; If he approve he shall sign it, but if not he shall return it, with his Objections to that House in which it shall have originated, who shall enter the Objections at large on their Journal, and proceed to reconsider it. If after such Reconsideration two thirds of that House shall agree to pass the Bill, it shall be sent, together with the Objections, to the other House, by which it shall likewise be reconsidered, and if approved by two thirds of that House, it shall become a Law. But in all such Cases the Votes of both Houses shall be determined by Yeas and Nays, and the Names of the Persons voting for and against the Bill shall be entered on the Journal of each House respectively. If any Bill shall not be returned by the President within ten Days (Sunday excepted) after it shall have been presented to him, the Same shall be a Law, in like Manner as if he had signed it, unless the Congress by their Adjournment prevent its Return, in which Case it shall not be a Law.

Every Order, Resolution, or Vote to which the Concurrence of the Senate and the House of Representatives may be necessary (except on a question of Adjournment) shall be presented to the President of the United States; and before the Same shall take Effect, shall be approved by him, or being disapproved by him, shall be repassed by two thirds of the Senate and House of Representatives, according to the Rules and Limitations prescribed in the Case of a Bill.

Section 8

The Congress shall have Power To lay and collect Taxes, Duties, Imposts and Excises, to pay the Debts and provide for the common Defense and general Welfare of the United States; but all Duties, Imposts and Excises shall be uniform throughout the United States;

To borrow money on the credit of the United States;

To regulate Commerce with foreign Nations, and among the several States, and with Indian Tribes;

To establish an uniform Rule of Naturalization, and uniform Laws on the subject of Bankruptcies throughout the United States;

To coin Money, regulate the Value thereof, and of foreign Coin, and fix the Standard of Weights and Measures;

To provide for the Punishment of counterfeiting the Securities and current Coin of the United States;

To establish Post Offices and post Roads;

To promote the Progress of Science and useful Arts, by securing for limited Times to Authors and Investors the exclusive Right to their respective Writings and Discoveries;

To constitute Tribunals inferior to the Supreme Court;

To define and punish Piracies and Felonies committed on the high Seas, and Offenses against the Law of Nations;

To declare War, grant Letters of Marque and Reprisal, and make Rules concerning Captures on Land and Water;

To raise and support Armies, but no Appropriation of Money to that Use shall be for a longer Term than two Years;

To provide and maintain a Navy;

To make Rules for the Government and Regulation of the land and naval Forces;

To provide for calling forth the Militia to execute the Laws of the Union, suppress Insurrections and repel Invasions;

To provide for organizing, arming, and disciplining the Militia, and for governing such Part of them as may be employed in the Service of the United States, reserving to the States respectively, the Appointment of the Officers, and the Authority of training the Militia according to the discipline prescribed by Congress.

To exercise exclusive Legislation in all Cases whatsoever, over such District (not exceeding ten Miles square) as may, by Cession of particular States, and the acceptance of Congress, become the Seat of the Government of the United States, and to exercise like Authority over all Places purchased by the Consent of the Legislature of the State in which the Same shall be, for the Erection of Forts, Magazines, Arsenals, dock-Yards, and other needful Buildings;—And

To make all Laws which shall be necessary and proper for carrying into Execution the foregoing Powers, and all other Powers vested by this Constitution in the Government of the United States, or in any Department or Officer thereof.

Section 9

The Migration or Importation of such Persons as any of the States now existing shall think proper to admit, shall not be prohibited by the Congress prior to the Year one thousand eight hundred and eight, but a tax or duty may be imposed on such Importation, not exceeding ten dollars for each Person.

The privilege of the Writ of Habeas Corpus shall not be suspended, unless when in Cases of Rebellion or Invasion the public Safety may require it.

No Bill of Attainder or ex post facto Law shall be passed.

No capitation, or other direct, Tax shall be laid, unless in Proportion to the Census or Enumeration herein before directed to be taken.

No Tax or Duty shall be laid on Articles exported from any State.

No Preference shall be given by any Regulation of Commerce or Revenue to the Ports of one State over those of another: nor shall Vessels bound to, or from, one State, be obliged to enter, clear, or pay Duties in another.

No Money shall be drawn from the Treasury, but in Consequence of Appropriations made by Law; and a regular Statement and Account of the Receipts and Expenditures of all public Money shall be published from time to time.

No title of Nobility shall be granted by the United States: And no Person holding any Office of Profit or Trust under them, shall, without the Consent of the Congress, accept of any present, Emolument, Office, or Title, of any kind whatever, from any King, Prince, or foreign State.

Section 10

No State shall enter into any Treaty, Alliance, or Confederation; grant Letters of Marque and Reprisal; coin Money; emit Bills of Credit; make any Thing but gold and silver Coin a Tender in Payment of Debts; pass any Bill of Attainder, ex post facto Law, or Law impairing the Obligation of Contracts, or grant any title of Nobility.

No State shall, without the Consent of the Congress, lay any Imposts or Duties on Imports or Exports, except what may be absolutely necessary for executing its inspection Laws: and the net Produce of all Duties and Imposts, laid by any State on Imports or Exports, shall be for the Use of the Treasury of the United States; and all such Laws shall be subject to the Revision and Controul of the Congress.

No State shall, without the consent of Congress, lay any duty of tonnage, keep Troops, or Ships of War in time of Peace, enter into any Agreement or Compact with another State, or with a foreign Power, or engage in War, unless actually invaded, or in such imminent Danger as will not admit of delay.

Article II

Section 1

The executive Power shall be vested in a President of the United States of America. He shall hold his Office during the Term of four Years, and, together with the Vice-President, chosen for the same Term, be elected, as follows.

Each State shall appoint, in such Manner as the Legislature thereof may direct, a Number of Electors, equal to the whole Number of Senators and Representatives to which the State may be entitled in the Congress: but no Senator or Representative, or Person holding an Office of Trust or Profit under the United States, shall be appointed an Elector.

The Electors shall meet in their respective States, and vote by Ballot for two persons, of whom one at least shall not be an Inhabitant of the same State with themselves. And they shall make a List of all the Persons voted for, and of the Number of Votes for each; which List they shall sign and certify, and transmit sealed to the Seat of the Government of the United States, directed to the President of the Senate. The President of the Senate shall, in the Presence of the Senate and House of Representatives, open all the Certificates, and the Votes shall then be counted. The Person having the greatest Number of Votes shall be the President, if such Number be a Majority of the whole Number of Electors appointed; and if there be more than one who have such Majority, and have an equal Number of Votes, then the House of Representatives shall immediately chuse by Ballot one of them for President; and if no Person have a Majority, then from the five highest on the List and the said House shall in like Manner chuse the President. But in chusing the President, the Votes shall be taken by States, the Representation from each State having one Vote; a quorum for this Purpose shall consist of a Member of Members from two thirds of the States, and a Majority of all the States shall be necessary to a Choice. In every Case, after the Choice of the President, the Person having the greatest Number of Votes of the Electors shall be the Vice President. But if there should remain two or more who have equal Votes, the Senate shall chuse from them by Ballot the Vice President.

The Congress may determine the Time of chusing the Electors, and the Day on which they shall give their Votes; which Day shall be the same throughout the United States.

No Person except a natural born Citizen, or a Citizen of the United States, at the time of the Adoption of this Constitution, shall be eligible to the Office of President; neither shall any Person be eligible to that Office who shall not have attained to the Age of thirty-five Years, and been fourteen Years a Resident within the United States.

In Case of the Removal of the President from Office, or of his Death, Resignation, or Inability to discharge the Powers and Duties of the said Office, the same shall devolve on the Vice President, and the Congress may by Law, provide for the Case of Removal, Death Resignation or Inability, both of the President and Vice president, declaring what Officer shall then act as President, and such Officer shall act accordingly, until the Disability be removed, or a President shall be elected.

The President shall, at stated Times, receive for his Services, a Compensation, which shall neither be encreased nor diminished during the Period for which he shall have been elected, and he shall not receive within that Period any other Emolument from the United States, or any of them.

Before he enter on the Execution of his Office, he shall take the following Oath or Affirmation:—"I do solemnly swear (or affirm) that I will faithfully execute the Office of President of the Unitied States, and will to the best of my Ability, preserve, protect and defend the Constitution of the United States."

Section 2

The President shall be Commander in Chief of the Army and Navy of the United States, and of the Militia of the several States, when called into the actual Service of the United States; he may require the Opinion in writing, of the principal Officer in each of the executive Departments, upon any subject relating to the Duties of their respective Offices, and he shall have Power to Grant Reprieves and Pardons for Offenses against the United States, except in Cases of Impeachment.

He shall have Power, by and with the Advice and Consent of the Senate, to make Treaties, provided two-thirds of the Senators present concur; and he shall nominate, and by and with the Advice and Consent of the Senate, shall appoint Ambassadors, other public ministers and Consuls, Judges of the supreme Court, and all other Officers of the United States, whose Appointments are not herein otherwise provided for, and which shall be established by Law: but the Congress may by Law vest the Appointment of such inferior Officers, as they think proper, in the President alone, in the Courts of Law, or in the Heads of Departments.

The President shall have Power to fill up all Vacancies that may happen during the Recess of the Senate, by granting Commissions which shall expire at the End of their next Session.

Section 3

He shall from time to time give to the Congress Information of the State of the Union, and recommend to their Consideration such Measures as he shall judge necessary and expedient; he may, on extraordinary Occasions, convene both Houses, or either of them, and in Case of Disagreement between them, with Respect to the Time of Adjournment, he may adjourn them to such Time as he shall think proper; he shall receive Ambassadors and other public Ministers; he shall take Care that the Laws be faithfully executed, and shall Commission all the Officers of the United States.

Section 4

The President, Vice President and all Civil Officers of the United States, shall be removed from Office on Impeachment for, and Conviction of, Treason, Bribery, or other high Crimes, and Misdemeanors.

Article III

Section 1

The judicial Power of the United States, shall be vested in one supreme Court, and in such inferior Courts as the Congress may from time to time ordain and establish. The Judges, both of the supreme and inferior Courts, shall hold their Offices during good Behaviour, and shall, at stated Times, receive for their Services, a Compensation, which shall not be diminished during their Continuance in Office.

Section 2

The judicial Power shall extend to all Cases, in Law and Equity, arising under this Constitution, the Laws of the United States, and Treaties made, or which shall be made, under their Authority;—to all Cases affecting Ambassadors, other public Ministers and Consuls;—to all Cases of admirality and maritime Jurisdiction;—to Controversies to which the United States shall be a Party;—to Controversies between two or more States;—between a State and Citizens of another State;—between Citizens of different States;—between Citizens of the same State claiming Lands under Grants of different States, and between a State, or the Citizens thereof, and foreign States, Citizens or Subjects.

In all Cases affecting Ambassadors, other public Ministers and Consuls, and those in which a State shall be Party, the supreme Court shall have original Jurisdiction. In all the other cases before mentioned, the supreme Court shall have appellate Jurisdiction, both as to Law and Fact, with such Exceptions, and under such Regulations as the Congress shall make.

The trial of all Crimes, except in Cases of Impeachment, shall be by Jury; and such Trial shall be held in the State where the said Crimes shall have been committed; but when not committed within any State, the Trial shall be at such Place or Places as the Congress may by Law have directed.

Section 3

Treason against the United States, shall consist only in levying War against them, or in adhering to their Enemies, giving them Aid and Comfort. No Person shall be convicted of Treason unless on the Testimony of two Witnesses to the save overt Act, or on Confession in open Court.

The Congress shall have Power to declare the Punishment of Treason, but no Attainder of Treason shall work Corruption of Blood, or Forfeiture except during the Life of the Person attainted.

Article IV

Section 1

Full Faith and Credit shall be given in each State to the public Acts, Records, and judicial Proceedings of every other State. And the Congress may by general Laws prescribe the Manner in which such Acts, Records and Proceedings shall be proved, and the Effect thereof.

Section 2

The Citizens of each State shall be entitled to all Privileges and Immunities of Citizens in the several States.

A Person charged in any State with Treason, Felony, or other Crime, who shall flee from Justice, and be found in another State, shall on demand of the executive Authority of the State from which he fled, be delivered up, to be removed to the State having Jurisdiction of the Crime.

No Person held to Service or Labour in one State, under the Laws thereof, escaping into another, shall, in Consequence of any Law or Regulation therein, be discharged from such Service or Labour, but shall be delivered up on Claim of the Party to whom such Service or Labour may be due.

Section 3

New States may be admitted by the Congress into this Union; but no new State shall be formed or erected within the Jurisdiction of any other State; nor any State be formed by the Junction of two or more States, or parts of States, without the Consent of the Legislatures of the States concerned as well as of the Congress.

The Congress shall have Power to dispose of and make all needful Rules and Regulations respecting the Territory or other Property belonging to the United States; and nothing in this Constitution shall be so construed as to Prejudice any Claims of the United States, or of any particular State.

Section 4

The United States shall guarantee to every State in this Union a Republican Form of Government, and shall protect each of them against Invasion; and on Application of the Legislature, or of the Executive (when the Legislature cannot be convened) against domestic Violence.

Article V

The Congress, whenever two-thirds of both Houses shall deem it necessary, shall propose Amendments to this Constitution, or, on the Application of the Legislatures of two-thirds of the several States, shall call a Convention for proposing Amendments, which, in either Case, shall be valid to all Intents and Purposes, as part of this Constitution, when ratified by the Legislatures of three-fourths of the several States, or by Conventions in three-fourths thereof, as the one or the other Mode of Ratification may be proposed by the Congress: Provided that no Amendment which may be made prior to the Year One thousand eight hundred and eight shall in any Manner affect the first and fourth Clauses in the Ninth Section of the first Article; and that no State without its Consent, shall be deprived of its equal Suffrage in the Senate.

Article VI

All Debts contracted and Engagements entered into, before the Adoption of this Constitution, shall be as valid against the United States under this Constitution, as under the Confederation.

This Constitution, and the Laws of the United States which shall be made in Pursuance thereof; and all Treaties made, or which shall be made, under the Authority of the United States, shall be the supreme Law of the Land, and the Judges in every State shall be bound thereby, any Thing in the Constitution or Laws of any State to the contrary notwithstanding.

The Senators and Representatives before mentioned, and the Members of the several State Legislatures, and all executive and judicial Officers, both of the United States and of the several States, shall be bound by Oath or Affirmation, to support this Constitution; but no religious Test shall ever be required as a Qualification to any Office or public Trust under the United States.

Article VII

The Ratification of the Conventions of nine States shall be sufficient for the Establishment of this Constitution between the States so ratifying the Same.

Done in Convention by the Unanimous Consent of the States present the Seventeenth Day of September in the Year of Our Lord one thousand seven hundred and Eighty seven and of the Independence of the United States of America the Twelfth.

In Witness whereof We have hereunto subscribed our Names.

Amendment I

Congress shall make no law respecting an establishment of religion, or prohibiting the free exercise thereof; or abridging the freedom of speech, or of the press; or the right of the people peaceably to assemble, and to petition the Government for a redress of grievances.

Amendment II

A well regulated Militia, being necessary to the security of a free State, the right of the people to keep and bear Arms, shall not be infringed.

Amendment III

No Soldier shall, in time of peace be quartered in any house, without the consent of the Owner, nor in time of war, but in a manner to be prescribed by law.

Amendment IV

The right of the people to be secure in their persons, houses, papers, and effects, against unreasonable searches and seizures, shall not be violated, and no Warrants shall issue, but upon probable cause, supported by Oath or affirmation, and particularly describing the place to be searched, and the persons or things to be seized.

Amendment V

No person shall be held to answer for a capital, or otherwise infamous crime, unless on presentment or indictment of a Grand Jury, except in cases arising in the land or naval forces, or in the Militia, when in actual service in time of War or public danger; nor shall any person be subject for the same offence to be twice put in jeopardy of life or limb; nor shall be compelled in any criminal case to be a witness against himself, nor be deprived of life, liberty, or property, without due process of law; nor shall private property be taken for public use, without just compensation.

Amendment VI

In all criminal prosecutions, the accused shall enjoy the right to a speedy and public trial, by an impartial jury of the State and district wherein the crime shall have been committed, which district shall have been previously ascertained by law, and to be informed of the nature and cause of the accusation; to be confronted with the witnesses against him; to have compulsory process for obtaining witnesses in his favor, and to have the Assistance of Counsel for his defence.

Amendment VII

In suits at common law, where the value in controversy shall exceed twenty dollars, the right of trial by jury shall be preserved, and no fact tried by a jury, shall be otherwise reexamined in any Court of the United States, than according to the rules of the common law.

Amendment VIII

Excessive bail shall not be required, nor excessive fines imposed, nor cruel and unusual punishments inflicted.

Amendment IX

The enumeration in the Constitution, of certain rights, shall not be construed to deny or disparage others retained by the people.

Amendment X

The powers not delegated to the United States by the Constitution, nor prohibited by it to the States, are reserved to the States respectively, or to the people.

Amendment XI

The Judicial power of the United States shall not be construed to extend to any suit in law or equity, commenced or prosecuted against one of the United States by Citizens of another State, or by Citizens or Subjects of any Foreign State.

Amendment XII

The Electors shall meet in their respective states and vote by ballot for President and Vice-President, one of whom, at least, shall not be an inhabitant of the same state with themselves; they shall name in their ballots the person voted for as President, and in distinct ballots the persons voted for as Vice-President, and they shall make distinct lists of all persons voted for as President, and of all persons voted for as Vice-President, and the number of votes for each, which lists they shall sign and certify, and transmit sealed to the seat of the government of the United States, directed to the President of the Senate;—The President of the Senate shall, in presence of the Senate and House of Representatives, open all the certificates and the votes shall then be counted;—The person having the greatest number of votes for President, shall be the President, if such number be a majority of the whole number of Electors appointed; and if no person have such majority, then from the persons having the highest numbers not exceeding three on the list of those voted for as President, the House of Representatives shall choose immediately, by ballot, the President. But in choosing the President, the votes shall be taken by states, the representation from each state having one vote; a quorum for this purpose shall consist of a member or members from two-thirds of the states, and a majority of all the states shall be necessary to a choice. And if the House of Representatives shall not choose a President whenever the right of choice shall devolve upon them, before the fourth day of March next following, then the Vice-President shall act as President, as in the case of the death or other constitutional disability of the President.—The person having the greatest number of votes as Vice-President, shall be the Vice-President, if such number be a majority of the whole number of Electors appointed, and if no person have a majority, then from the two highest numbers on the list, the Senate shall choose the Vice-President; a quorum for the purpose shall consist of two-thirds of the whole number of Senators, and a majority of the whole number shall be necessary to a choice. But no person constitutionally ineligible to the office of President shall be eligible to that of Vice-President of the United States.

Amendment XIII

Section 1

Neither slavery nor involuntary servitude, except as a punishment for crime whereof the party shall have been duly convicted, shall exist within the United States, or any place subject to their jurisdiction.

Section 2

Congress shall have power to enforce this article by appropriate legislation.

Amendment XIV

Section 1

All persons born or naturalized in the United States, and subject to the jurisdiction thereof, are citizens of the United States and of the State wherein they reside. No State shall make or enforce any law which shall abridge the privileges or immunities of citizens of the United States; nor shall any State deprive any person of life, liberty, or property, without due process of law; nor deny to any person within its jurisdictioin equal protection of the laws.

Section 2

Representatives shall be apportioned among the several States according to their respective numbers, counting the whole number of persons in each State, excluding Indians not taxed. But when the right to vote at any election for the choice of electors for President and Vice-President of the United States, Representatives in Congress, the Executive and Judicial officers of a State, or the members of the Legislature thereof, is denied to any of the male inhabitants of such State, being twenty-one years of age, and citizens of the United States, or in any way abridged, except for participation in rebellion, or other crime, the basis of representation therein shall be reduced in the proportion which the number of such male citizens shall bear to the whole number of male citizens twenty-one years of age in such State.

Section 3

No person shall be a Senator or Representative in Congress, or elector of President and Vice-President, or hold any office, civil or military, under the United States, or under any State, who, having previously taken an oath, as a member of Congress, or as an officer of the United States, or as a member of any State legislature, or as an executive or judicial officer of any State, to support the Constitution of the United States, shall have engaged in insurrection or rebellion against the same, or given aid or comfort to the enemies thereof. But Congress may by a vote of two-thirds of each House, remove such disability.

Section 4

The validity of the public debt of the United States, authorized by law, including debts incurred for payment of pensions and bounties for services in suppressing insurrection or rebellion, shall not be questioned. But neither the United States nor any other State shall assume or pay any debt or obligation incurred in aid of insurrection or rebellion against the United States, or any claim for the loss or emancipation of any slave; but all such debts, obligations and claims shall be held illegal and void.

Section 5

The Congress shall have power to enforce, by appropriate legislation, the provisions of this article.

Amendment XV

Section 1

The right of citizens of the United States to vote shall not be denied or abridged by the Unitied States or by any State on account of race, color, or previous condition of servitude.

Section 2

The Congress shall have power to enforce this article by appropriate legislation.

Amendment XVI

The Congress shall have power to lay and collect taxes on incomes, from whatever source derived, without apportionment among the several States, and without regard to any census or enumeration.

Amendment XVII

The Senate of the United States shall be composed of two Senators from each State, elected by the people thereof, for six years; and each Senator shall have one vote. The electors in each State shall have the qualifications requisite for electors of the most numerous branch of the State legislatures.

When vacancies happen in the representation of any State in the Senate, the executive authority of such State shall issue writs of election to fill such vacancies: *Provided,* That the legislature of any State may empower the executive thereof to make temporary appointments until the people fill the vacancies by election as the legislature may direct.

This amendment shall not be so construed as to affect the election or term of any Senator chosen before it becomes valid as part of the Constitution.

Amendment XVIII

Section 1

After one year from the ratification of this article the manufacture, sale, or transportation of intoxicating liquors within, the importation thereof into, or the exportation thereof from the United States and all territory subject to the jurisdiction thereof for beverage purposes is hereby prohibited.

Section 2

The Congress and the several States shall have concurrent power to enforce this article by appropriate legislation.

Section 3

This article shall be inoperative unless it shall have been ratified as an amendment to the Constitution by the legislatures of the several States as provided in the Constitution, within seven years from the date of the submision hereof to the States by the Congress.

Amendment XIX

The right of citizens of the United States to vote shall not be denied or abridged by the United States or by any State on account of sex.

Congress shall have power to enforce this article by appropriate legislation.

Amendment XX

Section 1

The terms of the President and Vice President shall end at noon on the 20th day of January, and the terms of Senators and Representatives at noon on the 3d day of January, of the years in which such terms would have ended if this article had not been ratified; and the terms of their successors shall then begin.

Section 2

The Congress shall assemble at least once in every year, and such meeting shall begin at noon on the 3d day of January, unless they shall by law appoint a different day.

Section 3

If, at the time fixed for the beginning of the term of the President, the President elect shall have died, the Vice President elect shall become President. If a President shall not have been chosen before the time fixed for the beginning of his term, or if the President elect shall have failed to qualify, then the Vice President elect shall act as President until a President shall have qualified; and the Congress may by law provide for the case wherein neither a President elect nor a Vice President elect shall have qualified, declaring who shall then act as President, or the manner in which one who is to act shall be selected, and such person shall act accordingly until a President or Vice President shall have qualified.

Section 4

The Congress may by law provide for the case of the death of any of the persons from whom the House of Representatives may choose a President whenever the right of choice shall have devolved upon them, and for the case of the death of any persons from whom the Senate may choose a Vice President whenever the right of choice shall have devolved upon them.

Section 5

Sections 1 and 2 shall take effect on the 15th day of October following the ratification of this article.

Section 6

This article shall be inoperative unless it shall have been ratified as an amendment to the Constitution by the legislatures of three-fourths of the several States within seven years from the date of its submission.

Amendment XXI

Section 1

The eighteenth article of amendment to the Constitution of the United States is hereby repealed.

Section 2

The transportation or importation into any State, Territory, or possession of the United States for delivery or use therein of intoxicating liquors, in violation of the laws thereof, is hereby prohibited.

Section 3

This article shall be inoperative unless it shall have been ratified as an amendment to the Constitution by conventions in the several States, as provided in the Constitution, within seven years from the date of the submission hereof to the States by the Congress.

Amendment XXII

Section 1

No person shall be elected to the office of the President more than twice, and no person who has held the office of President, or acted as President, for more than two years of a term to which some other person was elected President shall be elected to the office of the President more than once. But this Article shall not apply to any person holding the office of President when this Article was proposed by the Congress, and shall not prevent any person who may be holding the office of President, or acting as President, during the term within which this Article becomes operative from holding the office of President or acting as President during the remainder of such term.

Section 2

This article shall be inoperative unless it shall have been ratified as an amendment to the Constitution by the legislatures of three-fourths of the several States within seven years from the date of its submission to the States by the Congress.

Amendment XXIII

Section 1

The District constituting the seat of Government of the United States shall appoint in such manner as the Congress may direct:

A number of electors of President and Vice President equal to the whole number of Senators and Representatives in Congress to which the District would be entitled if it were a State, but in no event more than the least populous State; they shall be in addition to those appointed by the States, but they shall be considered, for the purposes of the election of President and Vice President, to be electors appointed by a State; and they shall meet in the District and perform such duties as provided by the twelfth article of amendment.

Section 2

The Congress shall have power to enforce this article by appropriate legislation.

Amendment XXIV

Section 1

The right of citizens of the United States to vote in any primary or other election for President or Vice President, for electors for President or Vice President, or for Senator or Representative in Congress, shall not be denied or abridged by the United States or any State by reason of failure to pay any poll tax or other tax.

Section 2

The Congress shall have power to enforce this article by appropriate legislation.

Amendment XXV

Section 1

In case of the removal of the President from office or of his death or resignation, the Vice President shall become President.

Section 2

Whenever there is a vacancy in the office of the Vice President, the President shall nominate a Vice President who shall take office upon confirmation by a majority vote of both Houses of Congress.

Section 3

Whenever the President transmits to the President pro tempore of the Senate and the Speaker of the House of Representatives his written declaration that he is unable to discharge the powers and duties of his office, and until he transmits to them a written declaration to the contrary, such powers and duties shall be discharged by the Vice President as Acting President.

Section 4

Whenever the Vice President and a majority of either the principal officers of the executive departments or of such other body as Congress may by law provide, transmit to the President pro tempore of the Senate and the Speaker of the House of Representatives their written declaration that the President is unable to discharge the powers and duties of his office, the Vice President shall immediately assume the powers and duties of the office as Acting President.

Thereafter, when the President transmits to the President pro tempore of the Senate and the Speaker of the House of Representatives his written declaration that no inability exists, he shall resume the powers and duties of his office unless the Vice President and a majority of either the principal officers of the executive department or of such other body as Congress may by law provide, transmit within four days to the President pro tempore of the Senate and the Speaker of the House of Representatives their written declaration that the President is unable to discharge the powers and duties of his office. Thereupon Congress shall decide the issue, assembling within forty-eight hours for that purpose if not in session. If the Congress, within twenty-one days after receipt of the latter written declaration, or, if Congress is not in session, within twenty-one days after Congress is required to assemble, determines by two-thirds vote of both Houses that the President is unable to discharge the powers and duties of his office, the Vice President shall continue to discharge the same as Acting President; otherwise, the President shall resume the powers and duties of his office.

Amendment XXVI

Section 1

The right of citizens of the United States, who are eighteen years of age or older, to vote shall not be denied or abridged by the United States or by any State on account of age.

Section 2

The Congress shall have power to enforce this article by appropriate legislation.

(The foregoing is copied from an edition of the Constitution published by the National Archives and Records Administration, Washington, D.C. 1986.)

Index

Index of Cases